Where the Animals Are

Where the Animals Are

A Guide to the Best Zoos,
Aquariums, and Wildlife Attractions
in North America

by Tim O'Brien

A Voyager Book

The
Globe
Pequot
Press

Old Saybrook, Connecticut

Library of Congress Cataloging-in-Publication Data

O'Brien, Tim.
  Where the animals are : a guide to the best zoos, aquariums, and wildlife attractions in North America / by Tim O'Brien. — 1st ed.
      p.   cm.
  "A Voyager Book."
  Includes index.
  ISBN 1-56440-077-8
     1. Zoos—North America—Guidebooks. 2. Aquariums, Public—North America— Guidebooks. 3. Wildlife refuges—North America—Guidebooks. I. Title.
  QL76.5.N7027   1992
  590'.74'473—dc20   92-20081
                                                              CIP

Manufactured in the United States of America
First Edition/First Printing

To my family: Rosi, Carrie, and Molly.
And to all the animals of the world, for without you,
this book wouldn't be necessary.

Contents

Foreword by Jack Hanna ix

Acknowledgments xiii

Introduction 1

How to Use This Book 4

Twenty Hints to Make Your Visit More Fun 6

The Zoos, Aquariums, and Wildlife Attractions

United States

Alabama 10

Alaska 13

Arizona 16

Arkansas 21

California 23

Colorado 43

Connecticut 47

Delaware 50

District of Columbia 52

Florida 55

Georgia 75

Hawaii 78

Idaho 82

Illinois 85

Indiana 95

Iowa 101

Kansas 103

Kentucky 109

Louisiana 111

Maine 116

Maryland 120

Massachusetts 125

Michigan 130

Minnesota 138

Mississippi 142

Missouri 144

Montana 149

CONTENTS

Nebraska 151
Nevada 156
New Hampshire 158
New Jersey 161
New Mexico 167
New York 169
North Carolina 186
North Dakota 190
Ohio 193
Oklahoma 203
Oregon 206
Pennsylvania 210
Rhode Island 221
South Carolina 223
South Dakota 226
Tennessee 229
Texas 237
Utah 254
Vermont 257
Virginia 259
Washington 263
West Virginia 269
Wisconsin 271
Wyoming 277

Canada

Alberta 279
British Columbia 281
Manitoba 284
New Brunswick 285
Nova Scotia 285
Ontario 286
Quebec 289
Saskatchewan 291

General index 293
Zoos, Aquariums, and Wildlife Attractions by State and Province 295

Foreword:
Why Zoos and Aquariums

by Jack Hanna

Writing an introduction that embraces all of the zoos and aquariums of North America is difficult, because no two of them are alike.

This diversity, however, is one of their major strengths. Each is unique and has its own personality. Each institution in this directory comes from different beginnings, from different forms of leadership, and different communities.

They have different operating styles and different philosophies. They emphasize different animals and different programs.

While not all of the listings in this book are accredited by the American Association of Zoological Parks and Aquariums (AAZPA), nearly 160 of the zoos and aquariums listed have this distinction. They share common standards and four basic goals: recreation, conservation, education, and scientific studies.

Recreation

From their beginnings as collections owned by royalty and the very wealthy—as long ago as 4500 B.C.—zoos were intended for the amusement of people. Even into this century, amusement was a primary function. Today zoos have assumed more serious roles while still functioning as major recreational sites for their communities.

That zoos rank high as wholesome family-oriented recreation is shown by the fact that more than 112 million people visit North American zoos and aquariums each year. This figure exceeds the total annual attendance of all professional football, basketball, and baseball games combined.

Our professionally run zoos and aquariums of the 1990s are a world apart from the cement-and-bar–caged menageries of earlier in this century. Today our visitors enjoy a combination of experiences. They see groupings of animals in displays that mimic the natural habitat. They are educated through attractive graphics and signage. They enjoy concerts and special events ranging from holiday festivals to birthday parties. Some zoos have achieved botanical-garden status and take pride in the appearance of their grounds and horticultural displays.

Visitors are our lifeblood, and few zoos are able to offer free admission. For most, admissions income is critical for operation. Even so, this charge is modest when compared to that of most theme parks, sporting events, and other public events. For most people, a visit to a local zoo is still the best recreational bargain in town.

Conservation and Scientific Study

At one time zoos and aquariums were consumers of wildlife. If an animal died, it was very easily replaced by another from the wild. Some zoos even operated their own animal collecting safaris.

Today when a zoo staffer embarks on safari, he or she has a more benevolent purpose. Along with conservation organizations, universities, and individual conservationists, zoos are assuming more and more responsibility in preserving wild places and wild things.

As we are all well aware, wild places are disappearing. Tropical forests are being cut down at an alarming rate. In North America, our wetlands and old-growth forests are at risk due to the demands of ever-expanding human populations. As these lands disappear, so do the plants and animals that make up the ecosystem.

Wildlife refuges have been created to protect specific ecosystems that would otherwise become extinct. Today more than 400 refuges in America alone provide protected natural habitat for approximately sixty endangered species and hundreds of species of birds, mammals, reptiles, amphibians, fish, and plants.

Zoos no longer empty the wild to fill their exhibits. In fact, more than 90 percent of mammals displayed in North American zoos are captive-born, and 50 percent of *these* are offspring of captive-born parents. Of all wildlife imported into the United States, less than one-tenth of one percent are destined for life in a zoo or aquarium. The majority of the rest go into the pet trade.

Today it's not unusual to find trained zoo staffers in the field conducting behavioral observations that will improve the life of captive animals or provide information that will lead to captive reproduction. These same people may also be found in preserves, helping to rehabilitate confiscated wildlife or replacing logged-out nesting sites with artificial nesting boxes for endangered parrots.

Although release projects are still relatively rare, zoos also have been instrumental in releasing several captive-born species into the wild: Arabian oryx into the Arabian deserts; golden lion tamarins in Brazil; Bali mynahs on

Bali; and California condors, black-footed ferrets, and red wolves in the United States. Loggerhead sea turtle hatchlings have been raised in "head start" programs to a size conducive to their survival before being released into the ocean.

Other species are the subjects of cooperative breeding programs, in which zoos exchange animals and expertise. They may even be part of the "frozen zoo," in which vials of frozen semen or embryos make the thousand-mile journeys rather more easily than a herd of their full-grown counterparts.

These breeding programs, or species survival plans (SSPs), now include some sixty endangered species. Through interzoo cooperation, under the leadership of the AAZPA, these animals are scientifically evaluated, identified individually, and put in breeding programs in an effort to maintain genetic diversity within the species.

The frozen zoo and the SSPs are the Noah's Ark of the twenty-first century. For even if animals can be prepared behaviorally to survive in the wild, there may or may not be a wild to which we can return them. In the meantime, scientific studies and selective breeding programs are maintaining these species for the future.

Education

What zoos and aquariums can do to preserve species and habitats is only the very small tip of a very large iceberg. But if people around the world can be educated about wildlife, then we have a true force for change. This is already being demonstrated in experimental projects worldwide.

The animals in our zoos and aquariums are ambassadors for their cousins in the wild. The visitor who stands in awe of a bull elephant will probably never again be tempted to buy ivory. Those who watch a mother tiger play with her young will never again covet an exotic fur coat. Our animals educate in a way that no other medium can. We, as educators, can only supplement their message.

We conduct adult education classes, but the heart of what we do is educating children about the wonders of wildlife. In animal facilities across the country, three- and four-year-olds enjoy classes and programs throughout the year. Saturday classes in the spring and fall and day camps in the summer fill up quickly. School groups enjoy programs during field trips.

Children study everything. They paint, they draw, they watch movies; they watch how rattlesnakes rattle and how sharks breathe. The lucky ones may witness a birth in the hoofstock yard or see how a keeper trims an elephant's toenails. Learning is fun at the zoo, and that's how we want it.

Our children are the future of wildlife, the captains of the next Ark. At zoos and aquariums, we are doing all we can to prepare the next generation to understand and respect wild life and wild places. With these tools will come preservation.

Who We Are and Where We're Going

As I mentioned previously, zoos and aquariums are a diverse group with a joint commitment to the welfare and well-being of wildlife.

Just like the three bears, some zoos are huge, some are medium, and some are small. Size in no way reflects quality. Some of our finest institutions cover only a few acres. For the most part, zoos and aquariums are staffed by caring people whose priority is the welfare of their animals.

The zoo staff of the future will become a little more sophisticated and probably hold more advanced degrees. Natural-habitat exhibits will increase and become even more innovative. Zoo staff will become increasingly involved in conservation programs in the wild, and the gap between captivity and the wild will become smaller and smaller. The one thing that won't change, however, is the dedication of our staffs and their determination to give their best to the captive animal population and to share this knowledge and respect with the public.

The zoos, aquariums, and wildlife attractions listed in this directory welcome you to their parks. I know you'll have a good time, and we all hope to see you soon and often.

Jack Hanna
Executive Director
Columbus Zoological Gardens
Columbus, Ohio

Acknowledgments

While researching this guide, I met a lot of very helpful and friendly "animal people." From owners of deer farms and small wildlife attractions to top executives at the major aquariums to secretaries at municipal zoos, everyone was most cooperative and made sure I received the information I needed. You all know who you are. Thanks again!

I'd especially like to thank Jack Hanna, executive director of the Columbus Zoological Gardens in Ohio, for agreeing to write the foreword. Since his zoo was the first one I ever visited as a child, it especially means a lot to me.

Also, special thanks go out to Julie Estadt of the Columbus Zoo for providing the animal "Fun Facts" that you'll see throughout the book.

This guide would not have come together as it did without the research assistance of my longtime journalistic colleague, Gale Cortelyou. Her contribution to this tome was most valuable. Thanks, Gale.

Where the Animals Are

Introduction

I remember my first visit to a zoo. It was during late spring, in 1957, and my grandparents took me to the Columbus Zoo to see Colo, the first gorilla born in captivity.

She was in a warm nursery and I remember standing out in the chilly weather, staring at the newborn through a window. I held Grandma's hand while Grandpa read the signs to us.

I don't remember much more about that visit, except that it's one of the happiest memories I have of my grandparents.

In the years since, I've grown up, moved away from Columbus, and now have two children. Colo still lives there and has three offspring and more than a dozen grandchildren. One of her grandkids is now the age I was when I first saw Colo. Quite a family she has created!

And speaking of families, it's the 1990s, the decade of family togetherness. And as more and more families play together, more and more are discovering the wonderful opportunities that zoos, aquariums, and other wildlife attractions offer for family outings.

The New Zoo

If you haven't been to a zoo in the last decade, you have quite a treat waiting for you. Over the years, zoo officials have been upgrading all facets of their facilities. Most have completely done away with bars and cages and are now providing natural habitats for their keepings. Botanical gardens, special events, and new approaches to signage and education have made zoos wonderfully diverse, fun places to visit.

It is also during the last ten years that large public aquariums have made a comeback in popularity. With state-of-the art-technology, flashy exhibits, and a focus on local and regional marine life, aquariums, whether newly built or recently updated, have become viable tourist attractions. They offer color, action, and a glimpse at the mysteries of the deep.

But zoos and aquariums aren't the only places where you'll find animals in North America. Drive-through safari parks allow you to see a variety of large animals of the Plains from the comfort of your car.

While most animal attractions offer wide variety, some specialize in only one or two types of animals. From monkeys to snakes, from alligators to butterflies, there are specialty attractions from coast to coast and from border to border.

Wildlife refuges also provide marvelous areas for animal viewing. While many refuges have comfortable walking paths and printed guide booklets, many are truly rough, natural areas. In fact, you need a boat or a plane to get to some of the refuges in the National Wildlife Refuge System.

Currently, there are more than 400 refuges in the United States alone, encompassing nearly ninety million acres in forty-nine states and five territories. They provide habitat—food, water, cover, and space—for approximately sixty endangered species as well as hundreds of other species of birds, mammals, reptiles, amphibians, fish, and plants.

Viewing animals in a refuge is viewing animals in their natural habitat, and that being the case, you may not always get to observe the animals you want to see. "We offer no guarantees," one ranger told me. But just think how much fun a family can have, all decked out in walking gear, with binoculars around their necks, in search of a glimpse of the animals.

Finding the Animals

Getting families to where the animals are is what this guide is all about. You'll see as you peruse the pages that this is much more than a listing of zoos and aquariums. You are holding the most comprehensive guide ever published on where to find wildlife in North America.

With diversity in mind, I have not only listed most of the zoos and aquariums in the United States, but also searched out wonderful little specialty zoos and wildlife attractions. In addition, I've listed a nice sampling of our country's wildlife refuges.

Although the separate listing for Canada doesn't include as many attractions, it does provide a good sampling of what the country offers.

While approximately 160 facilities listed in this book are accredited by the American Association of Zoological Parks and Aquariums (AAZPA), the rest are not. Accreditation means that the facility has met specific industry standards set by the association. When you visit an accredited zoo or aquarium you can pretty much expect top quality across the line, from management to facility maintenance to animal care.

It's important, however, to point out that just because an attraction is not accredited doesn't mean that the facility is necessarily substandard. Some establishments choose, for one reason or another, not to become "officially" accredited, even though they could qualify.

Visiting Many Zoos—Cheap

If you travel a lot and enjoy visiting zoos and aquariums wherever you go, or if you're loading up the family for a coast-to-coast zoo party, there's a way to save on admission prices.

A reciprocation policy exists among nearly 150 North American zoos and aquariums. If you're a member of any one such facility, you get in to all of the others for free or at a reduced rate.

To obtain a current list of reciprocating facilities, contact Judy Blackstock, P.O. Box 1861, Asheboro, NC 27204, or call her at (919) 625–4245.

In the meantime, enjoy and support your local zoo and aquarium. Buy a family membership, visit often, and take advantage of the educational opportunities each facility offers.

And if you're going on a trip, make sure you take a copy of this book with you. It will guide you to Where the Animals Are.

Happy Trails!

How to Use This Book

In an effort to be as thorough as possible, and to paint a realistic picture of *Where the Animals Are,* I've listed not only the larger, better-known animal facilities, but many small-town zoos, roadside animal attractions, and wildlife refuges as well. As a result, you will find two types of listings in this book: major and minor.

The Minor Listings

These brief listings include the attractions that I feel are special or different enough to be included in the book even though they don't necessarily have as much to offer as the major parks. Some minor listings may not have a great many species to offer or a lot of extra action taking place, but they'll have at least one distinct aspect that convinced me to give them a spot in my book.

As you no doubt will discover, some of the neatest places around are the ones with just a few exhibits and a great deal of atmosphere.

The Major Listings

Most of the categories in the major listing are self-evident, but for a better overview, here are a few additional comments:

- To list in detail what each exhibit contains would take too much space, so, for brevity's sake, in most cases only the name of the exhibit has been listed—in the section called "The animals."

  Generally, however, you should be able to figure out what type of animals and ecosystems each exhibit has simply from its name.

  The listing of animals and exhibits is not meant to be all-inclusive and in most cases is only a sampling of what the facility offers.

- Most entertainment shows in wildlife facilities are animal- or environment-oriented. Few have song-and-dance or variety shows. In some cases, the only entertainment offered is

animal feeding, which can be quite educational as well as fun.

- Zoos probably offer more creative special events than any other type of attraction in the world. From clever Halloween events to Christmas celebrations to spring and Easter parties, many zoos promote special fun activities for the entire family. Some attractions will have none, but others will have something going on every weekend. For the sake of space, only a sampling has been given.

- Length of stay listed for a facility is based on how long it will take a family of four to walk the grounds, see the shows, and partake of most of the activities.

- Many of the smaller facilities are located in city parks, and I've listed what the adjacent park has to offer in addition to the zoo itself. Many city parks were built with the zoo as one element of an entire inner-city entertainment zone.

- If a specific category isn't provided in a listing, it's not applicable to that particular facility and has been omitted.

- While the hours of operation and the admission prices listed in this book were confirmed at press time, it's generally a good idea to call ahead for the most current information before traveling a great distance.

Twenty Hints to Make Your Visit More Fun

1. Be kind to your feet. Wear well-broken-in athletic shoes, since you'll probably be doing quite a bit of walking. Many zoos and wildlife parks are located in wooded, hilly locations, so be prepared to do some hill walking.

2. Pick up a guide book and entertainment schedule at the gate. Since many of the animal shows are performed only once or twice daily, it's wise to plan your visit around the specific times of the shows and demonstrations. Make a list of must-see's and plan your route so you won't be needing to do a lot of time-consuming backtracking.

3. If you're with a crowd or you have kids who are old enough to go off on their own, give them a marked map or a sheet of paper with a specific meeting place and time. In the excitement of the day, kids (and others) have a way of forgetting directions.

4. Make sure you're dressed for the day. Take along a rain parka or a folded-up trash bag to use in case of a sudden shower. It's also wise to take along sweaters or jackets and leave them in the car, just in case.

5. If you plan on eating at the zoo, try to beat the lunch rush and eat before noon or after 2:30 P.M. Zoos usually have enough food service and food outlets, but it seems everyone wants to eat during "lunch" time. If you take a picnic lunch, stake out a shaded picnic table early in the day.

6. If the facility that you're visiting doesn't allow food to be brought onto the grounds, it still makes sense to take along an apple or two to hold you over. This point is especially important if you have children.

7. Wash your hands before eating! You've probably touched or petted something you normally don't touch.

8. If it's a hot, sunny day, make sure you wear a hat, apply sunscreen, and drink a lot of fluid. If you start feeling bad, report immediately to the first-aid station.

9. Even if you don't have children with you, consider renting a stroller or a wagon to hold your camera equipment, lunch, etc. A camera bag gets awfully heavy by mid-afternoon.

10. Souvenirs are great, but don't buy them before you're ready to leave. Hauling around some breakable item or a large teddy bear all day isn't too much fun. Tell the children that each can pick out one thing to buy just before you leave—but not before then.

11. Many of the larger facilities have rental lockers. If you have a lot of stuff and don't want to leave it in your car, rent a locker.

12. If you have medication that needs refrigeration, most first-aid stations should be able to keep it for you. If not, ask at the office: all facilities with any sort of food service have large coolers.

13. Live animal shows are very popular and there's usually a crowd at most of the performances. Get there early and pick out a good (shady) seat for yourself. (NOTE: Most marine mammal shows have wet-zone seating, areas where you might get splashed during the show. Believe the signs—you'll probably get soaked!)

14. If you want to leave for a while, to go to lunch or back to the hotel for a rest, make sure to get your hand stamped before leaving. Most facilities will allow you same-day reentry privileges if you are stamped.

15. It sounds simple, but make sure you remember where you parked. Whether it's on the facility's grounds or in a public parking lot, it's very easy to jump out of the car and head to the gate without noting your exact location. After a long day, it's no fun to spend an hour hunting for your car.

16. Many of the larger zoos, aquariums, and wildlife parks also sell their tickets at hotels, rental-car agencies, local ticket agencies, and the like. If you can buy your tickets before you get there, you've already eliminated one line to stand in.

17. Most rules are made for safety—both yours and the animals' you've come to visit. Please pay attention to posted regulations. Probably the most common rule concerns feeding the animals. Animals are usually on strict diets and if you feed them something, you can make them seriously ill. The same goes for air quality in some exhibits. If it says no smoking, officials are probably concerned with the animals' health, not necessarily yours.

18. Animals bite! Believe the signs and keep your hands and fingers to yourself! And never make a quick motion toward the head of any animal—it will frighten them.

19. Trainers, handlers, and keepers are wonderful sources of information about animals. Feel free to ask them questions following a show or as you see them throughout the day.

20. Treat the animals and their surroundings with respect. Remember, they live here, it's their home. You're just a visitor.

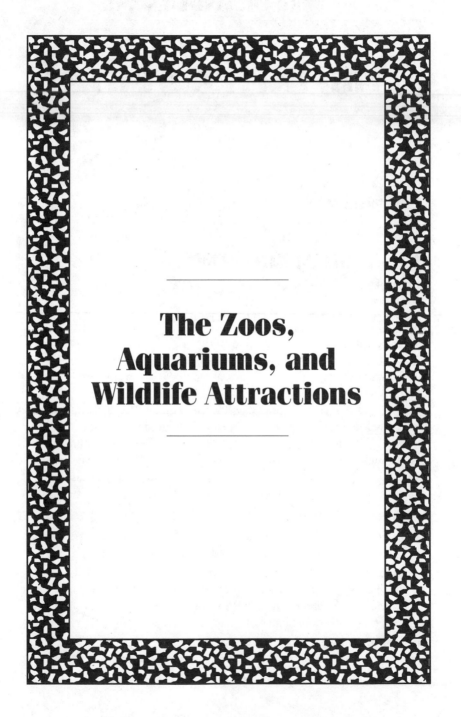

The Zoos, Aquariums, and Wildlife Attractions

THE UNITED STATES

Alabama

BIRMINGHAM ZOO

In Lane Park
2630 Cahaba Road
Birmingham, AL (205) 879–0408 (recording); (205) 879–0409

Established in 1955, this is the oldest zoo in the state of Alabama, and its hundred-acre site in Lane Park also makes it the largest. Shaded paths wind through the trees and landscaping, creating a peaceful respite from the hubbub of downtown Birmingham, a few miles to the north.

During late April and early May, the city is noted for its beautiful roses and dogwood trees, which are used extensively in the zoo's landscaping.

One of the highlights of a visit here is the train ride around the grounds and through the woods. Make sure you plan to eat lunch at the zoo's neat little sit-down restaurant, located in a converted railroad dining car.

Season: Year-round. Closed Thanksgiving and Christmas.

Hours: 9:30 A.M. to 5:00 P.M.

Admission: Adults, under $6; ages 2–17 and over 64, under $3; under age 2, free. Additional fee: train ride, under $3.

The animals: More than 750 animals representing more than 200 species are displayed in naturalistic outdoor habitats. Highlights include a rare white rhino, a Siberian tiger, and exhibits on red wolves, the rain forest, predators, and social animals.

Entertainment: No regularly scheduled entertainment, but the education department does conduct tours and demonstrations during special events.

Extras: Train ride around grounds; outdoor learning center, with children's zoo.

Special events: Zoobilee Day, at the end of September.

Food service: One sit-down restaurant in a converted railroad dining car; 2 fast-food concessions.

Plan to stay: 2 hours.

Directions: Take U.S. Route 280 to Mountain Brook Parkway exit. Zoo is at the end of the exit ramp, to the left.

Nearby attractions: Birmingham Botanical Gardens; Red Mountain Museum.

MONTGOMERY ZOO

329 Vandiver Boulevard
Montgomery, AL (205) 240-4900

As you enter the gates here, you'll be greeted by a family of elephants, but don't get out the peanuts, they're not real. These full-sized pachyderms are lifelike sculptures, and you won't be the first to do a double-take when you see them.

Before beginning your visit to the various exhibits, stop for a moment at the overlook area, just inside the entrance, and catch the panoramic view of the continental habitats that were opened in the fall of 1991.

Season: Year-round, closed Christmas and New Year's Day.

Hours: During daylight savings time: 9:30 A.M. to 5:00 P.M.; the remainder of the year: 9:30 A.M. to 4:30 P.M.

Admission: Adults, under $5; ages 4–12 and seniors, under $3; under age 4, free. Additional fee: train ride, under $2.

The animals: More than 800 animals representing more than 250 species. Animals are housed in both cages and naturalistic outdoor habitats separated from visitors by moats. Highlights include the North American, African, Asian, and Australian exhibits.

Entertainment: No regularly scheduled entertainment except during special events.

Extras: McMonty Express, a narrated, one-mile train tour of the continental exhibits. Playgrounds and athletic fields are located at the adjacent city community center.

Special events: Zoo Weekend, in late February or early March; Easter Egg Hunt, around Easter; Ballet and the Beasts, in June; Alabama Children's

Festival, in early June; Picnics at the Zoo, during warmer weather; Friday night concerts, in July; Zoo Boo, in late October; Christmas Nights at the Zoo, in December.

Food service: The full-service cafe in the center of the zoo has an outdoor dining area that overlooks the continental exhibit areas and serves fast-food meals, snacks, ice cream, and beverages. Small snack stands are located throughout the park. You may bring food into the park.

Plan to stay: 2 hours.

Directions: Located in the northern outskirts of the city. Take I–65 to the Northern Bypass (Route 152). Take the Bypass north to the Lower Wetumpka Road exit. Go south and follow signs to zoo entrance, about a mile on the left.

Nearby attractions: First White House of the Confederacy; W. A. Gayle Transit Planetarium; Ordeman-Shaw Complex, restored townhouses with guided tours; Jasmine Hill Gardens.

TOM MANN'S FISH WORLD AQUARIUM

Route 431
Eufaula, AL (205) 687–3655

When Tom Mann talks about fish, you listen. The legendary bass fisherman and lure inventor who now hosts *Tom Mann's Outdoor Show* on television, opened this aquarium complex to display the freshwater fish found in nearby Lake Eufaula.

Tim's Trivia

The North American Air Defense Command is hidden deep in the mountain below the Cheyenne Mountain Zoo in Colorado Springs, Colorado.

The main 38,000-gallon tank, which is just inside the front door, offers twelve underwater windows to view the large selection of fish. Ten additional 1,500-gallon aquariums display more fish as well as some turtles and baby alligators.

Additional displays include Indian relics of the area, the trophies Mann has won over the years, and an antique fishing lure collection.

Outside, a gazebo-topped tank allows you to feed the fish from the surface and then walk down and watch them through underwater windows as they eat. All sorts of fish are in the outside tank, including some catfish of up to fifty pounds.

The complex, which is adjacent to Tom Mann's Outdoors Pro-Shop and across the street from his farm, is open year-round. February through December, open 8:00 A.M. to 5:00 P.M. daily; January, open Fridays, Saturdays, and Sundays only, 9:00 A.M. to 4:00 P.M. Adult admission, under $3; grades 1–12 and senior citizens, $1. The pro-shop has a small restaurant, and when Mann is in town, he'll drop by to talk with guests and give casting demonstrations.

Located 4 miles north of downtown Eufaula on Highway 431, 20 miles north of Dothan, Alabama, in the southeast part of the state.

Alaska

ADMIRALTY ISLAND NATIONAL MONUMENT

Visitor Center, Centennial Hall
101 Egan Drive
Juneau, AK (907) 586–8751

Also known as the "Fortress of the Bears," the one-million-acre Admiralty Island preserve is a part of the sixteen-million-acre Tongass National Forest. With a population of one Alaskan brown bear per square mile, bears usually outnumber the people on the island.

Located south of Juneau, the island is a temperate rain forest and offers the highest density of brown bear population anywhere in the world. There's not a huge diversity of other animals out here due to the climate, but the animals that are native to the area are here in great numbers, including bald eagles, Sitka black-tailed deer, swans, beavers, river otters, and weasels.

Although most of the bears aren't used to humans, there's one area where up-close viewing is possible. The rest of the national forest also offers a great deal of animal watching potential throughout its acreage. A canoe portage trail connects nine freshwater lakes, which an abundance of waterfowl call home.

The best place to start a visit here is at the visitor's center in Juneau. The folks there will help you decide where to go in order to see what you're after. This isn't a place where you just go out and walk and hope to find something. Camping is permitted and there are a few rustic cabins on the freshwater lakes available for renting.

Access to the island is by boat and floatplane, reservations for which can be made at the visitor's center. Private boats are permitted to moor along the island, and a ferry runs from the small community of Angoon.

ALASKA ZOO

4731 O'Malley Road
Anchorage, AK (907) 346–2133

Officials here believe their facility is the northernmost zoo in the world. Specializing in indigenous animals, you'll find just about all species that survive in Alaska living here. From the glacier (blue) bear to the bearded musk-ox, the Alaskan wild is captured in naturalistic surroundings.

There are, however, two residents here who are a long way from home. Annabelle is an Asian elephant and Maggie is an African elephant. It's a treat to watch their trainer work with them. Currently one paints pictures, which are for sale in the gift shop, while the other is learning to play the harmonica and drums.

None of the residents of this zoo, which occupies twenty-five wooded hillside acres, was captured for display. They are rehabilitated, formerly injured animals and orphans raised from the wild. Facilities include a log-cabin admission and concession area, a sheltered picnic area, a gift shop, an education building, and the heated elephant house with indoor viewing.

Among other residents here are golden and bald eagles; horned and snowy owls; river otters; seals; brown, black, and polar bears; and hoofstock that includes reindeer, moose, and Sitka deer. It's also the only zoo in the world with an arctic marmot.

Open year-round; closed Thanksgiving, Christmas Day, and Tuesdays from October through April. Opens daily at 10:00 A.M., closing time varies with season and weather. Admission: adults, under $6; ages 13–18, under $4; ages 3–12, under $3; seniors, under $5; 2 and under, free.

Located about fifteen minutes from downtown, in South Anchorage. From the city, take New Seward Highway to O'Malley Road, turn left, and the zoo is on your left several blocks down.

CHILKAT BALD EAGLE PRESERVE

Haines Highway
Haines, AK (907) 766-2234

The tasty salmon in the Chilkat River are the main draw for the eagles here, and a lot of them obviously love this salmon. From mid-September through January, this is the largest gathering point for bald eagles in North America.

Groves of cottonwood trees growing next to the river are literally laden with the great winged creatures. As many as 4,000 may congregate here in any given season. The area is so unique that the Alaska legislature has designated it a "critical habitat area," which means that any activities incompatible with the eagle population or salmon rearing are prohibited.

And the best part is, it's not even necessary to leave your car or the highway to see the birds. The 49,000-acre preserve is located between mile 10 and mile 28 on Haines Highway. But, the grounds most favored by the eagles, where you'll probably see the largest concentration, are located 18 to 22 miles north of Haines, right beside the paved, all-weather highway, which parallels the river.

There are several pull-off areas along the highway, and for your own safety it is recommended that you use those and stay off the road. The preserve is an undeveloped site and there are no visitor facilities.

Haines is located north of Juneau in the southeast part of the state. To get there, take an air-taxi service from Juneau, or come via ferry on the Alaska Marine Highway.

KODIAK NATIONAL WILDLIFE REFUGE

1390 Buskin River Road
Kodiak Island
Kodiak, AK (907) 487-2600

Occupying two-thirds of Kodiak Island, this isolated wilderness in the Northern Gulf of Alaska is visited by people from all over the world for its beauty and its wildlife. Fishing, photography, and sightseeing are the dominant activities here.

The 1.8-million-acre refuge was established to preserve the natural habitat of the Kodiak bear, some of which grow to be 1,500 pounds. Rangers estimate that up to 3,000 of the creatures live on the refuge along with large populations of Sitka black-tailed deer, mountain goats, tundra voles, and red foxes. Along the rocky shores and in the bays, you'll spot seals, sea otters, sea lions, porpoises, and whales.

The visitor's center, in the town of Kodiak, is open daily year-round, until 4:30 P.M.; closed on holidays. There you'll see films and displays describing the refuge. You'll also get advice on transportation and camping, and other pertinent information for a trip into the wilderness.

Access to the island and to the refuge is by boat and floatplane only. Direct ferry access is from Seward and Homer, as part of the Alaska Marine Highway System.

Arizona

ARIZONA-SONORA DESERT MUSEUM

2021 North Kinney Road
Tucson, AZ (602) 883–1380

This is a case where instead of bringing the animals to the zoo, the zoo went to the animals.

Consistently rated among the ten best in the world, this zoo is located on 186 acres of desert, about fifteen minutes west of downtown Tucson. Actually it is much more than a zoo; it's an on-site natural-history museum that provides visitors with a unique view of desert life.

You can walk through a simulated limestone cave, a cactus garden, or a huge aviary—you'll find that there's a lot more to a desert than sand.

When you visit, try to come early in the day and make sure you wear comfortable shoes, cool clothing, and some protection from the sun. There are covered ramadas scattered along the miles of paths that snake through the various exhibit areas, as well as drinking fountains and beverage vending machines, to help you keep cool in the desert sun.

Season: Year-round, holidays too.

Hours: March through September, 7:30 A.M. to 6:00 P.M.; October through February, 8:30 A.M. to 5:00 P.M.

Admission: Adults, under $8; ages 6–12, under $3; under age 6, free.

▼▼▼▼▼▼▼▼▼▼▼▼▼▼▼▼▼▼▼▼▼▼▼▼▼▼▼▼▼▼▼▼▼▼▼▼▼▼

Fauna Fun Facts

A giraffe's tongue may grow to 18 inches long, allowing it to reach far into the trees for leaves to eat. The tongue is blue, perhaps to protect it from sunburn while gathering food.

The animals: More than 4,000 animals, more than 250 species, all native to Arizona and the adjacent Mexican states of Sonora and Baja California. Highlights include the underground Earth Sciences Cave and Exhibit; Riparian Habitat, with two-level viewing; Walk-In Aviary; Mountain Habitat; Hummingbird Exhibit.

Entertainment: No regularly scheduled entertainment, but docents conduct interpretive activities throughout the day at different exhibits.

Extras: Demonstration Garden, where you can learn how to create an attractive desert landscape at home; mineral exhibit in Earth History Gallery.

Special events: Desert Harvest Celebration, in the fall; Plant Sale, in the spring.

Food service: 1 indoor restaurant; snack bars scattered throughout the park.

Plan to stay: 3 hours.

Directions: I–19 to State Route 86 (Ajo Way). Go west on Route 86 to Kinney Road, about 5 miles. Turn right on Kinney and follow it about 10 miles to entrance, on the left.

Nearby attractions: Old Tucson, a former movie set that has been converted to an amusement park; Old West Wax Museum; Pima Air Museum, vintage aircraft.

GRAND CANYON DEER FARM

100 Deer Farm Road
Williams, AZ (800) 926–DEER

This is where the deer and the antelope *and* Marianne the Buffalo play. They live on ten acres, among goats, sheep, donkeys, a zebra, and the owners of the complex, the George family.

Through this large forest of ponderosa pines and aspen trees, you're allowed to wander among the animals who will more than happily eat out of your hand. "When you walk in there with a red cup of food in your hand, the deer will find you, no problem," said the owner. There are seven types of deer, and they number about 110 during most of the year.

You're liable to see a few deer births if you show up in June or July. Up to forty births take place here in a season, in the large pens, right in front of guests. It's a bit cooler here than the surrounding areas in mid-summer, so don't let the hot temperatures scare you off.

Located an hour's drive south from the Grand Canyon, off I–40. Take exit 171 (Deer Farm Road) and follow the service road and the signs. Open year-round, closing each day at dusk: spring and fall, open at 9:00 A.M.; June through August, 8:00 A.M.; November through February, 10:00 A.M. Closed Thanksgiving and Christmas Day.

Adults, under $5; ages 3–13, under $2.50; 2 and under, free.

PHOENIX ZOO

5810 East Van Buren Street
Phoenix, AZ (602) 273–1341

Opened in 1962 on the site of a former Arizona Game and Fish Department hatchery, this zoo has several lakes on its 125-acre property. All the lakes, the largest of which is 2 miles around, are connected to the canal system that runs through the city.

Each year nearly a million people visit the zoo, which consists of a grouping of low buildings set amid the lushness and greenery of Papago Park. Several migratory ducks also stop by on a regular basis to swim in the lakes and watch the visitors who fish there.

Season: Year-round, closed Christmas morning.

Hours: September through April, daily 9:00 A.M. to 5:00 P.M.; May through August, 7:00 A.M. to 4:00 P.M.

Admission: Adults, under $8; ages 4–12, under $5; under age 4, free. Children must be with an adult. Additional fee: Train tour, under $5 per person.

The animals: More than 1,300 animals, more than 300 species, in open habitat displays. Outstanding exhibits include the African Veldt, Arizona Exhibit, and a herd of rare Arabian oryx.

Extras: Children's petting zoo; playground; Safari Train tours.

Special events: Earth Day, in April; Boo at the Zoo, in October; Zoofari, in November; Zoobilee, in early December.

Food service: 5 snack bars are located throughout the zoo, offering a variety of fast-food sandwiches, snacks, and beverages.

Plan to stay: 2 hours.

Directions: I–10 to Papago Freeway, eastbound. Get off Papago at the 44th Street exit, at intersection go east on Van Buren. About a mile down the road, turn left onto Galvin Parkway, which leads to zoo entrance.

Nearby attractions: Hall of Flame Museum, history of fire fighting; Desert Botanical Garden; Castles N Coasters, amusement park; Metrocenter Mall, shopping and indoor midway rides.

REID PARK ZOO

22nd Street and Country Club Road
Tucson, AZ (602) 791–3204

An oasis in the desert. That's what all this greenery and lushness make you think of! This sixteen-acre zoo is located in Gene C. Reid Park, the largest park within the city of Tucson. Opened in 1967, the zoo also contains a rose garden and two lakes.

Season: Year-round, closed Christmas.

Hours: Mid-March through mid-September, weekdays 8:30 A.M. to 4:30 P.M., closing 1 hour later on weekends and holidays. Remainder of year, opens an hour later, daily.

Admission: Adults, under $4; ages 5–14, under $2; seniors, under $3; under age 5, free.

The animals: More than 800 animals, more than 100 species, displayed in naturalistic habitats. Outstanding exhibits include a giant anteater, Grévy's zebra, and a Big Cats area.

Entertainment: No regular daily shows, but there are special events scheduled on a monthly basis. The schedule is posted at the entrance.

Extras: In the park adjoining the zoo, there is a playground, tennis courts, a fishing lake, and Hi Corbett Field, where Triple-A baseball games are played.

Food service: 1 full-service snack bar, and 2 seasonal concessions offer a variety of fast foods, snacks, and beverages.

Plan to stay: 2 hours.

Directions: I–10 to 22nd Street exit. Go east on 22nd Street for 15 miles to Country Club Road. Park and zoo are on left side at the intersection.

Nearby attractions: Colossal Cave, underground cave; Old Tucson, former movie set, now an amusement park; Arizona-Sonora Desert Museum.

WILDLIFE WORLD ZOO

16501 West Northern Avenue
Litchfield Park, AZ (602) 935–WILD

There are several smaller exhibit areas included in this thirty-eight-acre facility, located in a western suburb of Phoenix. Among them are an aviary and small aquarium, allowing you to see a lot of animals in a short period of time, and with a minimum amount of walking.

Established in 1974 as a breeding farm for rare and endangered species, this zoo was opened to the public in 1984 and continues to supply animals to other zoos in the country.

Season: Year-round, holidays too.

Hours: Opens daily at 9:00 A.M. Closes: mid-June through mid-September, weekdays at 3:00 P.M., weekends at 5:00 P.M.; mid-September through mid-June, 5:00 P.M., daily.

Admission: Adults, under $7; ages 3–12, under $5; under age 3, free.

The animals: More than 1,200 animals, more than 300 species, displayed in outdoor enclosures and some natural habitats. Outstanding displays include Tropics of the World, Arizona's only exotic reptile exhibit; Waters of the World, with the state's first aquarium; walk-through aviary; and all five of the world's ostrich species.

Entertainment: Public feeding of the lory parrot, twice daily on weekdays, three times on weekends.

Extras: Children's petting zoo.

Food service: 2 snack bars offer a variety of fast food, snacks, and beverages.

Plan to stay: 2 hours.

Directions: I–10 West to Cotton Lane exit. After exiting, turn right on Northern Avenue. Zoo is about half a mile on the right.

Nearby attractions: Castles N Coasters, amusement park; Arizona Mineral Museum; Pioneer Arizona Living History Museum, a historic village; Phoenix Zoo.

Arkansas

ARKANSAS ALLIGATOR FARM

847 Whittington Avenue
Hot Springs, AR (501) 623–6172

Alligators, lots of them, are the star attractions, but they're definitely not the only animals you'll see. In addition to the four ponds full of gators, five species of primates call this place home—plus, there are mountain lions, an albino raccoon, turkeys, white German chickens, llamas, and ostriches, among others.

Some are in a contact area, where they can be petted. In the spring there are plenty of young fawns around that guarantee to bring thoughts of Bambi to mind.

Christmas Day is the only day the farm is closed. Hours: Memorial Day to Labor Day, 8:00 A.M. to 8:00 P.M.; rest of the year, 9:30 A.M. to 5:00 P.M.

To get there, take U.S. 70 or U.S. 270 to Highway 7. Travel 1 mile north on Highway 7 to Whittington Avenue. Make a left on Whittington (Majestic Lanai Towers Hotel is on the corner) and travel about 8 blocks. Entrance will be on the left.

EDUCATED ANIMAL ZOO

380 Whittington Avenue
Hot Springs, AR (501) 623–4311

As we all know, animals can be very intelligent as well as entertaining, and this zoo proves it by presenting one of the largest trained-animal stage shows in the country. Here you won't find animals in passive enclosed settings, they're usually on stage, demonstrating how clever they can be.

More than eight species of domestic and exotic animals and birds provide continuous entertainment for visitors. Vietnamese potbelly pigs who drive cars, basketball-playing raccoons, a goat fire chief, macaws doing headstands, and a variety of animals playing musical instruments are among the thirty different acts presented each day.

Continuous shows mean no waiting, which only adds to the enjoyment of a visit here. After the shows, you can pet and take pictures with some of the star performers.

Hours: Memorial Day through Labor Day, daily, 9:30 A.M. to 5:30 P.M.; March 1 to Memorial Day and between Labor Day and the end of November, Friday through Wednesday, 9:30 A.M. to 4:00 P.M. Between December 26 and 30, from 9:30 A.M. to 4:00 P.M., you can catch previews of the new shows for the coming year.

Admission: adults, under $3; ages 4–12, under $2; and ages 3 and under, free.

Directions: Located in the heart of the city, which is completely surrounded by the Hot Springs National Park, the zoo can be reached by taking U.S. 70 or U.S. 270 to Highway 7. Travel 1 mile north on Highway 7 to Whittington Avenue. Make a left on Whittington (Majestic Lanai Towers Hotel is on the corner), and travel 3½ blocks to zoo entrance on the right.

LITTLE ROCK ZOOLOGICAL GARDENS

1 Jonesboro Drive
Little Rock, AR (501) 666–2406

A pleasing blend of past and present, this zoo is owned and operated by the city of Little Rock. Although, like most zoos, it is moving toward having all its animals displayed in native outdoor habitats, a few are still housed in ornate stone buildings that were constructed during the 1930s as a WPA project, under President Franklin D. Roosevelt.

The facility occupies thirty-five rolling acres of War Memorial Park, in the heart of the state's capital city. Established in 1926 as Fair Park, it is the only accredited zoo in the state and draws nearly half a million visitors each year.

Season: Year-round. Closed Thanksgiving, Christmas, and New Year's Day.

Hours: During daylight saving time, hours are 9:30 A.M. to 5:00 P.M., daily. The rest of the year, closes at 4:30 P.M., daily.

Admission: Adults, under $5; ages 1–12, under $3; under age 1, free. Additional fee: Train ride, under $3 per person.

The animals: More than 600 animals, more than 200 species, most of which are in barless exhibits that provide naturalistic habitats. The more outstanding displays are the Great Ape Compound and the Big Cat display, where visitors can find jaguars and other large felines lounging around their own pool and waterfall.

Entertainment: Seasonally scheduled slide shows and animal demonstrations. Information is posted at the gate.

Extras: Train ride around the property gives visitors a scenic overview of the park's gently sloping terrain and large pond with waterfall. Children's zoo gives youngsters a chance to pet and feed small mammals, including baby bobcats and red deer.

Special events: Earth Day, in April; Zoo's Birthday, in June; Zoo Days, in late August.

Food service: Zoopermarket Restaurant overlooks duck pond and has indoor and outdoor seating. Additional concession stands are open daily in summer and on nice weekends the rest of the year. There is also a picnic area.

Plan to stay: 2 hours.

Directions: From I–30 take I–630 westbound to Fair Park exit. Exit ramp leads directly into park. Follow road around to parking area.

Nearby attractions: In other areas of the park, there are elephant rides, a small amusement park, and a golf course. Also, Ray Winter Field, home of the Arkansas Travelers (the St. Louis Cardinals' minor-league baseball team) is on the grounds.

California

CHAFFEE ZOOLOGICAL GARDENS OF FRESNO

In Roeding Park
894 West Belmont Avenue
Fresno, CA (209) 488–1549

When you walk through the thatched-hut entrance of this zoo, you enter eighteen of the most scenic acres the city of Fresno has to offer. Set in Roeding Park, this facility offers something for everyone. All the animals, except for certain birds, are permanently exhibited in outdoor habitats.

It's also a favorite spot for children's birthday parties.

Season: Year-round, holidays too.

Hours: April through September, 10:00 A.M. to 6:30 P.M., daily; Remainder of year, 10:00 A.M. to 5:00 P.M.

Admission: Adults, under $5; ages 4–14, under $3; over age 62, under $4; under age 4 and handicapped, free. Additional fees: parking in Roeding Park, under $2 per car, March through October only.

The animals: More than 650 animals, more than 200 species, in naturalistic outdoor settings. Outstanding exhibits include walk-through outdoor rain forest; Asian elephant area; Reptile House, with computer-controlled light and temperature; and small Australian animal exhibit.

Entertainment: Unscheduled demonstrations by keepers; prearranged guided tours.

Extras: In an adjoining section of Roeding Park, there is a small amusement park with kiddie rides, a museum, and a lake where several types of boats can be rented.

Special events: Safari Night, next-to-last Saturday in June; Singles Night, in July.

Food service: 1 concession sells fast food, snacks, and beverages. Picnics are permitted.

Plan to stay: 2 hours.

Directions: U.S. 99 to either Olive Avenue or Belmont Avenue exit to Roeding Park; zoo is about 200 feet from either highway exit.

Nearby attractions: Playland and Storyland amusement areas in Roeding Park; Kearney Mansion Museum; Golden Eagle Air Tours; Sequoia National Forest.

FOLSOM CITY PARK ZOO

Natoma and Stafford streets
Folsom, CA (916) 355–7200

Most of the approximately fifty animals displayed in this small city-park zoo are native to North America and are either physically handicapped or are pets that were discarded by their human families.

Histories of the raccoon, bear, fox, mountain lion, and other animals are displayed to teach children about the care of animals, both in the wild and at home. The park also contains a playground and picnic area.

Open Tuesday through Sunday, year-round, including holidays. Admission is under $2.50 for adults, under $2 for ages 5–12. Children under 5, free.

Take U.S. Route 50 to the Folsom Boulevard exit. Turn left on Folsom, and at the fourth traffic light go right on Natoma Street. After you pass two traffic lights, the first stop sign will be at Stafford Street. The park will be on the right side, immediately behind the City Hall complex.

HAPPY HOLLOW PARK AND ZOO

In Kelley Park
1300 Senter Road
San Jose, CA (408) 295–8383

Talk about cozy! With more than 200 animals exhibited on less than four acres, this is one intimate place, which is wonderful because there's so much to see and you don't have to walk much to see it. Located in Kelley Park, in downtown San Jose, this place has everything from guinea pigs to bears.

As an added bonus, there's a small kiddie park adjacent to the zoo with rides, a treehouse, and a riverboat replica. To get to either area, you walk across a drawbridge and through a small castle.

Season: Year-round, holidays too.

Hours: 10:00 A.M. to 5:00 P.M., daily. Last admission at 4:00 P.M.

Admission: Adults, under $4; ages 2–14 and seniors, under $3; under age 2, free. Admission ticket covers both zoo and amusement park. Additional fees: City park entrance fee, under $3 per car. There is also a charge for each of the amusement park rides.

The animals: 200 animals, 65 species, displayed in outdoor exhibits. The most popular include American black bears, a llama, exotic birds, sea lions, and a pygmy hippo.

Entertainment: No animal shows or demonstrations in the zoo, but there is a puppet show in the amusement area.

Extras: Petting zoo. In other areas of the park are the Japanese Friend-

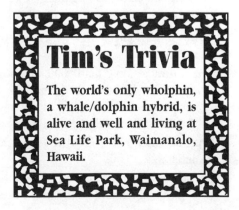

Tim's Trivia

The world's only wholphin, a whale/dolphin hybrid, is alive and well and living at Sea Life Park, Waimanalo, Hawaii.

ship Garden and Teahouse, and the San Jose Historical Museum.

Special events: Events are scheduled annually around Easter and Christmas.

Food service: No food concessions in the zoo, but picnics are permitted. Snack items can be purchased in the amusement area.

Plan to stay: 1 hour.

Directions: I–280 to exit for 10th Street and 11th Street. Go right on 10th Street (one-way) to Keyes Street. Follow Keyes to Senter Street, and the zoo is right there.

Nearby attractions: Raging Waters, water theme park; Winchester Mystery House, with guided tours through the 160-room mansion; Rosicrucian Egyptian Museum.

THE LIVING DESERT

47-900 Portola Avenue
Palm Desert, CA (619) 346–5694

Aptly named, this zoo is located on the outskirts of the Mojave Desert, in the Coachella Valley at the base of the Santa Rose Mountains. Dedicated to the interpretation of deserts of the world, this is a one-of-a-kind wildlife and botanical park occupying about 200 acres of a 1,200-acre permanent national preservation area.

There are shady areas within the park, but it's hot here. So hot, in fact, that it is closed during the summer months when temperatures regularly reach one hundred degrees or better. Dress coolly and don't forget your sunblock.

Season: September through mid-June. Closed during the summer.

Hours: 9:00 A.M. to 5:00 P.M., daily. Last admission at 4:30 P.M.

Admission: Adults, under $8; ages 3–15, under $5; seniors, under $6; under age 3, free.

The animals: More than 800 animals, more than 120 species, all native to desert areas of the world, and all in natural outdoor habitats that are interspersed with botanical planting areas. Scheduled to open in 1993 is Eagle Canyon, with a central aviary and a running stream.

Entertainment: Daily guided tours, and interpretive talks at the various exhibit areas.

Extras: Discovery Room, an interpretive center for the whole family; outdoor three-dimensional Native American exhibits; hiking trails.

Special events: Native American events, in February; plant sales, in the spring; Earth Day, in June; and monthly "pizza concerts" in the evening, year-round.

Food service: No food concessions, but picnics are permitted. A cafeteria may be added to the Eagle Canyon exhibit in the future.

Plan to stay: 2 hours.

Directions: I–10 to Monterey Avenue exit. Go south on Monterey to State Route 111. Turn left on Route 111 and travel for 1 mile to Portola Avenue. Turn right on Portola and entrance is 1½ miles on left.

Nearby attractions: In Palm Springs: Palm Spring Desert Classic Golf Tournament, in mid-January; Dinah Shore–Colgate Winners Circle Invitational Golf Tournament, in early April; Oasis Waterpark; Palm Springs Aerial Tramway, goes up and over the San Jacinto Mountains; Moorten Botanical Garden; Palm Canyon, on the Agua Caliente Indian Reservation, has 2,000-year-old palm trees and spectacular views of the canyon.

LOS ANGELES ZOO

In Griffith Park
5333 Zoo Drive
Los Angeles, CA (213) 666–4650 (recording); (213) 666–4090

Once you enter the gates here, you'll quickly leave the hustle and bustle of downtown L.A. behind. Located in 4,107-acre Griffith Park, in the foothills of the Santa Monica Mountains, the carefully landscaped hills of the zoo provide a natural oasis in the middle of the city. Animals from five continents roam freely in natural habitats.

Season: Year-round, closed Christmas.

Hours: Memorial Day through Labor Day, 10:00 A.M. to 6:00 P.M. daily. Remainder of the year, closes an hour earlier.

Admission: Adults, under $8, ages 2–12, under $5; seniors, under $7; under age 2, free.

The animals: More than 2,000 animals, more than 500 species, displayed in outdoor habitats corresponding to the five major continents. Highlights include Ahmanson Koala House, with five species of koala; Reptile House; aquatic exhibit.

Entertainment: World of Birds, Wild in the City, several times daily in Wildlife Theater.

┌───┐

Fauna Fun Facts

Each hair of a polar bear is hollow. The air in the middle of each hair
helps insulate the bear from the cold.

└───┘

Extras: Animal and horticultural tours; Adventure Island, a children's area,
with animals native to the southwestern United States, a petting zoo and
animal nursery.

Special events: Rhino Walk, in May; summer concerts; Zoo and Aquarium
Month activities, in June.

Food service: Several snack stands are located on zoo grounds, offering a
variety of fast foods, snacks, and beverages. There are also picnic areas.

Plan to stay: 3 hours.

Directions: Griffith Park is located in the southwest corner of the junction
of the Ventura Freeway (U.S. 101) and the Golden State Freeway (I–5).
On I–5, the first exit south of the junction, Colorado Boulevard, leads
right to park and zoo. Follow the signs.

Nearby attractions: In other areas of Griffith Park are pony rides, miniature
stagecoach and a one-third scale model steam engine, guided nature
hikes, Griffith Observatory and Planetarium, and the Los Angeles Eques-
trian Center, which rents horses. Nearby are the NBC studio tour and Universal Studios Hollywood; LaBrea Tar Pits; Hollywood; and Beverly Hills.

MARINE WORLD/AFRICA USA

Marine World Parkway
Vallejo, CA (707) 644–4000

Whatever type of animal you like, you'll probably find it here. More than a
wildlife park, more than an aquarium, and more than a marine park, this
place is a combination of all three, making it unique among animal attractions in the world.

All sorts of animals are showcased here, from killer whales to endangered tigers to butterflies. Add to this variety the shows, educational ex-

hibits, playful activities, and special events, and you've found yourself in animal heaven!

Season: Year-round. Open daily in the summer, Wednesday through Sundays the rest of the year. Closed Thanksgiving and Christmas Day.

Hours: 9:30 A.M. to 6:30 P.M. in summer, closes at 5:00 P.M. the rest of the year.

Admission: Adults, under $23; ages 4–12, under $17; ages 3 and under, free. Additional fees: animal rides, parking.

The animals: More than 325 species, more than 2,500 animals. Exhibits include: Aquarium, housing 180 species and 1,715 specimens of fish; Seal Cove; Flamingo Falls; Whale and Dolphins; Tiger Island; Butterfly World, walk-through exhibit; Lorikeet Aviary, walk-through exotic bird exhibit where you can feed the birds; Shark Experience, where visitors enter the 300,000 gallon habitat on a moving walkway through a clear acrylic tunnel.

Entertainment: 7 major animal shows daily, featuring tigers, elephants, killer whales, dolphins, sea lions, chimpanzees, and exotic birds; water ski and boat show; Elephant Encounter, watch and participate in elephant training.

Extras: Gentle Jungle children's area features a small petting zoo, a prairie crawl where children can crawl through tunnels and pop up in the middle of a prairie dog town, and a reptile discovery area where kids get to meet and learn about reptiles; Backyard Habitat, a display garden showing how you can plant your backyard to attract wildlife; animal nursery; and the giraffe dock, where guests are allowed to feed giraffes from a tall, eye-level platform.

Special events: Spring Break Celebration, new shows premiere first week of April; Water Ski Championships, first week of June; July Fourth fireworks, hours extended in park; Safeway Snow World, last week in December, when 600 tons of artificial snow are provided for sledding, snow play, and ski lessons.

Food service: The Lakeside Market is a food court featuring eateries that sell everything from fried chicken, deli sandwiches, and corn dogs—to beer and margaritas. Other restaurants include: The Broiler, hamburgers, fries, and milk shakes; Captain Mobe's Sea Food; Pizza Safari; and Clocktower Cafe, serving soups and salads. Additional food kiosks throughout the park.

Plan to stay: 6 hours.

Directions: Located 30 miles northeast of San Francisco. Off I–80, take the Marine World Parkway (Highway 37) exit. Or take Highway 37 East off Highway 101, to Marine World Parkway.

Nearby attractions: Napa Valley vineyards; shopping, dining, and attractions in San Francisco.

MICKE GROVE ZOO

In Micke Grove Regional Park
11793 North Micke Grove Road
Lodi, CA (209) 331–7270

One of the last remaining stands of oak trees in San Joaquin County is the setting for this zoo, which is located in the heart of one of the state's important wine-producing centers.

Only five acres in size, the zoo is part of the 600-acre Micke Grove Regional Park that was deeded to the county by William G. Micke, who once farmed the property. It's a comfortable flat and shady walk on a paved path to the indoor and outdoor animal exhibits.

Season: Year-round, closed Christmas Day.

Hours: 10:00 A.M. to 4:45 P.M., daily.

Admission: Adults, under $2; ages 13–19 and seniors, under $1.50; ages 6–12 under $1; under age 6, free. Additional fees: vehicle entry fee of $2 per car on weekdays; $3 per car on weekends and holidays.

The animals: More than 250 animals, more than 90 species, including lots of birds. Outstanding exhibits include Island Lost in Time, which features some of the only black-and-white-ruffed Madagascar lemurs in captivity; and the Indoor Tropical Forest, which includes squirrels and endangered golden lion tamarins.

Entertainment: On weekends, from Memorial Day to Labor Day, there are animal shows in Wildlife Theater. Shows are on a rotating basis, featuring such animal groups as Magnificent Mammals, Reptile Rendezvous, and Birds of a Feather.

Extras: Docents lead tours by reservation. In other areas of the park you will find Japanese gardens; Funderwoods, a small amusement park; a swimming pool; and the California Central Agricultural Museum.

Special events: Bunny Run, at Easter; Scout Day, in March; Conservation Fair, in early October; Christmas at the Zoo, in December.

Food service: 1 snack bar is located within the zoo, and picnics are permitted.

Plan to stay: 1 hour.

Directions: Located about a half-hour south of Sacramento. Take Highway 99 (South Sacramento Freeway) to the Armstrong Road exit. Go west on Armstrong for a half-mile to Micke Grove Road. Go south on Micke Grove Road for 1 mile. Park entrance will be on west side.

Nearby attractions: Oak Ridge Vineyards, with guided tours and tastings. In Stockton, Pixie Woods wonderland, located in Louis Park, is a children's playland featuring amusement rides, animal petting area, theater programs, and nursery-rhyme characters.

MONTEREY BAY AQUARIUM

886 Cannery Row
Monterey, CA (408) 648–4888

Here's your chance to get a nice, clear, up-close view of the creatures that live underwater in Monterey Bay. And quite a varied group of creatures it is! The bay ranks among the world's most diverse marine regions. From late winter through early fall, currents carry an upwelling of cold, nutrient-rich water into the bay.

This influx of nutrients is the basis of a food chain that supports the sea life found in habitats that range from mudflats and kelp forests to a 10,000-foot-deep submarine canyon, all of which are re-created in exhibits at the aquarium.

In all, there are more than a hundred galleries, with exhibits to please just about everyone in the family.

Season: Year-round, closed Christmas Day.

Hours: 10:00 A.M. to 6:00 P.M., daily.

Admission: Adults, under $11; ages 3–12, under $5; under 3, free; students and seniors, under $8.

The animals: More than 525 species, more than 6,500 animals, including fish, invertebrates, mammals, birds, and plants found in and around Monterey Bay. Top exhibits include: Kelp Forest, a 3-story, 335,000-gallon display of giant kelp in which sardines, leopard sharks, and others live; Monterey Bay Habitats, a 326,000-gallon tank comprising 4 major habitats; Sea Otters; and The Great Tide Pool.

Entertainment: On the outside deck overlooking the Great Tide Pool, aquarium officials give "deck talks" on various topics. Sea otter feedings take place three times daily; and divers can be seen hand-feeding fish in the Kelp Forest twice daily. A 15-minute video about research deep in the bay runs continuously.

Extras: The facility rests on the location of one of the largest canneries on the row. It was also the last to close, in 1972. The Boiler House displays the restored boilers from the old Hovden Cannery and details the entire canning process. Cannery Row artifacts and a film recall the history of the street built by sardines and made famous by John Steinbeck.

Special events: Short-term special events are booked throughout the year.

Food service: The Portola Cafe offers 2 dining options: a sit-down, full-service section, and a cafeteria section.

Plan to stay: 4 hours.

Directions: Located 100 miles south of San Francisco, along historic Cannery Row in Monterey.

Nearby attractions: Pebble Beach golf course; sightseeing, shopping, and dining along Cannery Row and in nearby Carmel.

OAKLAND ZOO

In Knowland Park
9777 Golf Links Road
Oakland, CA (415) 632–9525

Nestled into the 525 hilly acres that make up Knowland Park, in the southeastern quadrant of Oakland, the zoo offers a taste of the wild for all members of the family. A trip on the Sky Ride gives you a panoramic view not only of the zoo, but also of the surrounding hills and nearby San Francisco Bay.

Upon entering the zoo, you'll be impressed first by the flamingo exhibit, complete with its own waterfalls. From there you can either get on one of the rides or walk the dogleg-shaped path through the animal exhibits.

Ongoing work in a twenty-year master plan is responsible for the transformation that is presently under way at this facility. Old display cages have been torn down and replaced with naturalistic habitats, where the animals can feel more at home.

Season: Year-round, closed Thanksgiving and Christmas Day.

Hours: 10:00 A.M. to 4:00 P.M. Hours are extended during summer weekends and holidays.

Admission: Adults, under $6; ages 2–14, under $4; seniors, under $3; under age 3, free. Additional fees: parking, under $4 per car, except on the first Monday of each month (holidays excluded), when parking is free; sky ride, under $2; train, under $2; carousel and other kiddie rides, under $2.

The animals: More than 330 animals, 80 species, exhibited in both indoor and outdoor settings. Highlights include North American Range; Australian Outback, Gibbon Island; African Lion Exhibit; and African Elephant Exhibit. Plans call for grouping animals into three natural settings: African savanna, rain forest, and pre–Gold Rush California.

Entertainment: No regularly scheduled entertainment, but prearranged tours are available, as are talks by docents at some of the exhibits.

Extras: Sky Ride, a 15-minute chairlift ride over the North American Range area; Streamliner, turn-of-the-century miniature train ride; Carousel and other kiddie rides; children's zoo; and education center.

Food service: There are 2 food concessions on the property, selling fast foods, beverages, ice cream, and snacks. Picnic facilities are also available.

Plan to stay: 2 hours.

Directions: I–580 to the Golf Links Road/98th Avenue exit. Go east on Golf Links Road directly to park and zoo entrance.

Nearby attractions: J. R. Knowland State Arboretum, also in Knowland Park; Oakland-Alameda County Coliseum Complex, home of the Oakland A's and Oakland Warriors; Bret Harte Boardwalk, a community of restored Victorian homes, including the author's boyhood home; Jack London Square, waterfront area that includes the author's favorite tavern; Mormon Temple, with guided tours of the gardens and worship houses, and a genealogical library that is open to the public.

SACRAMENTO ZOO

In William Land Park
3930 West Land Park Drive
Sacramento, CA (916) 449–5885 (recording); (916) 449–5166

Lots of trees, gardens, and green lawns add to the lush atmosphere here. Visitors can stroll through an indoor tropical rain forest and snake-shaped reptile house, or just sit and enjoy the scenery in this residential suburb of California's capital city.

Situated on land that was occupied by a Union Army training ground during the Civil War, this is a nice little zoo contained within the 230-acre city-owned William Land Park.

Season: Year-round, closed Christmas Day.

Hours: 9:00 A.M. to 4:00 P.M., daily.

Admission: Adults, under $5; ages 3–12, under $3; under age 3, free. Combination tickets to the zoo and Fairy Tale Town are available. On weekends and holidays, admission fees to both attractions are slightly higher.

The animals: More than 500 animals, more than 100 species, displayed in indoor and outdoor habitats. Highlights include Sumatran orangutans, chimpanzees (which are part of a species survival program), and a rain forest with three species of rare South American cats.

Entertainment: In the spring and summer, docents conduct live animal demonstrations, as well as conservation and recycling programs. Animals used in presentations are those which have been injured and cannot return to the wild. Throughout the year, docents are also located throughout the park in Wildlife Wagons, where they lead hands-on demonstrations featuring feathers, eggshells, bones, and other items.

Extras: In other areas of the park are Fairy Tale Town and Funderland, with a carousel and other rides, a playground, and puppet shows. There are also athletic fields, a 9-hole golf course, and fitness trail.

Food service: 1 fast-food snack bar in the zoo. Picnics are permitted.

Plan to stay: 2 hours.

Directions: I–5 to the Sutterville Road exit. Travel east on Sutterville for a quarter-mile to zoo entrance on left.

Nearby attractions: Waterworld USA, water park; Towe Ford Museum, displaying every year and model Ford from 1903 to 1952; Sutter's Fort, containing relics of Gold Rush days; M/V *Matthew McKinley,* an 80-foot paddleboat that conducts tour cruises on the Sacramento River; California State Railroad Museum.

SAN DIEGO WILD ANIMAL PARK

15500 San Pasqual Valley Road
Escondido, CA (619) 747–8702

Africa is alive and well at the San Diego Wild Animal Park. Opened in 1972, this 2,100-acre facility offers plenty of room for all creatures—animal and human, great and small. Nearly everything in the park is geared to an African theme, with some Asian and Australian atmosphere thrown in to balance things out.

Whether you walk or take the Wgasa Bush Line monorail, you can visit such exotic places as Kupanda Falls, Nairobi Village, and the Kilimanjaro Trail.

Recognized worldwide for its animal preservation efforts, the San Diego Wild Animal Park is affiliated with the well-known San Diego Zoo, and was planned by that zoo's former director, Dr. Charles Schroeder, to be "the zoo of the future, where wildlife runs free and people are enclosed in a quiet monorail."

Season: Year-round, holidays too.

Hours: Mid-June through Labor Day, 9:00 A.M. to 6:00 P.M. Remainder of year, 9:00 A.M. to 4:00 P.M.

Admission: Adults, under $20; ages 3–15, under $12; seniors, under $18; under age 3, free. Additional fee: parking, $1 per car.

The animals: More than 2,500 animals, more than 400 species, most of which roam free in natural outdoor habitats. Some of the expansive exhibits are home to herds of zebras, giraffes, tigers, and rhinos, while smaller display areas house small mammal exhibits and aviaries.

Entertainment: Rare and Wild America Show, features unusual animals; Critter Encounters, bird shows, elephant demonstrations.

Extras: The Wgasa Bush Line monorail provides visitors with a 50-minute guided tour of the plains and savanna regions of the park; The Petting Kraal (African for "corral"); a children's zoo; 2-mile Kilimanjaro hiking trail..

Tim's Trivia

Two of the United States' largest butterfly atriums were made possible by two well-known (and rich) people. The Day Butterfly Center at Callaway Gardens in Pine Mountain, GA, was built in honor of the late Cecil B. Day, Jr., founder of the Days Inn motel chain. Country superstar Dolly Parton has a colorful atrium at her Dollywood theme park in Pigeon Forge, Tennessee.

Food service: Several fast-food restaurants, serving a variety of cuisine, including Mexican food. Picnics are permitted.

Plan to stay: 3 hours.

Directions: Located approximately 30 miles north of San Diego. Take I–15 to State Route 78 (Via Rancho Parkway). Go east on Route 78 for approximately 6 miles. Park entrance is on the left.

Nearby attractions: Mount Palomar Observatory; Camp Pendleton Army Museum; several Indian reservations in surrounding area.

SAN DIEGO ZOO

Zoo Place and Park Boulevard
San Diego, CA (619) 234–3153; (619) 231–1515

Consistently rated among the top zoos in the world, this is 125 acres of pure animal delight. The zoo is constructed on two levels—"mesas" and "canyons," connected by moving sidewalks—and is a must-see for the entire family. This tropical garden setting is home to many rare and exotic species of wildlife. In addition to cuddly Australian koalas, wild Przewalski's horses from Mongolia, rare Sichuan takins from China, and long-billed New Zealand kiwis, you will also see one of the largest collections of parrots and parrotlike birds ever assembled in one location.

The San Diego Zoo began with a scattering of specimens left in Balboa Park at the close of the 1915–16 Panama–California International Exposition and was chartered as a zoological park in 1922.

Season: Year-round, holidays too.

Hours: 9:00 A.M. to 5:00 P.M., daily. Last admission at 4:00 P.M.

Admission: Adults, under $12; ages 3–15, under $6; under age 3 and military in uniform, free. Additional fees: bus tour of grounds: adults, under $5; children, under $3. Or combination ticket, including admission and bus tour: adults, under $16; children, under $8.

The animals: More than 3,800 animals, more than 800 species, arranged in a sprawling array of indoor and outdoor naturalistic habitats. Other outstanding exhibits include the Tiger River Tropical Rain Forest, complete with a moving sidewalk and computer-controlled fogging system to provide a natural home for crocodiles, Chinese war dragons, tapirs, pythons, tarsiers, and several marsh-loving bird species; and Sun Bear Forest, with trickling brooks, cascading waterfalls, rocks, and lush foliage, provides a first-class home for Malayan sun bears, lion-tailed macaques, and many other tropical animal and plant species.

Entertainment: Channel Islands Sea Lion Show, 3 times daily; Animals in Action, 2 shows daily; and Animal Chit-Chat Show, twice daily.

Extras: Guided bus tours take visitors for a 40-minute tour of the zoo in double-decker buses; Skyfari Aerial Tram provides an overhead view of the southern portion of the park; children's zoo lets youngsters meet young animals face-to-face.

Food service: There are numerous places to eat here, including the Peacock and Raven, an indoor restaurant; the outdoor Lagoon Terrace just next door; Canyon Cafe, which specializes in Mexican food; five fast-food snack bars; and several vending carts.

Plan to stay: All day to see and do everything.

Directions: I–5 to Park Boulevard exit. Go north on Park, straight to zoo entrance.

Nearby attractions: Balboa Park museum complex, including aerospace, photographic arts, natural history, model railroad, and sports museums; Sea World of California; Maritime Museum of San Diego; Seaport Village; and Old Town San Diego Historical Park, the site of the city's first settlement.

SAN FRANCISCO ZOOLOGICAL GARDENS

1 Zoo Road
(at Sloat Boulevard and 45th Avenue)
San Francisco, CA (415) 753–7080

Zip around on the Zebra Zephyr, buzz on over to the Insect Zoo, marvel at Musk-Ox Meadow, or congregate at Koala Crossing. There's plenty to see here on the sixty-five acres that make up the San Francisco Zoo, and make sure you wear a comfortable pair of shoes!

Established in 1928, the zoo is still growing, with only about one-third of the master plan complete. Vintage Depression-era buildings alternate with modern indoor and outdoor animal habitats, but one of the first things you'll notice when entering the main gate is an old wooden carousel.

Built in 1921 by William H. Dentzel, the carousel came to the zoo in 1925 from the defunct Pacific City Amusement Park and was restored in 1978.

Another eye-catcher is the Mothers Building, which dates back to 1925. Brothers Herbert and Mortimer Fleishhacker, who were involved with creating the zoo, commissioned the Renaissance-style building in honor of their mother, Delia. It was originally designed as a place where mothers could relax and care for their children. This National Historic Landmark, now occupied by the Zoo Shop, is slated for restoration as a museum. The outside of the building contains mosaics that were done by the Bruton sisters as a WPA project during the 1930s.

Season: Year-round, holidays too.

Hours: 10:00 A.M. to 5:00 P.M., daily.

Admission: Adults, under $8; ages 12–15, under $5; under age 12 and over 64, free. Additional fees: children's zoo, under $2; Zephyr train, under $3; carousel, under $2. There is no parking lot on the zoo property, but there is ample public parking on the surrounding streets, where you'll find innovative parking meters with hummingbirds instead of the familiar red violation flags. Funds collected from the meters will be used for the future purchase of a Central American rain forest-habitat for the zoo.

The animals: More than 6,800 animals, more than 350 species, in indoor and outdoor natural habitats. Highlights include Koala Crossing, an Australian outback exhibit, one of only five in the country to display koalas; Penguin Island, the largest captive penguin breeding colony in the world; the Lion House, home of Prince Charles, a rare white tiger; Musk-Ox Meadow, where the first zoo births for white-fronted musk-oxen took place in 1986; and an Insect Zoo, one of only four "insectariums" in the United States.

Entertainment: From June 1 through Labor Day there is a variety of shows and demonstrations, including a daily livestock stampede and animal brunch in the Barnyard; a Nature Trail petting zoo, twice a day, Tuesday through Sunday; a one-hour parrot program each day in the Nature Theater; a hands-on livestock demonstration each day in the Barnyard; Wildlife Theater presentations featuring birds, amphibians, and small mammals, twice a day, Tuesday through Sunday; and a daily encounter, called Incredible Insects in Action, at the Insect Zoo.

Extras: Zebra Zephyr safari train, a 30-minute guided tour of the zoo, daily in summer, spring, and fall, weekends in the winter; free docent-guided walking tour of the zoo leaves from Koala Crossing every Saturday and Sunday at 1:00 P.M.; Antique Carousel rides; and unscheduled informal talks at exhibits around the zoo. Look for the docents' bright green and yellow "Ask Me" buttons.

Special events: Zoo Run, in January; What's Bugging You Day, in May, features close encounters with tarantulas and rare insects, and an edible insect tasting; Holiday Magic/Christmas at the Zoo, where animals open their gifts and artificial snow covers the playfield.

Food service: 4 cafes and 3 smaller concessions offer a wide variety of fast foods, beverages, and snacks, from chimichangas to gyros to fish and chips, popcorn and lollipops. The Polish sausage at the Plaza Cafe is quite popular, as are the specially topped baked potatoes.

Plan to stay: All day if you want to see and do everything.

Directions: Located in the southwest corner of the city, the zoo can be reached from I–280. Get off at the Ocean Avenue (west) exit. Turn right onto Junipero Serra Boulevard and continue to Sloat Boulevard. Turn left at Sloat and keep going west to 45th Street. Zoo entrance is on the left.

Nearby attractions: Golden Gate Park, contains a Japanese Tea Garden, Asian Art Museum, Conservatory of Flowers, California Academy of Sciences Natural History Museum, aquarium and planetarium, buffalo paddock and boat rentals; San Francisco Fire Department Museum; Golden Gate Bridge; Chinatown; Fisherman's Wharf; Cable Car Barn Museum; and the American Carousel Museum.

SANTA ANA ZOO

In Prentice Park
1801 East Chestnut Avenue
Santa Ana, CA (714) 836–4000

Built on an old orange grove that was donated to the city in 1952 by J. E. Prentice, the zoo is located in the middle of metropolitan Orange County and is centered around a pond with a small waterfall. Most animals are currently housed in individual exhibits set amid plantings of exotic trees and shrubs. In 1992 the zoo opened its first major exhibit, Amazon's Edge, which combines several species in a naturalistic setting.

Season: Year-round, closed Christmas and New Year's Day.

Hours: 10:00 A.M. to 6:00 P.M., Memorial Day through Labor Day. Closes 1 hour earlier the remainder of the year, and the last ticket is always sold 1 hour before closing.

Admission: Adults, under $3; ages 3–12 and seniors, under $1.50; under age 3 and handicapped, free. Additional fee: elephant ride, under $3.

The animals: More than 300 animals, more than 90 species, displayed in individual outdoor habitats. Highlights include Amazon's Edge, which features the zoo's extensive primate collection and several aviaries.

Entertainment: No tours or scheduled entertainments, but the zoo has plans to add a show or two.

Extras: Elephant rides; playground; children's zoo in a domestic barnyard setting.

Special events: Zoo Birthday, in March; Cookie Safari, end of September; Halloween Festival, in October; Christmas event in December.

Food service: There is 1 food concession on the grounds, which offers a variety of fast-food meals, snacks, sweets, and beverages. Picnics are not permitted in the zoo itself, but there are picnic areas in the adjoining park.

Plan to stay: 2 hours.

Directions: Due to extensive reconstruction of the interchange at I–5 and State Route 55, there will be intermittent road and ramp closings through the mid-1990s. The zoo is located off I–5 at 1st Street, but it would be best to call for the easiest way to get there when you plan to visit.

Nearby attractions: Goodwill Industries rehabilitation center and workshop offers free tours of their facility. Disneyland is in nearby Anaheim, as is the Hobby City Doll and Toy Museum, where more then 3,000 dolls and toys are housed in a half-scale model of the White House.

SANTA BARBARA ZOOLOGICAL GARDENS

500 Ninos Drive
Santa Barbara, CA (805) 962–5339

Only a few zoos offer breathtaking views of the Pacific Ocean, and this one offers one of the best. This privately operated zoo opened in 1963 and offers visitors a peaceful escape from everyday life.

Located on a hillside, the large facility is still being developed, but you'll find acres of manicured lawns for spreading out a picnic or just enjoying the wonderful climate. A trip here wouldn't be complete, though, without a ride around the property on the miniature railroad.

Season: Year-round, closed Thanksgiving and Christmas Day.

▼▼▼▼▼▼▼▼▼▼▼▼▼▼▼▼▼▼▼▼▼▼▼▼▼▼▼▼▼▼▼▼▼▼▼▼▼

Fauna Fun Facts

The cheetah is the fastest mammal on earth. It can attain a velocity of 70 mph very quickly and can maintain that speed for about 300 yards.

Hours: 9:00 A.M. to 6:00 P.M., from mid-June to Labor Day. Remainder of the year, 10:00 A.M. to 5:00 P.M.

Admission: Adults, under $6; ages 2–12 and seniors, under $4; under age 2, free. Additional fees: train ride: adults, under $2; children, under $1.50. Carousel (children only), under $1.50.

The animals: More than 500 animals, more than 150 species, mostly birds. Animals are displayed in both indoor and outdoor naturalistic habitats. Highlights include an African veldt with free-roaming Baringo giraffes; and a three-part walk-through exhibit that includes Tropical Aviary, Aquarium, and Nocturnal Hall.

Entertainment: At 2:00 P.M., on weekends only, visitors can watch elephant training demonstrations.

Extras: Miniature train ride; miniature carousel; playground.

Special events: Conservation Day, in the spring; Zoo Barbecue, in the fall; Zoofari Ball, in the fall; Sing to the Animals, in December. Other events are held on an occasional basis.

Food service: There are several food concessions around the grounds that carry a variety of fast foods, snacks, ice cream, and beverages.

Plan to stay: 2 hours.

Directions: I–101 to Cabrillo Boulevard exit. Go west on Cabrillo to Ninos Drive. Turn right on Ninos. Zoo entrance will be on the right, ocean on the left. Follow signs.

Nearby attractions: Santa Barbara Mission, built in 1786; El Presidio de Santa Barbara State Historic Park, a restored Spanish military outpost; Botanic Garden; Stearns Wharf, an 1872 landmark now occupied by specialty shops, restaurants, and fishing pier.

SEA WORLD OF CALIFORNIA

1720 South Shores Road
San Diego, CA (619) 226–3901

Marine parks and animal shows have not been the same since Sea World came onto the scene in 1964 with its professional staff of animal experts and a show-business approach to educating the masses. This is the original Sea World, located on 150 acres on Mission Bay.

As at its three sister parks, the cornerstone of this Sea World's collection, and perhaps its most popular feature, is its marine mammals. From killer whales to a group of Alaskan sea otters rehabilitated from the 1989 *Valdez* oil spill, marine animals make their presence known here through educational shows and exhibits.

Season: Open 365 days a year.

Hours: 9:00 A.M. to dusk, with extended hours during summer and holiday periods.

Admission: Adults, under $25; ages 3–11, under $18; ages 3 and under, free. Additional fees: both the Skytower and the Skyride over Mission Bay, under $2 each.

The animals: More than 18,000 animals, more than 570 species, mostly consisting of invertebrates and fish, displayed in aquariums and open pools. Exhibits include: Shark Exhibit, a 400,000-gallon aquarium housing pelagic sharks; Marine Aquarium, 25 displays feature fish from around the world; Freshwater Aquarium, 25 aquariums feature fish from Africa, Asia, and the Amazon basin; Dolphin Pool, where touching and feeding are encouraged; seals, sea lions, and walruses; Penguin Encounter, features 350 penguins representing 7 species.

Entertainment: 7 shows, including the major Shamu the Killer Whale production. Other shows feature whales and dolphins, and sea lions and otters. There's also a water-skiing presentation and a musical variety show.

Extras: Skyride, enclosed gondola cable cars cross Mission Bay at a height of 100 feet; Skytower, a 320-foot tower, gives guests a view of the park and the San Diego skyline; Cap'n Kid's World, a participatory play area; Gardens, where more than 3,500 plant species thrive.

Food service: 2 cafeteria-style and 3 fast-food restaurants serve up a wide variety of foods. Plus, there's a bakery and a candy store, and various portable stands throughout the park.

Plan to stay: 7 hours.

Directions: Take the Sea World Drive exit off I–5 and follow signs west to the park.

Nearby attractions: San Diego Zoo; San Diego Wild Animal Park; Marshal Scotty's, an amusement and water park; Belmont Park, with Giant Dipper roller coaster and carousel.

Colorado

CHEYENNE MOUNTAIN ZOOLOGICAL PARK

4250 Cheyenne Mountain Zoo Road
Colorado Springs, CO (719) 633–0917

It's not every day you come across a zoo that's nestled in the side of a mountain. Opened in 1926, this is the second-oldest zoo in Colorado, and officials say it's the only true mountain zoo in the United States.

The entrance gate is quite unique, as it serves for both pedestrians and vehicles. Those on foot will be walking around to the various animal exhibits, while those in cars are following a 2-mile scenic highway that takes them to the Will Rogers Shrine of the Sun, at the top of Cheyenne Mountain. From 8,000 feet above sea level the view is breathtaking.

Evergreens and aspens grow in and around the 150-acre zoo, where you can burn up a few calories as you follow the looping walkway on the slightly rugged terrain of the mountain's lower slopes.

Unbeknownst to most visitors is the fact that the North American Air Defense Command is hidden away inside the mountain.

Season: Year-round, holidays too.

Hours: Memorial Day through Labor Day, 9:00 A.M. to 5:30 P.M.; remainder of year, 9:00 A.M. to 4:00 P.M.

Admission: Adults, under $7; ages 3–11, under $4; seniors, under $6; under age 3, free. Access road to Shrine of the Sun is included in zoo admission. Additional fee: elephant ride (in summer), under $3.

The animals: Nearly 500 animals, more than 100 species, displayed in both indoor and outdoor exhibits. Highlights include Eyrie, the birds-of-prey exhibit; Rocky Cliffs, goat and marmot exhibit; Primate World; and a herd of giraffes.

Entertainment: Elephant demonstration daily; public feeding for penguins, monkeys, big cats, and birds of prey, daily. (Birds and cats are not fed on Monday and Friday.)

Extras: Elephant rides, during the summer; antique carousel; children's contact area; conservation center; self-guided nature trail; playground; Will Rogers Shrine of the Sun.

Special events: The Wildest Race in Town, annual foot race, in August.

Food service: 1 main food concession at the main entry building offers fast foods, snacks, ice cream, and beverages; 3 seasonal snack bars are also located in the zoo. Picnics are permitted.

Plan to stay: 3 hours.

Directions: I–25 to exit 138 (Circle Drive). Follow Circle Drive west; it will become Lake Avenue. Continue west on Lake until you get to the Broadmoor Hotel. Turn right and follow signs that will lead you to the zoo entrance, about a 5-minute drive.

Nearby attractions: World Figure Skating Hall of Fame; Broadmoor Ski Area; El Pomar Carriage House Museum; Hall of Presidents Wax Museum; Museum of American Numismatic Association; Pro Rodeo Hall of Champions; Ghost Town Museum; U.S. Olympic Complex.

DENVER ZOOLOGICAL GARDENS

In City Park
(at 23rd Avenue, between Colorado Boulevard and York Street)
Denver, CO (303) 331–4100

Once a sagebrush flatland, the Denver Zoo began in 1896, when a bear cub was given to then-mayor Thomas S. McMurray. The bear, named Billy Bryan, was tethered near a haystack in City Park, and the zoo was literally built around him.

Today the facility covers seventy-six acres in downtown Denver and is one of the most modern in the country, taking an active part in the movement to protect the rain forests, rivers, forests, swampland, and other critical habitats of the world that are threatened by overdevelopment.

When you enter through Pronghorn Plaza you follow a path that makes its way in an oval loop amid the dozens of buildings, ponds, and outdoor animal exhibits. Walking is easy, but if you get tired you can always take the Zooliner tour train around the grounds, or the Pioneer Train around the children's zoo.

Season: Year-round, holidays too.

Hours: Opens at 10:00 A.M., daily, year-round. Closing time varies.

Admission: Adults, under $6; ages 6–15 and seniors, under $4; under age 6, free. Additional fees: Zooliner Train, under $2; Miniature Train, under $1.50.

The animals: More than 1,300 animals, more than 300 species, displayed in both indoor and outdoor naturalistic habitats. Popular exhibits include the Bird World Aviary and Northern Shores, with its underwater viewing of sea lions and polar bears. In late 1993 the first phase of the conservatory-type Tropical Discovery will open. It will be a re-creation of the critical habitats of the world that are now threatened.

Entertainment: No regularly scheduled shows, but visitors may watch some of the animals being fed. Felines are fed once a day, excluding Mondays; sea lions and penguins, twice a day; primates, once a day.

Extras: Zooliner, a rubber-tired train that tours the entire zoo; Pioneer Train, a miniature train that skirts the perimeter of the children's zoo; and the children's zoo, with a duck pond, education center, and contact area.

Special events: Throughout the year there are special events, including a summer concert series.

Food service: The Hungry Elephant Restaurant serves fast food and snacks cafeteria-style, as does the Northern Shores Cafe. Both have outdoor terraces where you can enjoy a tasty hamburger, hot dog, sandwich, or your own picnic lunch. There are also snack bars located throughout.

Plan to stay: 3 hours.

Directions: I–70 to Colorado Boulevard exit. Go south on Colorado to 23rd Avenue. Turn right, and in about 1 block you'll see the zoo entrance on the left, across from the golf course.

Nearby attractions: Denver Museum of Natural History, adjacent to the zoo; Molly Brown House Museum; U.S. Mint, with free tours (but no samples); Denver Botanic Gardens; Elitch Gardens and Lakeside amusement parks.

PUEBLO ZOO

In Pueblo City Park
Pueblo Boulevard and Goodnight Avenue
Pueblo, CO (719) 561–9664

Educational exhibits can sometimes get a little dry, but not here. Learning about animals and the environment at the Pueblo Zoo is fun—especially in such a pretty setting. The park is located within the city but is full of shade trees, flower gardens, and a stream.

Tim's Trivia

The Alaska Zoo, in Anchorage, is the northernmost zoo in the world.

Although only ten acres in size, this zoo has a lot of activities to hold children's (and adults') interest. They can look at insect wings through microscopes, touch skeletons, put on animal masks, and make animal footprints, in addition to seeing their favorite animals up close.

Season: Year-round, holidays too.

Hours: Memorial Day through Labor Day, 10:00 A.M. to 5:00 P.M.; remainder of the year, 9:00 A.M. to 4:00 P.M.

Admission: Adults, under $2; ages 5–12, under $1; under age 5, free.

The animals: More than 70 species displayed in both indoor and outdoor enclosures and habitats. Highlights include the hamadryas baboons, Bengal tigers, the Small Mammal House, and the Cold-Blooded Creatures Herpetarium. Don't miss Solar Sue, the sun bear, or J.R., the bobcat.

Entertainment: No regularly scheduled entertainment, but programs are run during special events.

Extras: White Discovery Room, features hands-on displays and an aquarium; Happy Time Ranch, a contact area. In other areas of the park are kiddie rides, a swimming pool, and a fishing lake.

Special events: Feast with Father, a Father's Day pancake breakfast; Zoofari, a summer barbecue; celebrations of animals' birthdays throughout the year.

Food service: 1 snack bar offers candy and soda. Picnics are permitted.

Plan to stay: 1 hour.

Directions: Located in the western part of the city. Take I–25 to Highway

50. Go west on Highway 50 to Pueblo Boulevard. Go south on Pueblo. After crossing the Arkansas River, make a left at the first light, onto Goodnight Avenue. Zoo entrance will be on the right.

Nearby attractions: Funputter Park, miniature golf; El Pueblo Museum, depicts history of the area and includes a full-size reproduction of Old Fort Pueblo; Rosemount, a Victorian mansion; Pueblo Greyhound Track, dog racing; Colorado State Fair, held at the fairgrounds in late August.

Connecticut

BEARDSLEY ZOOLOGICAL GARDENS

In Beardsley Park
1875 Noble Avenue
Bridgeport, CT (203) 576–8126

This relatively small zoo of 35 acres is situated among the gently rolling hills that make up Beardsley Park in the wooded suburbs of bustling Bridgeport, home of the late showman P. T. Barnum.

The turn-of-the-century greenhouse, where tropical plants are grown for the zoo's landscape, is a beautiful feature of the facility.

Season: Year-round, closed Thanksgiving, Christmas Day, and New Year's Day.

Hours: 9:00 A.M. to 4:00 P.M., daily.

Admission: Adults, under $6; ages 5–12 and seniors, under $4; under age 3, free. Additional fees: parking, under $4; pony ride, under $3.

The animals: More than 300 animals, more than 100 species, primarily native to the Americas, displayed in indoor and outdoor habitats. Outstanding exhibits include World Tropics Building, with a walk-through jungle that is unique in the New England area; the aquatic exhibit; and the hoofstock.

Entertainment: There is no regularly scheduled entertainment, but weekend animal programs are sometimes conducted by the education department in conjunction with special events.

Extras: New England Farmyard, a children's zoo; pony rides.

Special events: There is usually a special event scheduled each month, geared to holiday and seasonal themes.

Food service: 1 snack shop and a picnic grove.

Plan to stay: 2 hours.

Directions: I–95 to exit 27A (Route 25). Go south on Route 25 to exit 5 (Boston Avenue). Make a left off the exit ramp onto Boston Avenue eastbound. At the fourth traffic light, make a left onto Noble Avenue. Park entrance is a quarter-mile on the left.

Nearby attractions: Barnum Circus Museum; Birdcraft Museum and Sanctuary, in Fairfield, has a collection of dinosaur footprints and live bee exhibits; American Festival Theatre in Stratford.

MARITIME CENTER

10 North Water Street
Norwalk, CT (203) 852–0700

The marine life and ecology of Long Island Sound is the focus here. Twenty tanks feature more than 125 indigenous species of marine life. When you visit, you'll learn about the Sound from the perspective of the scientist, diver, marine historian, fisherman, sailor, and even the fish.

One of the main attractions is a 110,000-gallon open ocean tank, featuring nine-foot sharks. Another popular exhibit is an indoor-outdoor pool which houses harbor seals.

Located in the historic oystering community of South Norwalk, the facility's home is a restored nineteenth-century foundry. In addition to its live attractions, there are interactive navigational exhibits where you can learn the use of the compass, map reading, and knot tying. An IMAX theater screens films daily, and (optional) river cruises provide firsthand information. A large variety of power and sailing vessels are on display, and there's an active boat-building center.

Open daily, Memorial Day through Labor Day, 10:00 A.M. to 6:00 P.M.; closes the rest of the year at 5:00 P.M. Closed Thanksgiving, Christmas Day and New Year's Day.

Admission: Adults, under $8; ages 3–12 and seniors, under $7; under 2, free. Additional price for IMAX: adults, under $6; 3–12 and seniors, under

$3. Combination ticket for aquarium and IMAX: adults, under $12; 3–12 and seniors, under $10.

Take exit 14 (northbound) off I–95, and go down the hill. Take a right onto West Avenue and bear left onto North Main Street when you see Professional Pharmacy. Take a left on Ann Street and follow signs to facility.

MYSTIC MARINELIFE AQUARIUM

55 Coogan Boulevard
Mystic, CT (203) 536–9631

Penguins, seals, whales, and dolphins are just a few of the stars you'll get a chance to see here at the state's most visited attraction. Actually, there are more than 6,000 marine creatures displayed in fifty exhibits.

A couple of the highlights include: the Penguin Pavilion, an exhibit that houses a breeding colony of African black-footed penguins; and Seal Island, a 2½-acre outdoor complex with four species of seals and sea lions in recreations of their natural habitats. More than fifty seals and sea lions, including the unusual northern fur seals, are on display.

In the main aquarium building are forty-eight exhibits featuring a variety of marine and freshwater life, including Atlantic Coral Reef, a colorful display of exotic fishes from the tropics. The whales and dolphins are housed in a 350,000-gallon pool and can be watched from below water level or from an observation deck above the tank. In the Marine Theater, there are marine mammal demonstrations.

The facility is open daily except for Thanksgiving Day, Christmas Day, New Year's Day, and the last full week of January. Times are 9:00 A.M. to 4:30 P.M., with extended closing time of 5:30 P.M. during summer. Visitors are permitted to stay in the Aquarium building one and a half hours past official closing time.

Admission: adults, under $9; children 5–12, under $5; 4 and under, free. No food service in the complex but the adjacent Old Mystic Village offers a variety of restaurants and shops.

Located at exit 90 on I–95, in historic Mystic.

WICKHAM PARK

1329 West Middle Turnpike
Manchester, CT (203) 528–0856

A small aviary and mini-zoo are located in this park, which is owned by the Connecticut National Bank. The resident species, including raccoons, ferrets, rabbits, pheasants, doves, peacocks, and ducks, are native to the area.

In addition to the animals, the park contains an Asian garden, athletic fields, and a walking-fitness trail. Opens each year on the first weekend in April and closes on the last Sunday in October. Operating hours are 9:30 A.M. till dusk. Admission on weekdays is $1 per vehicle; $2 per vehicle on weekends.

To get there take I–84 to exit 60. Get on U.S. 6/44 West, to West Middle Turnpike; go about a half-mile to the park entrance.

Delaware

BRANDYWINE ZOO

In Brandywine Park
1001 North Park Drive
Wilmington, DE (302) 571–7788

The only zoo in the state, Brandywine is a tranquil respite just a few minutes from busy downtown Wilmington. The facility is tucked away on twelve of the 180 acres that make up Brandywine Park, one of the several green spaces in this part of the country that was designed by renowned nineteenth-century landscape architect Frederick Law Olmsted.

Here you can stroll along the banks of the Brandywine River, which flows through the park near the zoo, meander through a free-flight aviary, or picnic in a shaded grove that connects the two ends of the barbell-shaped animal exhibit area.

Season: Year-round, including holidays.

Hours: 10:00 A.M. to 4:00 P.M., daily.

Admission: Adults, under $5; ages 3–12 and seniors, under $3; under age

3, free. Admission is charged only from April 1 through October. The rest of the year, everyone gets in free.

The animals: More than 100 animals, more than 50 species, primarily from North and South America, are exhibited in both indoor and outdoor habitats. Siberian tiger, North American river otter, and Florida bobcat exhibits are among the most popular.

Entertainment: No regularly scheduled entertainment, but there are animal-related educational demonstrations during special events.

Extras: In other areas of the park, you'll find a children's playground and the Josephine Garden, which contains more than 100 Japanese cherry trees, an impressive display when in flower each spring.

Special events: Spring Fling, in April; Conservation Day, in June; Zippity Zoo Days, in September.

Food service: 1 concession stand sells a variety of fast foods, beverages, ice cream, and snacks. Picnics are permitted in both zoo and park.

Plan to stay: 2 hours.

Directions: From I–95, get off at exit 8. Go south on Route 202 (Concord Pike). Concord turns into Bayard Boulevard. Continue south on Bayard to North Park Drive, just before the Brandywine River. Go right on North Park Drive. Zoo entrance will be less than a mile on the right.

Nearby attractions: Longwood Gardens, former estate of Pierre S. Du Pont; Winterthur Museum and Gardens, including 200-acre estate and largest collection of decorative American arts from 1640 to 1840; Hagley Museum, site of original Du Pont Mills; Brandywine River Museum, a restored gristmill housing paintings by the Wyeth family.

Fauna Fun Facts

Bears don't really hibernate. Instead, they go into a deep sleep from which they occasionally awake. If they find some food, they may eat during the winter, but they mostly live on body fat built up in the warmer months.

PRIME HOOK
NATIONAL WILDLIFE REFUGE
Broadkill Beach Road
Lewes, DE (302) 684–8419

Located on the Atlantic Flyway, these 9,000 acres on Delaware Bay attract numerous species of migrating and year-round wildlife. You'll find heavy concentrations of Canada geese, snow geese, black ducks, mallards, wood ducks, and other waterfowl throughout the spring and fall. The best time to see the migration is during mid- to late October.

In the spring, several species of reptiles and amphibians can be seen in great numbers, including red-bellied and painted turtles, frogs, salamanders, toads, and snakes. Four short trails can be followed through the refuge, which is made up mostly of marshland, with some forested and grassy areas.

The refuge is open year-round, from sunrise to sunset, and is free. Office hours of the headquarters are 7:30 A.M. to 4:00 P.M., Monday through Friday, closed on holidays.

To get there, take U.S. Route 1 to Route 16 (Broadkill Beach Road), and then go east on Route 16 for 1 mile. Make a left into the refuge entrance and proceed 1.6 miles to the headquarters.

District of Columbia

NATIONAL AQUARIUM
Department of Commerce Building
14th Street and Constitution Avenue NW
Washington, DC (202) 377–2825

It's fitting that the oldest public aquarium in the United States—and the third-oldest in the world (circa 1873)—should be located in our nation's capital.

Located in the lower level of the Department of Commerce Building, the surroundings make you feel like you're actually below sea level. Marine sounds can be heard as you enter the facility, and a mini-theater offers slide shows and a guide to the undersea life that you're likely to meet.

The most popular exhibits here feature sharks and sea turtles.

Season: Year-round, closed Christmas Day.

Hours: 9:00 A.M. to 5:00 P.M., daily.

Admission: Adults, under $3; ages 4–12 and seniors, under $1. Metered parking is available on 14th and 15th streets.

The animals: More than 250 species, more than 1,200 specimens, including alligator, sea turtle, moray eel, piranha, lemon shark, yellow-head jawfish, trigger fish, and a touch tank with horseshoe crabs and sea urchins, among others.

Entertainment: Shark feedings, on Monday, Wednesday, and Saturday, 2:00 P.M.; piranha feedings, Tuesday, Thursday, and Sunday, 2:00 P.M.

Special events: Special programs include Shark Day, cosponsored by The Discovery Channel; special activities around Christmas usually include crafts show fashioned around fish and water themes.

Food service: A cafe adjacent to the gift shop.

Plan to stay: 1 hour.

Directions: East of Washington Monument, across from Plaza and across from National Theater, in lower level of the U.S. Department of Commerce Building, 14th Street between Constitution and Pennsylvania avenues, NW.

Nearby attractions: One block from Washington Monument and the Mall; two blocks from White House, and near the Natural History Museum.

NATIONAL ZOOLOGICAL PARK

3000 Connecticut Avenue NW
Washington, DC (202) 673–4800

A trip to the nation's capital wouldn't be complete without a stop at the National Zoo. Not only is it home to the country's only giant pandas, but it is among the oldest zoological parks in the United States.

Located on 163 gently rolling acres in Rock Creek Park, in the northwestern section of the city, it was designed by world-renowned landscape architect Frederick Law Olmsted and is now well into its metamorphosis into a "biopark," in which form it will integrate the major elements of natural history museums, botanical gardens, and zoos.

Season: Year-round, closed Christmas Day.

Hours: Buildings: May through mid-September, 9:00 A.M. to 6:00 P.M.; mid-

September through April, 9:00 A.M. to 4:30 P.M. Grounds: mid-April through mid-October, 8:00 A.M. to 8:00 P.M.; mid-October through April, 8:00 A.M. to 6:00 P.M.

Admission: Free. Additional fees: parking (in public garage), $5–$10, depending on length of stay. Free parking can be found on the streets adjacent to the zoo.

The animals: More than 4,500 animals, about 500 species, in both indoor and outdoor settings. Outstanding exhibits include giant pandas; Amazonia, a two-level viewing area of South American river and forest; Komodo Dragons; Wetlands Habitat.

Entertainment: Sea lion training demonstrations once a day; panda feedings, twice a day; elephant training demonstrations once a day.

Extras: Botanical gardens.

Special events: Concerts, lectures, and films, also scheduled monthly. Call for schedule.

Food service: Mane Restaurant, near lion exhibit; Panda Cafe, a pizza parlor located on top of the panda house; several snack bars located throughout park.

Plan to stay: 4 hours.

Directions: I–95 South to I–495 West. Get off at Connecticut Avenue exit and go south, toward Chevy Chase. Zoo entrance is the second traffic light after crossing the bridge, about 4.5 miles from I–495.

Nearby attractions: White House; U.S. Capitol; Smithsonian Institution; Washington Monument; Lincoln Memorial; Arlington National Cemetery.

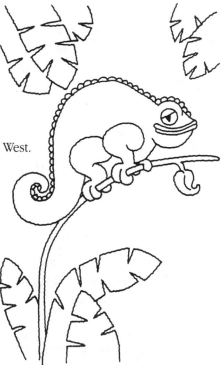

Florida

BLUE SPRING STATE PARK

Highway 17/92
Orange City, FL (904) 775–3663

Here's a great place to view those wonderful manatees up close. In fact, this is one of several places in the state where you can see these majestic animals from the shore. When the water temperature of St. Johns River drops in the winter, manatees take refuge from the cold in a warm, spring-fed tributary of the river.

They usually start arriving in mid-November, and the last of them are gone by March. Their appearance is directly related to the weather, and at the peak, you'll usually see a population of about seventy-five. Two observation platforms and a boardwalk along the warm spring-run (72°F) provide perfect viewing stations for the antics of the manatees as they swim about in the crystal-clear water.

Also in the park is a Sand Pine Scrub, one of the state's unique plant communities. In the scrub are several threatened species of animals, including the Florida mouse and the gopher frog. Ranger programs and slide presentations take place several times daily.

There are camping sites, a concessions building, and picnic pavilions. Admission is $3.50 per car. The park is located along the St. Johns River, 2 miles west of Orange City on Highway 17/92. It's 25 miles to Daytona Beach to the east, and 25 miles to Orlando to the south.

BUSCH GARDENS

3000 Busch Boulevard
Tampa, FL (813) 971–8282

The diversity of this 300-acre family park is awesome. Not only does it have twenty-three amusement rides, a beer brewery, and a full array of shows and other entertainment attractions, it is also considered one of the nation's top zoos.

And the truly amazing thing about this place is that all of its seemingly contrasting elements meld together to present a very convincing African theme. The restaurants, animal exhibits, rides, shows, and shopping bazaars are all at home together in the eight themed areas of the park.

Season: Open 365 days a year.

Hours: 9:30 A.M. to 6:00 P.M., with extended hours during parts of the summer season and holiday periods.

Admission: Under $26; age 2 and under, free. Additional fee: parking, under $4.

The animals: More than 3,300 animals. Exhibits include: Eagle Canyon, a natural habitat for golden and bald eagles; Myombe Reserve—The Great Ape Domain; Koala Exhibit in the Bird Gardens; Serengeti Plain, an 80-acre setting with 500 African animals, including hippos, antelope, black rhinos, Asian elephants; Nairobi Field Station, an animal nursery with petting zoo and reptile displays; Nocturnal Mountain, where a simulated environment allows guests to observe nocturnal species; Claw Island, featuring white Bengal tigers; and the world-famous Budweiser Clydesdales.

Entertainment: Several musical shows plus a dolphin show, bird shows, snake charmer, and Animal Tales, an educational show about animals.

Extras: Monorail, steam locomotive, and skyride take guests over and through the Serengeti Plain; self-guided tours of the adjacent Anheuser-Busch Brewery.

Food service: The Crown Colony House is a full-service restaurant overlooking the Serengeti Plain; Das Festhaus is an authentic German beer hall, complete with big mugs of beer and an oompah band. Additional food outlets appear throughout the park.

Plan to stay: 8 hours if you want to see the animals and take in the rides and shows.

Tim's Trivia

The flight cage that housed the bird exhibit at the 1904 World's Fair is now the aviary at the St. Louis Zoo.

Directions: Located at the corner of Busch Boulevard and 40th Street, 8 miles northeast of downtown. Take exit 33 (Busch Boulevard) off I–75 and go east 2 miles to the park. Or take exit 54 (Fowler Avenue) off I–75, go west 2 miles and follow the signs.

Nearby attractions: Adventure Island water park; Alessi Farmers Market; Ybor City, a historic Latin community.

CENTRAL FLORIDA ZOOLOGICAL PARK

U.S. Highway 17/92 at Interstate 4
Monroe, FL (407) 323–4450

A good part of your walk through this zoo is on a boardwalk over the wetlands that border scenic Lake Monroe. Located about ten minutes north of Orlando, this 109-acre facility is close to central Florida's other major tourist attractions.

The animals here are a blend of native and exotic species, and are all exhibited outdoors. It's best to come here on the weekend; that's when all activities are in full swing.

Season: Year-round, closed Thanksgiving and Christmas Day.

Hours: 9:00 A.M. to 5:00 P.M., daily.

Admission: Adults, under $6; ages 3–12, under $4; age 60 and over, under $5; under age 3, free. Additional fees: elephant ride, under $2.50; pony ride, under $2.

The animals: More than 400 animals, more than 170 species, displayed in outdoor exhibits. Highlights include the Herpetarium, which houses Florida's native snakes and lizards; and the big cat collection.

Entertainment: On weekends there are feeding demonstrations for primates, otters, and felines.

Extras: Children's zoo, with contact area; elephant rides, on weekends; pony rides, on weekends. In the adjoining park are kiddie rides.

Special events: Easter Egg Hunt, the Saturday before Easter; Reptile Day, in the spring; Young Artists Day, one Saturday in spring; Conservation and Earth Day activities, in April and June; and a Halloween event, in October.

Food service: 1 concession stand offers a variety of fast foods, snacks, ice cream, and beverages. Picnics are permitted.

Plan to stay: 2 hours.

Directions: I–4 to exit 52. When you get off the exit ramp, go east; zoo entrance is one-tenth of a mile, on your left.

Nearby attractions: The Big Tree, a cypress believed to be 3,500 years old, with a circumference of 47 feet; Captain Hoy's Riverboat Fleet, narrated cruises on the St. Johns River aboard a sternwheeler; nearby Orlando, and its myriad of attractions.

DISCOVERY ISLAND ZOOLOGICAL PARK

Walt Disney World
Lake Buena Vista, FL (407) 824–2875

Imagine what it would be like to live on an undeveloped tropical island, amid thickets of bamboo, sweet-smelling, brightly colored flowers, and acres of lush vegetation, with the sound of hundreds of birds filling the air around you.

That's what you'll find on Discovery Island, an 11.5-acre island near the southeast shore of Bay Lake in Walt Disney World, where paths and board-walks wind through tropical forests, swamps, and sandy beach areas. From several viewing areas along the trail you can see both flora and fauna native to the tropical areas of the world.

Season: Year-round, holidays too.

Hours: 10:00 A.M. to 6:00 P.M., daily. During summer months, closing time is an hour later.

Admission: Adults (10 and older), under $10; ages 3–9, under $6; under 3, free. Combination tickets that include River Country water park admission are under $18 for adults, and under $14 for ages 3–9.

The animals: More than 500 animals, more than 100 species, all native to tropical areas of Africa, Asia, South America, and the South Pacific. The island is one large natural habitat with 9 designated points of interest where concentrations of particular species are housed.

Entertainment: Discovery Island Bird Show, in which trained macaws, cockatoos, and other birds do individual tricks. Visitor participation is encouraged in these presentations, which run continually during operating hours.

Food service: Thirsty Perch sells snacks, ice cream, and soft drinks. Picnics are also permitted on the beach or down by the docking area.

Plan to stay: At least 1 hour.

Directions: Access is only by watercraft from Magic Kingdom, the Fort Wilderness campground, and River Country, as well as from the Polynesian, Contemporary, and Grand Floridian resorts, all on Disney property.

Nearby attractions: Magic Kingdom, Epcot Center, Pleasure Island, River Country, Typhoon Lagoon, and other Walt Disney World attractions; also other points of interest in central Florida.

DREHER PARK ZOO

1301 Summit Boulevard
West Palm Beach, FL (407) 533–0887

Palm trees and huge hibiscus plants abound amid the lush foliage found here, where winding pathways lead visitors to the various animal exhibits. A series of canals also snake through the flora, adding to the feeling of being in a tropical paradise.

Here and there, as you stroll down the paths, you will probably encounter some free-roaming ducks, peacocks, and guinea fowl, who either live here year-round or migrate from northern regions during the cooler weather.

Season: Year-round, holidays too.

Hours: 9:00 A.M. to 5:00 P.M., daily.

Admission: Adults, under $6; ages 3–12, under $4.50, seniors, under $5.50; under age 3, free.

The animals: 400 animals, 100 species, displayed in natural settings. Highlights include a pair of Bengal tigers; the Australia exhibits, with a Bennett wallaby family, red kangaroos, and a black swan; the endangered marmoset monkeys; a Florida panther; and giant Aldabra tortoises.

Entertainment: There are no animal shows or rides, but there are occasional animal encounters, in which a keeper or docent will bring a bird, a small mammal, or a reptile out of its exhibit to give visitors a close-up look and answer any questions. These are unscheduled.

Extras: Domestic yard with animal contact area. Also in Dreher Park is the South Florida Science Museum, Planetarium, and Aquarium.

Special events: There are several special events held throughout the year, usually in conjunction with a particular holiday, such as Valentine's Day, Halloween, Thanksgiving, and Christmas. On Feb. 2, the zoo usually holds Sun Bear Day, during which Spanky the Sun Bear determines whether or not there will be six more weeks of winter in West Palm Beach.

Food service: 1 snack stand on the grounds, and picnics are permitted.

Plan to stay: 2 hours.

Directions: I–95 to U.S. 98 (Southern Boulevard). Go west on Southern about 2 miles to State Route 807 (Congress Avenue). Go south on 807 and follow signs into the park.

Nearby attractions: Lion Country Safari, animal preserve and amusement park; Municipal Stadium, where the Atlanta Braves and Montreal Expos play their spring training baseball games; Greyhound races at the Palm Beach Kennel Club; jai alai at the Palm Beach Fronton; and polo matches in nearby Wellington.

GATORLAND

South Orange Blossom Trail
Kissimmee, FL (407) 855–5496

To enter here, you'll have to walk through the jaws of a giant alligator, a toothsome portal that has become a Florida landmark and a popular photo spot. It also identifies the largest alligator breeding farm in the world.

Although their specialty is gators, the Godwin family, which has owned Gatorland since it opened, in 1949, has turned the property into a preserve for other forms of Florida wildlife as well. The native cypress swamp, with its half-mile of covered bridges and walkways, has become a rookery for many varieties of birds, including the endangered green heron.

Located in the high-tech tourist area dominated by Disney and Universal, Gatorland is a good place to see what Florida was like in the pre–theme park era. While you're visiting, don't pass up some great opportunities to have your picture taken with a boa constrictor, a baby alligator, or Albert the Galapagos turtle.

If you're really observant, you'll recognize this as the place where scenes from two feature films, *National Lampoon's Vacation* and *Indiana Jones and the Temple of Doom,* were photographed.

Season: Year-round, holidays too.

Hours: 8:00 A.M. until dusk, daily.

Admission: Adults, under $15; ages 3–11, under $12; under age 3, free.

The animals: More than 5,000 alligators and crocodiles, as well as other reptiles, small mammals, and birds. All are displayed outdoors in natural settings.

Entertainment: Two shows are presented several times each day. Gator Jumparoo features alligators that jump several feet to get their food;

while Gator Wrestling is just that—trainers wrestling the reptiles as part of an educational demonstration.

Extras: A 10-minute narrated tour of the facility via narrow-gauge railroad; contact area; alligator incubator.

Food service: 1 snack bar sells snack items, but a visit to Pearl's Smokehouse is a must. That's where you'll find the tasty gator nuggets and smoked gator ribs. These items are genuine alligator meat, which is tender and has a taste somewhere between chicken and veal. Picnics are permitted.

Plan to stay: 4 hours.

Directions: Located on the South Orange Blossom Trail (U.S. Routes 17, 92, and 441), about 3 miles south of the Beeline Expressway, and 8 miles from I–4, between Orlando and Kissimmee.

Nearby attractions: Walt Disney World; Universal Studios Florida; Sea World of Florida; Wet 'n Wild, a water park; and a bevy of other tourist attractions in the Orlando area.

JACKSONVILLE ZOOLOGICAL PARK

8605 Zoo Road
Jacksonville, FL (904) 757–4463

Perched at the conjunction point of the Trout and St. Johns rivers, the Jacksonville Zoo is one of the oldest in the state, and one of the prettiest.

This zoo has it all: expansive habitats, animal shows and rides, and boat rides on the river. You can escape to the wilds of Africa, wind your way through Florida wetlands without getting your feet wet, or walk through an outdoor aviary and see the only Pondicherry vultures bred in captivity in the Western Hemisphere, and see a breeding pair of marabou storks.

Season: Year-round, closed Thanksgiving, Christmas Day, and New Year's Day.

Hours: 9:00 A.M.. to 5:00 P.M., daily.

Admission: Adults, under $5; ages 4–12, under $3.50; under age 4, free; discount for seniors. Additional fees: train ride, under $2; camel rides (age limit), under $2.50; river cruises, under $4 per half-hour; ecology tours, under $4.

The animals: More than 700 animals, more than 200 species, including lots of birds. All animals are in outdoor natural exhibits. There's an 11-acre African veldt area, with an adjoining lion exhibit; a free-flight aviary, with rare Pondicherry vultures; and a natural Florida wetlands area.

Entertainment: On weekends, a variety of animal shows are performed 3 times a day. Elephant Encounters are held twice a day on weekends and holidays, once a day during the week.

Extras: Okavango Train Ride through the African exhibit leaves from Okavango Village, where there is a petting zoo and a pier where you can take cruises on the Trout and St. Johns rivers. There are also ecology tours, which last 2 to 3 hours.

Special events: Teddy Bear Fair, in April; Halloween activities, in October; Christmas events, in December. There are other events as well, including free admission days.

Food service: In addition to snack carts, there is the Botswana Burger Company, a cafeteria-style restaurant in Okavango Village. As its name suggests, the specialty is burgers, although other fast foods, snacks, ice cream, and beverages are also available.

Plan to stay: 3 hours.

Directions: I–95 to exit 124A (Heckscher Drive). Take Heckscher Drive east for about 1 mile. Zoo entrance will be on the right. Billboards direct you.

Nearby attractions: Anheuser-Busch Brewery, offers self-guiding tours and samples; Museum of Science and History; Mayport Naval Station usually has a ship open for tours; dog racing at St. Johns Greyhound Park.

JUNGLE LARRY'S ZOOLOGICAL PARK

1590 Goodlette Road
Naples, FL (813) 262–5409

Jungle Larry Tetzlaff, who died in 1984, was a colorful character who loved animals and practiced conservation long before it was in vogue. In his long career as a wildlife photographer, lecturer, and author of many current animal-exhibit standards, he also found time to stand in as Johnny Weissmuller's double in the famous Tarzan movies.

Located on the grounds of the historic Caribbean Botanical Gardens,

Jungle Larry's boasts a lush, tropical setting with many varieties of palm trees, bamboo, and rare, single-specimen trees. It even has one of the largest collection of bromeliads in the country, and is still owned and operated by the family.

During the summer months, the Jungle Larry's at Cedar Point Amusement Park in Sandusky, Ohio, is also open. For more information on that facility, see the Ohio section of this book.

Season: Year-round, closed Thanksgiving and Christmas Day.

Hours: 9:30 A.M. to 5:30 P.M., daily.

Admission: Adults, under $12; ages 3–15, under $8, under age 3, free. Discounts for seniors. Additional fee: Safari Island Cruise.

The animals: Several hundred mammals, reptiles, and birds in outdoor enclosures and habitats. Highlights include the anteaters, primates, and big cats.

Entertainment: Alligator lecture and feeding, twice a day; Bird Circus, twice a day; Wildlife Encounters, twice a day; and arena shows featuring tigers and leopards.

Extras: Elephant demonstrations and rides; narrated tram ride around the park; Safari Island Cruise; playgrounds; walking trails; petting zoo.

Special events: Tarzan Yell Contest, in May; Santa's arrival by elephant, in December; Easter events.

Food service: 1 snack bar offers sandwiches, beverages, and Carvel ice cream. Picnics are permitted.

Plan to stay: 4 hours.

Directions: I–75 to exit 16. Travel west 3 miles to Goodlette Road. Turn left onto Goodlette and travel 3 miles south to park entrance on left.

Nearby attractions: Collier Automotive Museum; Island Nature Cruises through the Everglades; Naples Nature Center; Rookery Bay National Estuarine Research Reserve.

Fauna Fun Facts

The king cobra, which grows up to 18 feet in length, is the largest poisonous snake in the world. It is also the only snake known to construct a nest for its eggs.

LOWRY PARK
ZOOLOGICAL GARDENS

7530 North Boulevard
Tampa, FL (813) 935–8552

Native Florida, before the tourist, before the mega-attraction . . . that's what you'll see here. There are more than seven acres devoted to native fauna, including fox, deer, black bear, panthers, and bison. Even the beloved endangered manatee has a home here in the aquatic building.

While you're here, make a special note of the landscaping. It's very impressive, not only in the visitor areas and the exhibits, but in the parking lot as well.

Season: Year-round, closed Christmas Day.

Hours: 9:30 A.M. to 6:00 P.M. during daylight saving time; Remainder of the year, closes an hour earlier.

Admission: Adults, under $6; ages 4–11, under $4; ages 65 and older, under $5; under age 4, free.

The animals: More than 500 animals, more than 170 species, including many birds. Animals are exhibited in natural habitats, some with moats, and some with overhead walkways cleverly incorporated into the scenery and landscaping. Highlights include Asian Domain; free-flight aviary; Primate World; and Manatee Center.

Entertainment: No regularly scheduled entertainment, but there are unscheduled demonstrations with animals in the petting zoo.

Extras: Children's petting zoo. Next to the zoo, in Lowry Park, there is an amusement area, with rides, playground, and carousel.

Special events: There are special events throughout the year, changing monthly. At Halloween and Christmas each year there are activities for children.

Food service: The Garden Cafe serves the standard fast-food fare of hamburgers, hot dogs, chicken nuggets, snacks, ice cream, and beverages, while the Key West Cafe offers rice, beans, and chicken dishes. Portable snack carts are also located throughout the zoo. Picnics are not permitted in the zoo, but are allowed in the adjoining park.

Plan to stay: 2 hours.

Directions: I–275 to exit 31 (Sly Avenue). Follow Sly Avenue west for 1 mile to North Boulevard and zoo entrance. Signs will direct you.

Nearby attractions: Adventure Island, a water park; Busch Gardens (The Dark Continent), African-theme amusement park and animal safari; Ybor City State Museum, in a former bakery with brick ovens, depicts the cigar industry in Cuba; Greyhound racing; the Gasparilla Pirate Invasion, in early February.

MIAMI METROZOO

12400 Southwest 152nd Street
Miami, FL (305) 251–0400

(Editor's Note: Hurricane Andrew severely damaged this facility in August 1992. Officials state that the zoo may remain closed until the spring of 1993. We suggest that you call this and other south Florida listings before visiting.)

Asia, Africa, and Australia provide the flora and fauna for the Metrozoo, which is located on 740 acres southwest of downtown Miami, not far from the Everglades. Since it is one of the newest zoos in the country, this facility has no cages for its animals, only natural outdoor habitats.

Koalas, white Bengal tigers, and flamingos are among the animals living here, along with small-clawed otters and clouded leopards, who are right at home in authentic re-creations of their native surroundings.

Season: Year-round, holidays too.

Hours: 9:30 A.M. to 5:30 A.M., daily. Last ticket sold at 4:00 P.M.

Admission: Adults, under $10; ages 3–12, under $6; under age 3, free. Reduced rates for Florida residents.

The animals: More than 3,000 animals, more than 250 species, in cageless exhibits. Outstanding exhibits include Asian River Life, a two-level exhibit of life under and above the water; Wings of Asia, a 1½-acre free-flight aviary; and Lowland Gorillas.

Entertainment: Elephant Show; Wildlife Show; Ecology Theater. Each performed three shows daily.

Extras: Monorail guided tours; Paws, a children's petting zoo with animal rides and kiddie rides.

Special events: Scheduled monthly, entertainment events are posted at gate and published in local newspapers and travel guides.

Food service: 1 lakefront restaurant and 2 snack bars. Picnic meals cannot be brought into the zoo.

Plan to stay: 2 hours.

Directions: Take the Florida Turnpike (West Dade Expressway) to Coral Reef Drive. Go west on Coral Reef. Zoo entrance is ahead three-quarters of a mile, on the left.

Nearby attractions: Everglades National Park; Monkey Jungle; Parrot Jungle; Miami Seaquarium; Planet Ocean, an educational ocean-science center; and Vizcaya, a museum on the former estate of industrialist James Deering.

MIAMI SEAQUARIUM

4400 Rickenbacker Causeway
Miami, FL (305) 361-5703

Remember Flipper, the dolphin star of the television show of the same name? Well, a Flipper descendant is living here in Flipper Lagoon and still performing. He's joined by a few of his friends for fun-filled shows several times each day. The television series was filmed here, as was the second Flipper movie.

But this facility has much more to offer than a glimpse at the famous dolphin. Education plays an important part of all the activities here, and the best part of it is you don't realize you're learning, you just think you're having fun.

One regularly scheduled show features a 10,000-pound killer whale, and another highlights sea lions. In all, six different shows are presented continuously. Exhibits include: the Lost Islands Habitat, where you'll see flamingos, sea turtles, and fish in a mangrove forest setting; Faces of the Rainforest, exotic birds and reptiles; Life on the Edge, a touch pool with a variety of marine life; and a special manatee presentation and discussion.

Open daily, 9:30 A.M. to 6:30 P.M. Admission: adult, under $18; 12 and under, under $13.

Food may not be brought into the facility, but a cafeteria and several specialty snack stands serve a wide variety of food and drink. Make sure you try the open-pit-barbecued ribs and chicken. Just follow your nose, and you'll find the appropriate eatery.

Located ten minutes from downtown Miami. Take the Key Biscayne exit off I–95; pick up the Rickenbacker Causeway and follow signs to the Seaquarium.

MONKEY JUNGLE

14805 Southwest 216th Street
Miami, FL (305) 235–1611

(Editor's Note: The jungle received severe damage from Hurricane Andrew in August 1992. Park officials estimate that complete restoration may take two years. Portions of the facility, however, will remain open. Call first.)

The traditional zoo roles are switched here. Once you enter, you'll be in the cage while the animals run free. Opened in 1935, Monkey Jungle was one of the first animal parks to exhibit animals in the wild while containing visitors in a wire mesh walkway.

You may not see Tarzan and Jane cavorting among the apes here, but you will enjoy the walk through thirty acres of lush tropical greenery as you observe hundreds of monkeys, chimps, orangs, and apes going about their everyday business in their native settings. Keep your camera ready, because if you're lucky you might come face-to-face with one of them.

Season: Year-round, holidays too.

Hours: 9:30 A.M. to 6:00 P.M., daily. Last ticket sold at 5:00 P.M.

Admission: Adults, under $12; ages 4–12, under $7; seniors, under $10; under age 4, free.

The animals: More than 1,600 mammals, fish, and reptiles, more than 50 species, displayed in outdoor naturalistic habitats. Highlights include the Asiatic ape compound and South American Rain Forest.

Entertainment: 1 of 3 different animal shows begins every 45 minutes, throughout the day. They include the Wild Monkey Swimming Pool, Amazonian Rain Forest, and Ape Encounter.

Extras: Self-guided tours through the display area.

Special events: There are occasional special weekend events scheduled throughout the year.

Food service: 1 snack bar on the grounds, and picnics are permitted.

Plan to stay: 2 hours.

Directions: Located southwest of downtown Miami. Take U.S. Route 1 to S.W. 216th Street. Go west on 216th for 3 miles to the entrance.

Nearby attractions: Parrot Jungle and Gardens; Miami MetroZoo; Hialeah Racetrack; Vizcaya, former estate of industrialist James Deering; Miami jai alai games; Joe Robbie Stadium, home of the Miami Dolphins football team and the Florida Marlins baseball team.

PARROT JUNGLE AND GARDENS

11000 Southwest 57th Avenue
Miami, FL (305) 666–7834

If you like big, brightly colored birds and flowers, this is the place for you. To walk through the imposing entrance of native coral is to embark on a mini-trip into a tropical jungle.

Here hundreds of parrots, macaws, cockatoos and other exotic birds fly freely about as you make your way along the trail through a lush jungle-river setting filled with blooming orchids, bromeliads, hibiscus, caladiums, and many, many trees and shrubs.

Season: Year-round, holidays too.

Hours: 9:30 A.M. to 6:00 P.M. Last admission at 5:00 P.M.

Admission: Adults, under $14; ages 3–12, under $9; under age 3, free.

The animals: More than 1,000 animals, more than 100 species, all in a natural outdoor setting. Living in harmony with the hundreds of tropical
birds are a handful of reptiles and small mammals. Highlights include a
large flock of flamingos in Flamingo Lake, and a major waterfowl display.

Entertainment: Macaws and cockatoos perform daily at the Parrot Bowl.
Shows run continuously throughout the day. At designated locations,
birds will also eat out of your hands and pose for pictures.

Extras: Baby-bird training arena; cactus garden.

Food service: Parrot Cafe offers a variety of rice and pasta dishes, chili, salads, and some fast-food items. It is also open for breakfast, at 8:00 A.M.,
offering some of the best omelets around. Snack bars are located
throughout the property, and picnics are permitted.

Plan to stay: At least 2 hours.

Directions: Located south of downtown Miami. Take U.S. 1 (Dixie Highway) to S.W. 57th Avenue (Red Road). Go south on Red Road for about
4 miles to S.W. 112th Street (Kilian Drive). Entrance will be on your
right.

Nearby attractions: Miami Seaquarium; Monkey Jungle; Vizcaya, former
estate of industrialist James Deering; Gold Coast Railroad Museum; HMS
Bounty, built for the movie *Mutiny on the Bounty;* Miami MetroZoo;
Miami Herald Building, offers free tours; Miami Jai Alai Fronton, where
jai alai games can be seen during the winter months.

ST. AUGUSTINE ALLIGATOR FARM

Route A1A South
St. Augustine, FL (904) 824-3337

Gomek, the largest crocodile in the Western Hemisphere, moved here a few years ago from his former home in the Fly River of New Guinea. Here in Florida you can see him from above and below in a special glass-walled exhibit.

The "Farm" has an interesting history that dates back to its founding in 1893, when George Reddington and Felix Fire operated a trolley between the city and the beaches. The two men often came upon alligators along the trolley route and captured the reptiles, placing them in an abandoned beach house.

As more people learned of their collection, Reddington and Fire decided to charge admission, thus creating one of Florida's earliest tourist attractions. Beach erosion forced the collection to be moved to its present location, where it occupies seventeen acres on Anastasia Island.

Also contained here is the largest crocodilian collection in the world, with representatives of twenty-one of the twenty-two existing species. There is also a bird rookery in the adjoining marshland that relies on the alligators to keep tree-climbing predators away.

Season: Year-round, holidays too.

Hours: June through August, 9:00 A.M. to 6:00 P.M., daily. Remainder of the year, closes at 5:00 P.M., daily.

Admission: Adults, under $10; ages 3–11, under $8; over age 55, under $9; under age 3, free.

The animals: Approximately 700 animals, 100 species, all in natural habitats. Highlights include Gomek; rookery in swamp area, inhabited by egrets, herons, ibis, and other native birds.

Entertainment: Wildlife shows every hour, from 10:00 A.M. to 5:00 P.M., daily; tours by reservation.

Extras: Self-guided trail through swamp on elevated walkway; animal petting area.

Food service: 1 snack bar offers a variety of fast foods, snacks, ice cream, and beverages. Picnics permitted.

Plan to stay: At least 1 hour.

Directions: Located on Anastasia Island. Take U.S. 1 (Dixie Highway) to

Route A1A East (Anastasia Boulevard). Cross waterway on Bridge of Lions. Alligator Farm is less than 2 miles ahead, on right, after crossing bridge. Follow signs.

Nearby attractions: Potter's Wax Museum; Castillo de San Marcos National Monument, an old Spanish fortress; Old St. Augustine, with buildings dating back to the 1700s, best viewed on a walking tour; Fountain of Youth Archaeological Park, contains spring reputed to be the one sought by Ponce de Leon.

SANTA FE TEACHING ZOO

3000 Northwest 83rd Street
Gainesville, FL (904) 395–5604

Unlike other listings in this book, this zoo does not exist primarily for the public. Its main purpose is to provide an environment where zoo keepers may learn their trade. Operation of this zoo is a required part of the curriculum of the Animal Technology Program at the Santa Fe Community College.

Set on fourteen wooded acres on the college campus, the zoo is a functioning biological and zoological garden and is open only at particular times to the public.

Season: Year-round. Closed the last two weeks of December and all major school holidays.

Hours: Weekends, 9:00 A.M. to 2:00 P.M.; weekdays by appointment only.

Admission: Free

The animals: More than 250 animals—mostly small animals—from over 70 species, all in naturalistic habitats.

Entertainment: Although there are no special events or entertainment here, free tours are available to all visitors.

Food service: A cafeteria is located elsewhere on the campus, and there are nearby picnic areas.

Plan to stay: 1 hour.

Tim's Trivia

Ninety percent of the mammals displayed in North American zoos are captive-born. Fifty percent of those are offspring of captive-born parents.

Directions: I–75 to exit 77. Make a right off the exit and follow signs to the college.

Nearby attractions: Devil's Millhopper State Geological Site, guided tours through a ravine formed in the 1800s when an underground cave collapsed; Florida Museum of Natural History, on University of Florida campus, contains large shell collection, mounted birds, Indian artifacts, and replicas of a Mayan temple and a Florida cave.

SEA WORLD OF FLORIDA
7007 Sea World Drive
Orlando, FL (407) 351–3600

Shamu is the star here, but as you'll see, there's a lot more to Sea World than killer whales. This particular marine park has gone down in the history books as the facility where the first killer whale was born and thrived in captivity. Since then, two other Sea World facilities have done the same.

Similar to the other Sea Worlds in Ohio, Texas, and California (the original), this 135-acre park features a variety of marine animals in theme productions and exhibits.

Season: Open 365 days a year.

Hours: 9:00 A.M. to 7:00 P.M., with closing extended during summer and holidays. Gates close one hour before park closes.

Admission: Adults, under $30; ages 3–9, under $25; under 3, free. Seniors and military receive a 15 percent discount.

The animals: More than 8,000 animals, more than 360 species, including mammals, birds, reptiles, and fish. Exhibits include Penguin Encounter, considered the world's largest and most advanced of its kind, home to hundreds of penguins and alcids native to the Arctic and Antarctic regions; Walrus Training, a facility and exhibit; Tropical Reef and Caribbean Tide Pool, featuring more than 1,000 tropical fish that inhabit a 160,000-gallon South Pacific coral reef display and 17 smaller aquariums; Sting Ray Lagoon, and the dolphin and seal community pools where people are allowed to interact with the animals; and Terrors of the Deep, featuring more than 1,000 of the most dangerous sea critters, from eels and venomous fish to barracuda and sharks.

Entertainment: 7 major shows include the major trademark production of all Sea Worlds, the killer whale show. Others include a whale and dolphin show; an otter, walrus, and sea lion presentation; and the Windows to the Sea, a multimedia presentation.

Extras: A 90-minute behind-the-scenes tour; sky tower, extra fee; Shamu's Happy Harbor, a 3-acre participatory playground for the kids; the Busch Hospitality Center, with exhibits and a history of the Busch family businesses; and Bermuda Triangle, a simulated sub-oceanic adventure.

Food service: 6 restaurants and numerous food, drink, and snack locations.

Plan to stay: 8 hours.

Directions: Located at the intersection of I–4 and the Bee Line Expressway, 10 minutes from downtown Orlando.

Nearby attractions: Wet 'N Wild water park; Water Mania water park; Universal Studios Florida; Gatorland zoo; Larzland family fun center; Walt Disney World.

SILVER SPRINGS

State Route 40
Ocala, FL (800) 274–SILVER

The advertisements for this venerable complex call it a peaceful paradise and a geological wonder. Few could find grounds for argument. It's a wonderful journey into what Florida once was.

Known for decades for its glass-bottom boat journeys, the park is also a great place to do some animal watching.

Season: Open 365 days a year.

Hours: 9:00 A.M. to 5:30 P.M., with extended hours during summer, holidays, and peak visitor seasons.

Admission: Adults, under $21; ages 3–10, under $15; under age 3, free.

The animals: Native and exotic animals in natural habitats.

Extras: Lost River Voyage, a boat trip on the Silver River, will show you an untouched area of Florida; Jeep Safari is a ride among free-roaming wildlife, from great horned owls to zebras to rhesus monkeys; Cypress Point is a 5-acre natural marsh with alligators, turtles, and flamingos; the Jungle Cruise, a narrated river safari passes Barbary sheep, llamas, giraffes, zebras, and ostriches; Doolittle's Petting Zoo.

Entertainment: 3 different shows, 3 times daily, featuring mammals, reptiles, and birds.

Special events: Photo Safari, in May; Chimpanzee Celebration, two weeks in June; Christmas Spectacular, entire month of December; and Light Up the Springs, one night in mid-December, featuring Santa and Florida "snow."

Food service: Several eateries, including Springside Pizzeria, Outback Restaurant, and Jungle Junction, serve up a wide array of food and beverages. There are also numerous snack spots.

Plan to stay: 5 hours.

Directions: Located 72 miles north of Orlando. Take exit 69 (U.S. 40) off I–75. Park is located one mile east of Ocala, on U.S. 40.

Nearby attractions: Wild Waters water park, which also has mechanical rides, directly adjacent to Silver Springs.

THE ZOO

5701 Gulf Breeze Parkway
Gulf Breeze, FL (904) 932–2229

As you walk through the gorilla exhibit here, don't be alarmed if you notice a very large pair of eyes staring back at you. They probably belong to Colossus, one of the largest gorillas in captivity, who lives here with his mate, Muke.

The Zoo, one of the newest in the country, occupies fifty acres in the western Florida panhandle, part of which is actually a thirty-acre wildlife preserve in its natural state. You can view much of it from the Safari Line Train; the remaining acreage contains a series of beautifully landscaped ponds and walkways, with lots of tropical flowers, shrubs, and trees.

Season: Year-round, closed Thanksgiving and Christmas Day.

Hours: During daylight saving time, 9:00 A.M. to 5:00 P.M. Remainder of the year, closes at 4:00 P.M. Visitors may remain on the grounds one hour after closing.

Admission: Adults, under $10; ages 3–11, under $6; seniors, under $8; handicapped, under $4; under age 3, free. Additional fees: elephant rides, under $3; Safari Line Train, under $2.50.

The animals: More than 600 animals, approximately 200 species, in naturalistic habitats. Highlights include the gorilla exhibit, with a circular overhead walkway; Australian exhibit; and the new cougar and jaguar area, opened in 1992.

Entertainment: Elephant shows twice daily; daily giraffe feedings.

Extras: Safari Line Train; elephant rides and picture-taking sessions; children's zoo with contact area.

Special events: Zoo Boo, at the end of October, is the only regularly scheduled event.

Food service: Jungle Cafe offers a complete line of fast foods, sandwiches, pizza, nachos, fries, beverages, ice cream, and snacks. Picnics are permitted.

Plan to stay: 3 hours.

Directions: Located in the westernmost area of the state, between Pensacola and Navarre Beach, on Highway 98 (Gulf Breeze Parkway), about 15 minutes south of the Pensacola Bay Bridge.

Nearby attractions: Gulf Islands National Seashore, with tours of Fort Pickens and parts of the Pensacola Naval Air Station; also several museums and shopping areas in Pensacola itself.

WEEKI WACHEE SPRING

State Route 50 and U.S. 19
Spring Hill, FL (904) 596–2062

Known for its beautiful mermaids, this 200-acre family park is much more than a place to watch the mythical creatures perform. The bird shows here are some of the best in the state. The Birds-of-Prey show features eagles, hawks, falcons, and vultures in free flight demonstrations. The Exotic Birds show highlights colorful macaws, parrots, and cockatoos.

The Wilderness River Cruise takes visitors on a silent, electric-powered boat down a winding river to get a good look at alligators, river otters, and raccoons in their natural habitats. The boat stops at the Pelican Preserve, where pelicans and other sea birds that are permanently injured and unable to survive in the wild live out their lives.

There's also a petting zoo and various other shows in the complex, which is considered to be America's only natural springwater park. Open daily, 9:30 A.M. to 5:30 P.M., with ticket booths closing one hour prior to park closing. Adults, under $15; ages 3–12, under $10; under 3 free. Free parking. Located forty-five minutes north of Tampa at the intersection of U.S. Highway 19 and State Road 50.

Georgia

AQUARIUM OF THE UNIVERSITY OF GEORGIA

On Skidaway Island
McWhorter Road
Savannah, GA (912) 598–2496

Admission is free at this facility, which is run by the Marine Extension Service of the university. Overlooking the Intracoastal Waterway, the building houses sixteen aquarium tanks, and outside are nature trails through the woods where you're likely to find quite a few native Georgian animals.

Most of the tanks are saltwater, featuring the marine life indigenous to the coastal areas of the state. One exhibit highlights the specimens found around Gray's Reef, a national marine sanctuary, 18 miles off the coast of Georgia. Elsewhere in the building is a small marine museum featuring shells, bones, and artifacts.

Open year-round, closed on Sundays and holidays. Hours: Monday through Friday, 9:00 A.M. to 4:00 P.M.; Saturdays, noon to 5:00 P.M. Picnic facilities are available.

Located 14 miles southeast of the city. Take Waters Avenue out of town, across the Skidaway Island Bridge to McWhorter. Take a left and go about 4½ miles. Facility is on your left.

DAY BUTTERFLY CENTER

In Callaway Gardens
Pine Mountain, GA (404) 663–2281

Referred to as "flowers of the air," more than 1,000 butterflies live harmoniously among hummingbirds, doves, ducks, and hundreds of tropical plants here in the largest free-flight, glass-enclosed conservatory in North America built especially for butterflies.

The 7,000-square-foot glass conservatory features more than fifty species of tropical butterflies. Outside the conservatory, special wildlife gardens have been designed and planted to attract more than seventy native species of butterflies.

▼▼▼▼▼▼▼▼▼▼▼▼▼▼▼▼▼▼▼▼▼▼▼▼▼▼▼▼▼▼▼▼▼▼▼

Fauna Fun Facts

An elephant's trunk contains 40,000 muscles and can pick up an object as small as a grain of rice or as large as a huge log.

Built in 1988, the octagonal building also houses a gift shop, educational exhibits, and a theater that offers a twelve-minute film on butterflies in continuous showing.

Located on four and a half acres, the butterfly center is a part of the 2,500-acre year-round horticultural display garden and resort collectively known as Callaway Gardens. There are hiking trails, horticulture exhibits, 700 varieties of azaleas, and the world's largest display of hollies.

Named in honor of Cecil B. Day, Sr., founder of Days Inns of America, the butterfly center is open year-round, seven days a week. Admission is included in general gate admission to the gardens: adults, under $8; children 6–11, $1; under 6, free. Hours are 8:00 A.M. to 5:00 P.M., with extended hours during summer months. Picnics may be brought in, and there are several family restaurants on the grounds.

Located seventy miles south of Atlanta. Take I–85 to exit 14 and follow signs to Callaway Gardens.

STONE MOUNTAIN PARK

Highway 78
Stone Mountain, GA (404) 498–5600

Miles of nature trails and twenty acres of natural woodlands housing bison, elk, waterfowl, bobcats, otters, hawks, and owls are just part of the attractions here at Stone Mountain Park. A petting area offers contact with chickens, ducks, baby goats and sheep, cows, and a variety of other animals. A self-guided tour will take you along paved walkways past the various wildlife areas, including one for newborns and a duck pond full of local as well as transient waterfowl.

In addition to the wildlife, make sure you see the huge carvings on the side of the mountain. That's what put this place on the map to start with.

The park is open year-round, 10:00 A.M. to 7:00 P.M. from Memorial Day through Labor Day, and 10:00 A.M. to 5:30 P.M. the rest of the year. A vehicle fee to the park is $5 per car, with admission to the woodland's area extra: adults, under $3; ages 3–11, under $2; 2 and under, free.

Stone Mountain is located 16 miles east of Atlanta on Highway 78. Look for the Stone Mountain exit and follow the signs.

ZOO ATLANTA

In Grant Park
800 Cherokee Avenue
Atlanta, GA (404) 624–5600

Peacocks roam the grounds and a beautiful butterfly garden is in full bloom during the summer months here on the zoo's thirty-seven acres in Atlanta's Grant Park. Exhibits are arranged in a circular pattern on low rolling hills, making it easy walking for the whole family.

Opened in 1889, the zoo began when Atlanta merchant G. V. Gress purchased a collection of animals from a traveling circus and donated them to the city. In 1935 the zoo was enlarged when Coca-Cola heir Asa Candler, Jr., donated his private animal collection to the city.

The facility is currently being redeveloped along the lines of a "biopark," with an integration of flora and fauna that will bring extensive botanical displays within the animal exhibits.

Season: Year-round, closed New Year's Day, Martin Luther King, Jr.'s Birthday, Thanksgiving, and Christmas Day.

Hours: Memorial Day through Labor Day, 10:00 A.M. to 6:00 P.M. Remainder of the year, closes at 5:00 P.M., daily.

Admission: Adults, under $9; ages 3–11, under $6; under age 3, free. Additional fee: train ride, under $2.

The animals: More than 900 animals, more than 200 species, in natural outdoor habitats. Highlights include Ford African Rain Forest, starring zoo mascot Willie B., an African gorilla brought to the zoo in 1961, when he was only 3 years old; Masai Mara, an East African Plains exhibit; Sheba Sumatran Tiger Forest; Okefenokee Swamp exhibit.

Entertainment: Elephant show, 3 times daily; Nature Quest, a wildlife animal show, 3 times daily; Gorilla feedings throughout the day.

Extras: Train ride; OK-to-Touch Corral, animal contact area.

Special events: On a changing basis, each month is devoted to a particular group of animals. At the end of that month there is a big event to wrap up the observation. Annual special events include the Aldabra 500 Tortoise Race, in May; Willie B.'s birthday and Conservation Day, both in June; the Great Halloween Caper, in October.

Food service: Okefenokee Cafe, a sit-down restaurant; Swahili Market snack bar; and smaller snack bars along the trails.

Plan to stay: 3 hours.

Directions: I–20 to Boulevard exit. Go south on Boulevard. Zoo entrance is a half-mile ahead on right side, next to the Atlanta Cyclorama.

Nearby attractions: Atlanta Cyclorama, a 360-degree painting of the Civil War; Six Flags Over Georgia, amusement park; Stone Mountain Memorial State Park, a Confederate memorial cut into the side of a mountain; Underground Atlanta, stores, restaurants, and nightclubs; The World of Coca-Cola museum.

Hawaii

HONOLULU ZOO

In Kapiolani Park
151 Kapahula Avenue
Honolulu, HI (808) 971–7171 (recording); (808) 971–7175

Barren brown mountains form a neutral background to the forty-two acres of lushness that makes up what officials here call "the biggest and the best zoo for 2,300 miles."

Since 1947 the facility has occupied formerly royal lands that were dedicated as a public park by King David Kalakaua in 1877. Today, the facility presents some of the world's vanishing wildlife, exhibiting them in a peaceful park setting, a virtual botanical garden.

You'll see lions, elephants, and bears here, but also rare wildlife like the nene (Hawaiian goose) and a collection of Hawaiian marsh birds.

Season: Year-round, closed Christmas Day and New Year's Day.

Hours: 8:30 A.M. to 4:00 P.M.

Admission: Adults, under $3.50; ages 12 and under, free when accompanied by an adult.

The animals: More than 300 species, more than 850 animals, featuring 15 endangered species of reptiles, 15 endangered species of birds, and 12 endangered species of mammals. Top exhibits include: a 10-acre African Savanna; Galapagos turtles, some of the first hatched in captivity; golden lion tamarins; white rhinoceri; and the Elephant Encounter.

Entertainment: Daily showcases of elephant behavior, intelligence, and care; conservation presentations; hands-on experiences at the children's petting zoo; animal demonstrations; and puppet shows.

Special events: On Wednesdays, June through August, everyone gets in free after 4:30 P.M. and local musicians perform Hawaiian music in the "Wildest Show in Town," starting at 6:00 P.M.

Food service: 1 snack bar. Picnics permitted.

Plan to stay: 2 hours.

Directions: Located at the southeast corner of Queen Kapiolani Park, at the Diamond Head end of Waikiki. Zoo entrance is at the corner of Kapahulu and Kalakaua avenues.

Nearby attractions: The famous Waikiki Beach is across the street from the park entrance; Waikiki Aquarium.

SEA LIFE PARK

Makapuu Point, Oahu
Waimanalo, HI (808) 259–7933

There are a great many attractions in the world that are located next to bodies of water, but it's hard to believe that any could be as beautifully situated as this marine park, which overlooks the blue Pacific at Makapuu Point, 15 miles from Waikiki.

And getting here is half the fun. The drive from Waikiki offers spectacular vistas, including natural lava-rock formations and the U.S. Coast Guard lighthouse atop the 600-foot cliffs at Makapuu Point, which also forms quite a backdrop to this park.

Among the multicolored fish on exhibit, the full array of shows and exhibits, and the world's only wholphin, you'll get a chance to look at Hawaii's state fish, the humuhumunukunukuapuaa. And believe it or not, they have another fish here with an even longer name!

Season: Open daily, year-round.

Hours: 9:30 A.M. to 5:00 P.M.; till 10:00 P.M. on Fridays.

Admission: Adults, under $16; ages 7–12, under $9; and ages six and under, free.

The animals: More than 270 species, more than 8,200 animals, including dolphins, monk seals, penguins, sea lions, eels, and the world's only wholphin, a unique whale/dolphin hybrid. Exhibits include: Penguin Habitat, a breeding colony of Humboldt penguins; Monk Seal Care Center, home to the engangered Hawaiian monk seal; Rocky Shores, a reproduction of the intertidal zone; Turtle Lagoon; and the Reef Tank, a 300,000-gallon aquarium that 4,000 specimens, including sharks, rays, and moray eels, call home.

Entertainment: Koloje Kai Sea Lion Show; Hawaii Ocean Theater, dolphin show; Sea Lion feeding pool; touch pool; mini-lectures, scheduled throughout the day; and behind-the-scenes tours (for an extra fee.) Friday night is Kamaaina Night, when island musicians take the stage at 8:30. (A Kamaaina is someone who was born in the islands or has lived here for so long they're Hawaiian at heart.)

Extras: The Pacific Whaling Museum features scrimshaw, historical whaling artifacts, and the skeletal system of a giant sperm whale. Make sure you pick up a "Wholphin Dollah" or a "Fat Fred Fiver." They're custom-minted souvenir coins that can be spent in the park or taken home as mementos.

Special events: February is Humpback Whale Awareness Month, and the park celebrates the annual return of the endangered humpback to Hawaiian waters; International Day of the Seal, March 8; and Easter Egg Hunts, around Easter. Plus, there are special single-session educational seminars scheduled throughout the year.

Food service: Sea Lion Cafe and Rabbit Island Bar and Grill, a sit-down eatery, serves a full line of island and stateside meals. While sitting at the Rabbit Island Bar, you can enjoy a mai tai while taking in a view of the park and offshore islands. Also in the park are 2 snack bars serving fast food and snacks.

Plan to stay: 3 hours.

Directions: Located on the ocean side of Highway 72, 15 miles from Waikiki.

Nearby attractions: Koko Head Park at Hanauma Bay, the beautiful location where the movies *From Here to Eternity* and *Blue Hawaii* were filmed; the Halona Blowhole; Sandy Beach, a popular bodysurfing site; and the offshore islands of Manana and Kaohikaipu, both sanctuaries where more than a quarter of a million birds nest and breed.

WAIKIKI AQUARIUM
2777 Kalakausa Avenue
Honolulu, HI (808) 923–9741

Author Jack London visited this aquarium in 1916 and raved at the beauty of its collection. "I never dreamed of so wonderful an orgy of color and form," he wrote of the experience. Today, that color and form still exist and still continue to fascinate visitors.

Founded in 1904, the 289 species and 1,200 specimens found here focus on the marine life of the Hawaiian Islands and the South Pacific. The live exhibit galleries follow a story line distinctive to its location in the mid-Pacific. Among the exhibits: Hawaiian Waters and Man; Hawaiian Marine Habitats; Hunters on the Reef; and South Pacific Marine Life.

An interesting historical exhibit is From the Sea, which illustrates some of the ways early Hawaiians used local marine life as an important source of food, materials, tools, and medicines.

Located adjacent to the beachwalk, the facility uses the blue waters of the Pacific as a backdrop to its outdoor exhibits, which include The Edge of the Reef, where you can explore the island's rocky shoreline and touch the living sea creatures. Especially nice is the Mahimahi Hatchery and Nursery Deck, an aquaculture exhibit featuring adult and juvenile Mahimahi, eggs, and the food web cultivated to feed the young fish.

Except for Thanksgiving and Christmas Day, open daily from 9:00 A.M. to 5:00 P.M. Admission is under $4 for adults, children under 16, free. Located across from the Honolulu Zoo and Kapiolani Park, adjacent to the Natatorium.

Idaho

DEER FLAT NATIONAL WILDLIFE REFUGE

13751 Upper Embankment Road
Nampa, ID (208) 467–9278 or (208) 888–5582

You get two popular bird watching havens at this refuge: Lake Lowell and the Snake River Islands.

At the lake there's usually a heavy winter concentration of waterfowl, including some 10,000 geese and 100,000 mallard, widgeon, teal, wood, merganser, and other species of ducks. The waterfowl, in turn, attract large numbers of raptors, including hawks, harriers, kestrels, eagles, falcons, and owls.

Tim's Trivia

The only family of white alligators known to exist in the world lives at the Audubon Zoo and the Aquarium of the Americas in New Orleans, Louisiana.

Canada geese nest on the 107 islands that make up the Snake River Islands, and they are joined by ducks, herons, gulls, and such native mammals as muskrat, beaver, raccoon, mule deer, rabbit, and coyote.

The best time to see the heavy concentrations are in the early spring (March and April) and late fall (October and November). The white pelicans, however, can be seen here only during the summer. The islands can be reached only by boat, and boating is limited to daylight hours, between April 15 and September 30.

No charge to enter the refuge, which is open year-round, from dawn to dusk. Headquarters, which includes a visitor's center, is open 7:30 A.M. to 4:00 P.M., Monday through Friday, except holidays.

Located in the southwestern part of the state, between Boise and the Oregon border. Take I–84/80N/U.S. 30 into Nampa, where the road is called Nampa-Caldwell Boulevard. Turn onto West Roosevelt Avenue, going west, and follow signs to Refuge Office and Visitor Center.

MINIDOKA NATIONAL WILDLIFE REFUGE

Route 4
Rupert, ID (208) 436–3589

Created after the Minidoka Dam was constructed on the Snake River in 1906, this refuge is a key habitat for colony-nesting birds, including the western grebe, the double-crested cormorant, the great blue heron, the snowy egret, the black-crowned night heron, and the California gull, as well as Idaho's only nesting white pelicans.

It is also an important stopover for waterfowl following the Pacific Flyway. During spring and fall migrations, up to 100,000 ducks and geese can be found here, with some 500 tundra swans which also stop by.

Bird watching is a do-it-yourself activity here, because there is no visitor's center and no guided tour. Boating is permitted on Lake Walcott, but boats are not permitted in areas of the lake that are inhabited by the birds, so it's best to bring your binoculars. There are some rough trails through the refuge, accessible by foot or in a four-wheel-drive vehicle, where you may be able to see some of the mule deer and pronghorn antelope.

The refuge is open year-round, from dawn to dusk, and the ranger's office is open Monday through Friday, except holidays, from 8:00 A.M. to 4:30 P.M. Admission is free.

Located in the south-central part of the state, east of Twin Falls. Take I–84 into Rupert, then turn onto Route 24 North and drive about 6½ miles, through Acequia. Turn right on County Road 400 and proceed for 5 miles to the refuge headquarters.

ZOO BOISE

In Julia Davis Park
Capitol Boulevard
Boise, ID (208) 384–4260

Located in downtown Boise, in part of the city's popular Julia Davis Park, this neat little ten-acre facility is the state's only accredited zoo.

The eighty-acre park is the city's year-round fun center and has a great deal to offer in addition to the animals. The park was built for Julia Davis by her husband, and the Davises' former home is now a museum in the park.

"Boise" means "wooded" in the French-Canadian dialect, and Zoo Boise lives up to the name. There are a lot of huge trees here, making the atmosphere shady and comfortable, even on the hottest of days.

Season: Year-round, closed Thanksgiving, Christmas Day, and New Year's Day.

Hours: 10:00 A.M. to 5:00 P.M., daily. During June, July, and August, open until 9:00 P.M.

Admission: Adults, under $3; ages 4–11 and seniors, under $2; under age 4, free. On Thursdays everyone gets in for half-price.

The animals: More than 200 animals, more than 90 species, displayed in indoor and outdoor settings. Highlights include the otter and moose exhibits. This is one of the few zoos in the country to feature the moose in its own exhibit.

Entertainment: On weekends, year-round, there are shows featuring birds of prey, small mammals, and reptiles.

Extras: Children's zoo. In other areas of the park are: Julia Davis Fun Depot, an amusement park with a train theme; playground; historical museum; art museum; paddleboats on the lagoon; a rose garden; and a tour train that provides 1-hour guided tours of downtown Boise.

Special events: Zoo Day, third Saturday in May; Zoolympics, second weekend in August; Boo at the Zoo, Saturday before Halloween; Christmas at the Zoo, Saturday before Christmas.

Food service: There is a small fast-food concession stand in the park, and picnics are permitted.

Plan to stay: 1 hour.

Directions: I–84 to the Vista Avenue exit. Follow Vista north about 2 miles. Vista then becomes Capitol Boulevard and the park/zoo entrance is about 1 block up, on the right.

Nearby attractions: Idaho Botanical Garden; the Old Idaho Penitentiary complex, which includes tours of the prison, the History of Electricity in Idaho Museum, and an Idaho Transportation Exhibit; Wild Waters water park; and the World Center for Birds of Prey.

Illinois

BROOKFIELD ZOO

3300 Golf Road
(31st Street and First Avenue)
Brookfield, IL (708) 485–0263

There's so much to see and do here, you'd better reserve a whole day so you'll be able to enjoy it to its fullest. Oh yes, and don't forget to wear comfortable shoes.

The zoo is situated on 215 beautifully manicured acres surrounding Indian Lake, in a suburb of Chicago. It's one of the most modern zoos in the country and ranks among the best in the world for naturalistic habitats and extensive environmental conservation and animal-breeding programs.

The first thing you should do when you enter the gate is check the schedule of events for that day, then plan your visit around those times. There are several shows and activities in both the main zoo area and the children's zoo.

While walking the grounds, make note of the extensive plantings in formal malls and gardens. More than 35,000 annuals bloom during the summer season.

Season: Year-round, holidays too.

Hours: Memorial Day through Labor Day, 9:30 A.M. to 5:30 P.M.; remainder of the year, 10:00 A.M. to 4:30 P.M., with extended hours on spring and fall weekends. Buildings close 30 minutes before the grounds. Both Tropic World and the children's zoo open at 10:00 A.M., year-round.

Admission: Adults, under $4; ages 3–11 and 65 and over, under $2; under age 3, free. Free admission for everyone on Tuesdays. Additional fees: parking, under $4 (slightly more on Tuesdays); children's zoo: adults, under $2; ages 3–11 and seniors, under $1.50; under age 3, free (free admission to children's zoo from November through February); Dolphin Shows: adults, under $3; ages 3–11 and seniors, under $2.50; under age 3, free; Motor Safari: adults, under $3; ages 3–11 and seniors, under $1.50; under age 3, free.

The animals: More than 2,500 animals, about 400 species, displayed in indoor and outdoor naturalistic habitats. Highlights include: Tropic World, one of the world's largest indoor rain-forest displays, where visitors walk a pathway that looks down into the exhibit; the Fragile Kingdom, which includes the Fragile Rain Forest, Fragile Hunters, and Fragile Desert areas of Africa and Asia; Aquatic Bird House, where you can learn how to fly like a bird; the Seven Seas Panorama; and the Walkabout in Australia House.

Entertainment: Elephant demonstrations daily (except Monday), from Memorial Day to Labor Day; Dolphin Shows; Animals in Action (Memorial Day to Labor Day), demonstrations with domestic animals at the children's zoo; daily cow and goat milkings, and wool spinning demonstrations on Tuesdays, also at the children's zoo. Daily feedings at the Bear Grottos and Aquatic Bird House.

Extras: Motor Safari, a narrated tram tour of the zoo, operates continuously each day from early spring through late fall, stopping at various points of interest, at which passengers can reboard; Discovery Center, a multimedia presentation about the zoo; and a hiking trail along Indian Lake.

Special events: Eggcitement, a weekend near Easter; Earth Day observance, in April; Mother's Day and Father's Day events; Affie the Elephant's birthday, in June; July Fourth celebration; Teddy Bear Picnic, in August; Zoo Run Run, in October; Boo at the Zoo, the weekend before Halloween; children's zoo Thanksgiving, on Thanksgiving Day; Breakfast with Santa, and Holiday Magic Festival, weekends in December.

Food service: There are 3 fast-food restaurants and 12 concession stands throughout, selling a complete range of food from hamburgers, fries, and salads, to frozen yogurt, popcorn, cotton candy, and soft drinks. Picnics are permitted.

Plan to stay: All day.

Directions: Brookfield is located 14 miles west of Chicago, at the intersection of 1st Avenue and 31st Street. Take I–294 to 31st Street exit. Travel east on 31st for about 5 miles and watch for signs that will direct you to the zoo, which will be on your right.

Nearby attractions: Kiddieland Amusement Park, in Melrose Park; home and studio of architect Frank Lloyd Wright, in Oak Park, has a visitor's center and architectural tours of homes in the area.

GLEN OAK ZOO

In Glen Oak Park
2218 North Prospect Road
Peoria, IL (309) 686-3365

Lots of big old oak trees provide a shady canopy for this compact zoo in the hills of northeastern Peoria. Although the facility itself is only seven acres in size, there's a lot to see here, including the peacocks that roam the grounds and mingle with the visitors.

The surrounding Glen Oak Park, which occupies 100 acres, is one of the busiest entertainment areas in Peoria, containing the Lucien Memorial Botanical Gardens and Conservatory, a century-old pavilion, athletic fields, lagoon, and amphitheater, where shows are presented regularly during the summer.

Season: Year-round, closed Thanksgiving, Christmas Day, and New Year's Day. Closes at noon on Christmas Eve and New Year's Eve.

Hours: Memorial Day through Labor Day, 10:00 A.M. to 7:30 P.M.; remainder of the year, closes at 3:30 P.M.

Admission: Adults, under $4; ages 4–12, under $3; under age 4, free. On Mondays, seniors are admitted at reduced rates. Additional fees: pony ride, under $2; camel ride, under $3.

The animals: More than 250 animals, more than 100 species, in both indoor and outdoor naturalistic habitats. Highlights include the African Plains, the big cat exhibit, and the reptile exhibit.

Entertainment: In the summer, during times of peak attendance, there are occasional animal and magic shows with a conservation theme.

Extras: Pony rides and camel rides, during the summer; Animal Ring contact area; World of Wonder, a hands-on play area.

Special events: Zoo Day, in August, features free admission and a running race; Halloween Party, in October; Christmas Party, in December. Other

Fauna Fun Facts

Sea turtles return to the same beach where they were hatched to lay their own eggs. The rest of the time they spend their lives at sea.

regular events include Teddy Bear Day and McZoo Day, which are scheduled on a different day each year.

Food service: During the summer, the Banana Cabana offers a good variety of fast foods, snacks, ice cream, and beverages. Picnics are permitted year-round.

Plan to stay: 1 hour.

Directions: Located in central Illinois. Take I–74 to the University Street North exit. Go north on University Street to McClure. Turn right on McClure and follow it to the end, at the park entrance.

Nearby attractions: The Boatworks, a restored riverfront area with museum, meals and cruises; Fort Creve Coeur Park, a reconstructed fort and museum where Rendezvous Days, a living history celebration, is held the fourth weekend in September; Wheels O' Time Museum, vintage autos and toys; Wildlife Prairie Park, nature preserve with museum and guided tours.

HENSON-ROBINSON ZOO

1100 East Lake Drive
Springfield, IL (217) 529–2097

Considered one of the shining jewels in the city's park district, this fourteen-acre zoo was once part of a duck farm owned by one of the area's oldest families.

Lush landscaping and a gardenlike setting make this facility one of the prettiest areas in the city. A large pond with a monkey island in the middle forms the centerpiece. From the grounds you can see Lake Springfield, a 4,235-acre lake that was constructed on the southeastern edge of town.

Season: Mid-April through mid-December, depending on the weather.

Hours: Mid-April through October, daily from 10:00 A.M. to 5:00 P.M.; nice weekends in November and December, 11:00 A.M. to 3:00 P.M.; In July and August, open until 8:00 P.M. on Tuesdays and Thursdays.

Admission: Adults, under $2.50; ages 3–12, under $1.25; seniors, under $1.50; under age 3, free.

The animals: More than 200 animals from 6 continents, approximately 85 species are displayed in enclosures and naturalistic habitats. Highlights include 3 species of endangered lemurs from Madagascar, 1 of only 3 such exhibits in the country; Indonesian binturong exhibit; and tamarins.

Entertainment: No regularly scheduled entertainment, but if you make a request at the gate, zookeepers and their assistants will present brief demonstrations at the various animal exhibits.

Extras: Animal contact area. In the adjoining park, you will find a playground, a beach, and a boat-watching dock.

Special events: Dr. Doolittle Day, in early May, marks the official opening of the season; Conservation Day, June 1; Zoolie Ghoulies, on Halloween.

Food service: Snack items are sold in vending machines. Picnics are encouraged.

Plan to stay: 1 hour.

Directions: I–55 to East Lake Drive/Stevenson Drive exit. Go south on East Lake. About 3 miles after passing the golf course, there will be a sign on the right that directs you to the zoo entrance. If you reach the Lincoln Memorial Garden, turn around, you've gone too far.

Nearby attractions: Lincoln Memorial Garden and Nature Center; Lincoln Depot Museum, where President Abraham Lincoln left for his inauguration; Lincoln Home National Historic Site; Lincoln's Tomb State Historic Site; Oliver P. Parks Telephone Museum; Thomas Rees Memorial Carillon, in Washington Park, has observation decks where visitors can get a close-up look at the bells.

LINCOLN PARK ZOOLOGICAL GARDENS

2200 North Cannon Drive
Chicago, IL (312) 294–4662

You'll be taking a trip back in time when you step into this charming zoo, located between the city skyline and the shores of Lake Michigan. Century-old brick buildings contain state-of-the-art animal exhibits, and the landscaped hillside, with lots of trees, provides a peaceful oasis in the middle of downtown Chicago.

Located on thirty-five acres within Lincoln Park, the city's largest park, this zoo is one of the oldest in the country, having opened in 1869. It has the highest attendance of any zoo in North America, with more than four million visitors each year. Indoor and outdoor animal exhibits, including a working farm, have undergone several renovations in the past fifteen years to keep pace with changing zoological standards.

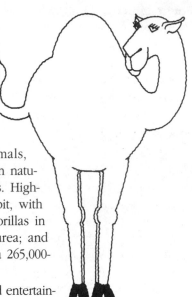

Season: Year-round, holidays too.

Hours: Park, 9:00 A.M. to 5:00 P.M.; animal buildings, 10:00 A.M. to 5:00 P.M.; farm, 10:00 A.M. to 4:00 P.M.

Admission: Free. Additional fee: metered parking on Cannon Drive, under 50 cents per hour.

The animals: More than 1,900 animals, more than 400 species, displayed in naturalistic indoor and outdoor habitats. Highlights include the Great Ape exhibit, with the largest captive collection of gorillas in the United States; Large Mammal area; and Polar Bear Habitat, complete with a 265,000-gallon pool.

Entertainment: No regularly scheduled entertainment, but visitors can watch animals being fed. Feeding times, which vary, are posted at the entrance gate each day.

Extras: Children's zoo, hands-on educational center; Farm-in-the-Zoo a 5-acre working farm.

Special events: Spooky Zoo Spectacular, one Saturday near Halloween; Caroling to the Animals, second Sunday in December.

Food service: Elephant Cafe in the oldest building on the grounds; Cafe Brauer; and Zoo Food Festival concessions at 3 locations in zoo. There is also a tent for picnics.

Plan to stay: 3 hours.

Directions: I–55 to U.S. 40 (Lake Shore Drive). Go north on Lake Shore Drive about 5 miles to Fullerton Avenue. Go west on Fullerton and make first left onto Cannon Drive.

Nearby attractions: In other parts of the park there are: a conservatory with year-round flower exhibits, beaches, playground, tennis courts, golf course, and a place where you can rent bicycles, in-line skates, tandems, and paddleboats. In other parts of Chicago are the John G. Shedd Aquarium, Adler Planetarium, Museum of Broadcast Communications, and Wrigley Field.

MILLER PARK ZOO

In Miller Park
1020 South Morris Avenue
Bloomington, IL (309) 823–4250

This small zoo's origins go back to 1891, when it was basically a collection of menagerie cages spread across Miller Park. About twenty years later, the red brick zoo building, with its ornate windows and turrets, was constructed as a nucleus for the six acres now occupied by the animal exhibits.

Season: Year-round, weather permitting.

Hours: Memorial Day through Labor Day, 10:00 A.M. to 6:30 P.M.; remainder of year, closes at 4:30 P.M.

Admission: Adults, under $2; ages 3–17 and over 60, under $1.50; under age 3, free.

The animals: More than 200 animals, nearly 100 species, displayed in both indoor and outdoor naturalistic habitats. Highlights include the walk-through Tropical Rain Forest, with more than two dozen bird species; river otters; sea lions; and harbor seals.

Entertainment: No regularly scheduled entertainment, but there are animal demonstrations during special events.

Extras: Farmyard-setting children's zoo; Education Building exhibits. In other areas of the park are a playground, tennis courts, outdoor theater, miniature golf, and a fifteen-acre lake where paddleboats and canoes can be rented.

Special events: Love Your Bear Day, in February; Roll into Spring, in mid-March; Conservation Day, on June 1; Zoo Birthday, on June 9; Ice Cream Safari, one Sunday in late June; Fireworks, on July Fourth; music concerts on Sundays in August; Flea Market/Crafts Fair, on Labor Day weekend; Boo at the Zoo, in late October; Holiday at the Zoo, in mid-December.

Food service: Inside the zoo there are snack and beverage vending machines, and picnics are permitted. Just outside the zoo entrance, in the park, there is a concession stand that offers a variety of fast foods, snacks, ice cream, and beverages.

Plan to stay: 1 hour.

Directions: Located in the center of the state, about an hour east of Peoria. Take I–74 to I–55 to Veterans Parkway. Get off at Morris Avenue and go north for about 1½ miles. Park/zoo entrance will be on the right.

Nearby attractions: Nestlé-Beich Candy Factory, offers free tours.

JOHN G. SHEDD AQUARIUM

1200 South Lake Shore Drive
Chicago, IL (312) 939–2438

Of all the attractions in downtown Chicago, none can compare with this facility when it comes to providing a fun and educational time for the entire family. Colorful fish, amazing mammals, playful penguins—they're all here, plus a whole lot more. In the original aquarium building, you'll see specimens ranging from the rare bonytongue fish of the Amazon basin to a Tahitian land snail, to an extensive collection of popular home aquarium fish. A 90,000-gallon coral reef exhibit features an assortment of fish, and a diver who hand-feeds them several times each day.

The new Oceanarium offers scenic re-creations of a rugged Pacific Northwest coastline, complete with mountains. The winding trails lead you past whales, dolphins, sea otters, and harbor seals and through a temperate rain forest. Downstairs, an underwater viewing area provides an up-close view of these mammals.

Season: Year-round, closed Christmas Day and New Year's Day.

Hours: 9:00 A.M. to 6:00 P.M. daily

Admission: Aquarium *and* Oceanarium: adults, under $8; ages 3–11, under $6; 3 and under, free. Aquarium *only:* adults, under $4; ages 3–11, under $3. Free admission to Aquarium every Thursday, with special rates to Oceanarium on that day. NOTE: To avoid long lines and sold-out situations, you can purchase tickets in advance that will give you a specific entry time and date. Definitely the way to go during busy periods. Call (312) 559–0200 for tickets.

The animals: More than 600 species, more than 6,000 animals, all exhibited in re-creations of natural habitats. Notable exhibits include: Animals of Cold Oceans; Animals of the Indo-Pacific; Animals of Warm Fresh Waters; Coral Reef; otters; seals; penguins.

Entertainment: Marine mammal shows in Oceanarium amphitheater, 5 times daily; fish-feeding by diver in Coral Reef exhibit, 2 or 3 times daily. Various interpretive exhibits are accompanied by audio presentations, and there are video presentations as well.

Food service: The Soundings restaurant provides sit-down dining with a panoramic view of Lake Michigan and the city's scenic lakefront. The Bubble Net cafeteria offers a variety of fast food and snack items. Both are located in the Oceanarium.

Plan to stay: 5 hours.

Directions: Located on Lake Shore Drive, near Grant Park and Field Museum. Easy access from the Stevenson I-55 and Eisenhower I-290 expressways. Parking lots are available at Soldier Field and off Solidarity Drive.

Nearby attractions: Field Museum; Adler Planetarium; Grant Park; Soldier Field.

WILDLIFE PRAIRIE PARK

Rural Route 2
Peoria, IL (309) 676-0998

Native Illinois wildlife openly roam these 2,000 lush acres—quite a contrast to what the land looked like but a few decades ago. A former strip mine, the decimated, barren acres were lovingly (and properly) reclaimed and now provide a good example of what can be done through environmentally sound reclamation projects.

This park, which is dotted with lakes and ringed with hiking trails, is now an intermingling of forests, wetlands, and prairies where animals can be see in their natural settings.

Tim's Trivia

More zoos have elephant rides than any other type of live-animal ride. Camels are next in popularity, then ponies. A few have turtle rides.

Season: Year-round, closed Christmas Day and New Year's Day.

Hours: May through October, 10:00 A.M. to 6:30 P.M. weekdays, opens at 9:00 A.M. on weekends; November and April, 11:00 A.M. to 4:00 P.M. weekdays, and 9:00 A.M. to 4:30 P.M. weekends; December through March, 11:00 A.M. to 4:00 P.M. weekdays, 10:00 A.M. to 4:00 P.M. on Sundays, closed Saturdays.

Admission: Weekdays: adults, under $5; ages 13–17, under $2.50; ages 5–12, under $2; under age 5, free. On weekends, rates are slightly higher. Every Wednesday is Carload Day, when up to 8 people enter for a total of less than $8. Every Thursday seniors enter for half-price. Additional fee: train ride, $2 per person over age 4.

The animals: There are more than 150 native Illinois animals in natural settings, which can be seen from elevated trails. Animals include bison, elk, black bears, badgers, wolves, and coyotes, among others.

Entertainment: From May through October, park naturalists present special programs along the various trails; free slide show is presented at visitor center on request.

Extras: Train ride, a 20-minute tour of the enclosed section of the park; walking trails; playgrounds, including one with a 50-foot sliding board; nature museum; country store; overnight accommodations available in log cabin or caboose; Pioneer Homestead contact area; orphan animal nursery.

Special events: Easter Brunch, the day before Easter, features an Easter egg hunt and breakfast at the zoo; Prairie Harvest Festival, in September, has bluegrass music, food, and crafts; Wildlife Scary Park, the three nights before Halloween, features a spooky train ride, costume parade, and trick-or-treating; Old Fashioned Christmas, in December, offers carriage rides, caroling, crafts, and Santa.

Food service: 1 sit-down restaurant is open for weekday lunches and Sunday brunch, serving home-cooked food and great desserts. The brunch consists of a 60-foot-long buffet table with practically anything you might want to eat. There is also a snack shop that offers standard fast-food fare, snacks, ice cream, and beverages.

Plan to stay: 3 hours.

Directions: Located west of Peoria. Take I–74 to exit 82. Follow the big black bear signs about 3 miles to park entrance.

Nearby attractions: Fort Creve Coeur Park, overlooks Illinois River and includes the reconstructed fort and trading post, as well as camping facilities; Steamboat Days Festival, along the waterfront in early June, when several restored boats are open to the public; Lakeview Planetarium.

Indiana

COLUMBIAN PARK ZOO

End of South Street
Lafayette, IN (317) 447–9353

There's a whole lot of family entertainment within the sixty acres of this city park. Among the activities is a small amusement park, a public swimming pool, lots of picnic space, a paddleboat lagoon, and the zoo. Although it has its own area, the zoo also has several attractions away from its central location in the park, including a monkey island and a petting zoo.

You'll find a good deal of stonework throughout the park, which began as a WPA project. The Animal House, the central building of the zoo, is a good example of this masonry. There are approximately seventy-five species, and more than 400 specimens of animals here, featuring one of the largest birds-of-prey collections in the Midwest. These raptors live in a large outdoor walk-through aviary.

Open year-round, free admission. Hours: Memorial Day through Labor Day, noon to 8:30 P.M.; rest of the year, noon to 4:30 P.M. Take exit 26 (South Street) off I–65 and follow it to the park.

FORT WAYNE CHILDREN'S ZOO

In Franke Park
3411 Sherman Boulevard
Fort Wayne, IN (219) 482–4610

Africa and Australia await you here. All you have to do is walk through the blockhouse-style front gate and you're on your way.

Located on thirty-eight gently rolling acres in Franke Park, this zoo is for children of all ages. A couple of interesting attractions here include an adventure-filled canoe ride through the Australian exhibit, and a ride through the African Veldt exhibit in an enclosed safari train.

Season: Mid-April to mid-October, daily. Also open on Halloween and Christmas Day.

Hours: Monday through Saturday, 9:00 A.M. to 5:00 P.M.; on Sundays, remains open an hour later.

Admission: Adults, under $5; ages 2–14, under $3.50; under age 2, free. Additional fees: train ride, pony ride, safari ride, and river ride, all less than $1.50. Horse rental, in Franke Park, is about $5 for a 20-minute ride.

The animals: More than 800 animals, approximately 200 species, displayed in both indoor and outdoor natural habitats. Highlights include the Australian Adventure, which also has a 17,000-gallon Great Barrier Reef aquarium exhibit; African Veldt; Amazon Rain Forest; and the nocturnal animals building.

Entertainment: Zoo docents conduct demonstrations in the amphitheater featuring some of the many animals on exhibit.

Extras: Australian Adventure canoe ride; African Safari ride; train ride, pony ride. In Franke Park there is a horse trail that goes around the zoo and park; playgrounds; a pond with an island containing Mother Goose figures.

Special events: Working for Wildlife Day, in June; The Great Zoo Halloween, in October; Christmas Time at the Zoo, in December.

Food service: 1 fast-food concession stand in the zoo. There's no picnicking in the zoo, but there are picnic areas in Franke Park.

Plan to stay: 2 hours.

Directions: I–69 to exit 109A (Highway 30). Take Highway 30 East, past Coliseum Boulevard, where Highway 30 becomes Goshen Avenue. Continue on Goshen to the third traffic light (Sherman Boulevard). Make a left on Sherman and park/zoo entrance is less than a mile on the left.

Nearby attractions: Historic Fort Wayne, a reconstruction of the original 1816 fort; Lincoln Museum, a collection of Abraham Lincoln memorabilia; The Landing, a shopping area featuring old gaslights and restored shops and restaurants bordering the Erie-Wabash Canal; Lakeside Rose Garden, one of the country's largest rose gardens; and Johnny Appleseed Park, where the annual Johnny Appleseed Festival is held in late September.

INDIANAPOLIS ZOO

In White River State Park
1200 West Washington Street
Indianapolis, IN (317) 630–2001

Not to be confused with the old one, the "*new* Indianapolis Zoo" is a state-of-the-art zoological park located on sixty-four acres on the west bank of the White River, in the southwestern quadrant of downtown Indianapolis.

It contains the state's first major aquarium, one of the world's largest totally enclosed, environmentally controlled whale and dolphin pavilions, and is three times larger than its previous location on the other side of town.

Situated amid the 276-acre White River State Park, which is undergoing extensive renovations, the new cageless zoo is made up of spacious natural habitats and attracts more than a million visitors annually.

Season: Year-round, holidays too.

Hours: Opens every day at 9:00 A.M. and closes either at 4:00 or 5:00 P.M., depending on the season.

Admission: Adults, under $9; ages 3–12, under $6; over age 62, under $7; under age 3, free. On the first Tuesday of each month, there is free parking and a reduced admission charge from 9:00 A.M. to noon. Additional fees: parking, under $3; carousel, under $1.50; pony and train rides, under $2; camel and elephant rides, under $3.

The animals: More than 2,000 animals, more than 300 species, in simulated natural habitats of the world's waters, deserts, plains and forests. Outstanding exhibits include the Waters Complex, with its large aquarium and huge whale and dolphin pavilion; a Deserts Conservatory, under an 80-foot diameter dome; and a Plains area, featuring a wide variety of mammals and a walk-through aviary.

Entertainment: Dolphin shows; daily animal programs and the feeding of dolphins and sea lions are also open to the public.

Extras: Antique carousel; pony, camel, and elephant rides; miniature train ride; Encounters area, with a discovery center and outdoor arena; horse-drawn streetcar in the plaza area.

Food service: Main restaurant with seating for 500 in the plaza, as well as snack and ice cream stands scattered throughout the grounds.

Plan to stay: 5 hours.

Directions: I–70/I–65 to Washington Street (U.S. 40). Go west on Washington for about 2 miles. Watch for signs directing you to zoo entrance on the right, just after crossing the bridge over the White River.

Nearby attractions: Home of Benjamin Harrison, 23rd President of the United States; Children's Museum of Indianapolis, featuring toys, science experiments, and computer discovery center; Indianapolis Motor Speedway, home of the Indy 500; James Irving Holcomb Observatory and Planetarium; and Indiana State Museum.

MESKER PARK ZOO

Bement Avenue at St. Joseph Street
Evansville, IN (812) 428–0715

The centerpiece of this sixty-seven-acre zoo is a large lake where you can paddle around in boats along with the swans and waterfowl. In the middle of the lake is an island containing a concrete replica of the *Santa Maria,* one of Christopher Columbus's three famous ships.

For a fun and a very different type of summer activity, come during August, when the zoo holds its famous Winter Carnival. Through the wonders of modern technology, visitors can take part in all sorts of winter activities, including snowball fights and ice sliding, in the dead of summer. There's even an iceberg floating in the lake, and local restaurants hold ice carving demonstrations.

Season: Year-round, holidays too.

Hours: Memorial Day through Labor Day, 9:00 A.M. to 7:00 P.M.; remainder of year, closes at 4:00 P.M.

Admission: Adults, under $5; ages 3–12 and seniors, under $3; under age 3, free. In December, January, and February, admission is free for everyone. Additional fees: paddleboats, under $2 per person per half-hour; train ride, under $2.

The animals: More than 650 animals, more than 200 species, displayed in naturalistic habitats according to continent of origin. Highlights include African Panorama, Asian exhibit, and the only pair of glacier blue bears on exhibit in the world.

Entertainment: No regularly scheduled entertainment except during special events. Occasionally, zoo volunteers will be stationed near exhibits to talk about the animals contained within.

Extras: Train ride around zoo; paddleboats on the lake; children's zoo, with contact area. There is also a playground in another part of the park.

Special events: Easter at the Zoo, in the spring; Zoo Day, in June; Winter Carnival, in August; Children's Art Fair, in September; Halloween at the Zoo, in late October; Christmas Light Festival, in December.

Food service: 1 concession stand offers a variety of fast foods, snacks, ice cream, and beverages. Picnics are permitted.

Plan to stay: 2 hours.

Directions: Located in the southwestern corner of the state. Take State

Route 31 to Diamond Avenue exit. Travel west on Diamond about 3½ miles to St. Joseph Street. Go south on St. Joseph for about a half-mile, then follow signs to park entrance.

Nearby attractions: Angel Mounds State Historic Site, contains a reconstructed ancient Indian village, with interpretive center and nature preserve; Evansville Museum of Arts and Science, contains antique railroad exhibits, reproduction of late 19th-century river town and art exhibits.

POTAWATOMI ZOO

In Potawatomi Park
500 South Greenlawn Boulevard
South Bend, IN (219) 284–9800

Named after a tribe of native Americans who once inhabited the area, this zoo is a nice little belt of green in downtown South Bend.

Here among the rolling hills you can stroll through Indiana's oldest zoo, which opened in 1917. One of the original buildings is still standing and is currently occupied by some of the big cats. Although there are several ponds on the zoo's twenty-two acres, don't miss the one with the spectacular fountain.

Season: Year-round, closed Thanksgiving, Christmas Day, and New Year's Day.

Hours: 10:00 A.M. to 5:00 P.M., daily.

Admission: Adults, under $4; ages 3–14 and over 62, under $2; under age 3, free. On Tuesday and Thursday afternoons, between 4:00 and 5:00, everyone gets in free. Additional fee: pony ride, under $2.

The animals: Nearly 300 animals, more than 50 species, grouped geographically and displayed in naturalistic habitats.

Entertainment: No regularly scheduled entertainment, but animal demonstrations are given by the education department during special events and by reservation.

Extras: Pony rides in summer; children's zoo/farm, with contact and feeding area. In other areas of the park are a pool, greenhouse, playground, tennis courts, and picnic area.

Special events: Zoofest, during the summer; Zoo Boo, at the end of October; Zooltide, Christmas lights and other holiday activities, in late

November and early December. Other special events are held, but not on a regular basis.

Food service: One concession stand offers standard fast-food fare, snacks, ice cream, and beverages. Picnics are not permitted in the zoo but can be held in the adjacent park.

Plan to stay: At least 1 hour.

Directions: Route 90 to exit 23 (Mishawaka). Take Highway 23 (South Bend Avenue) south to Ironwood Drive. Follow Ironwood south to Jefferson. Make a right turn and travel 1 block to the traffic light at Greenlawn Boulevard. Turn left on Greenlawn. Zoo entrance will be on the left after crossing the railroad tracks.

Nearby attractions: Studebaker Archives Center and Century Center, displays related to history of automobile; on the grounds of the University of Notre Dame is a reproduction of the Grotto of Lourdes, along with a replica of the log chapel built in 1830 by the first Catholic priest ordained in the United States, and the Snite Museum of Art.

WASHINGTON PARK ZOO

In Washington Park
Lakefront
Michigan City, IN (219) 873–1510

Built on the dunes of Lake Michigan as a WPA project, this ten-acre zoo has a great deal of stonework from that era throughout the facility, visible in fences, walls, and buildings.

The centerpiece of the zoo is a tall stone observation tower. A walk up its 150 steps takes you to a deck where on a good clear day you can make out Chicago across the lake, about 100 miles away. Being situated on the dunes, the zoo enjoys a nice rolling terrain and is colorfully landscaped.

There are about 200 animals here, representing 100 species. Among the favorites are the Kodiak bear, buffalo, camel, and Siberian tigers. There's also a reptile house and a petting zoo. The zoo hosts an Easter Egg Hunt, and a big celebration on Earth Day each April. Open daily from mid-March through Labor Day.

Hours: March through Memorial Day, 10:30 to 3:00 P.M.; summer months, stays open until 6:00 P.M. Admission: adults, under $3; ages 3–12 and seniors, under $2; under age 3, free. During the summer there's a parking charge, which also includes access to the swimming beach. There are concession stands in the park as well as picnic facilities.

Iowa

BLANK PARK ZOO OF DES MOINES

7401 Southwest Ninth Street
Des Moines, IA (515) 285–4722

As Iowa's only accredited zoo, this one has a great deal going for it. Here you can get up-close and personal with an emu or a peacock, as the path in the Australian Walkabout winds through the habitat at ground level. Also, there's a good chance you'll meet a white swan face-to-face sometime during your visit. They love to mingle.

Located on twenty-two acres just south of downtown Des Moines, the facility has a few midwestern farm-style buildings and a lot of greenery.

Season: May through mid-October.

Hours: 10:00 A.M. to 5:00 P.M., daily.

Admission: Adults, under $4; ages 2–11, under $2.50; seniors, under $3; under age 2, free. Additional fee: train ride, under $2.

The animals: More than 800 animals, more than 120 species, displayed in natural outdoor habitats. Highlights include Australian Walkabout; African Safari; sea lion pool; and macaque (snow monkey) exhibit.

Entertainment: No animal shows are scheduled, but there are interpretive demonstrations in the Australian Walkabout.

Extras: Train ride around the Australian and African exhibits; Discovery Center, with hands-on activities; barnyard, where visitors can feed the goats. Just outside the zoo, in the adjacent park, is a small playground.

Special events: Double Delight Day, end of June, contests for twins; Celebrate Seniors Day, in July, free admission for seniors; Zoo Keeper Weekend, end of July, with keepers out front to answer questions; Bring Your Can to the Zoo Day, in October, children who bring canned goods for the Iowa Food Shelter get in free; Night Eyes, in October, a not-too-scary Halloween event for children.

Food service: Several concession stands offer hamburgers, hot dogs, corn dogs, fries, yogurt, beverages, and some great pizza.

Plan to stay: 2 hours.

Directions: From downtown area, take S.W. 9th Street about 5 miles, and zoo will be on the left. From I–35, take exit 68 to S.W. 64th Avenue. Follow 64th Avenue east to S.W. 9th Street (about 6 miles). Turn right on S.W. 9th and the zoo is on the left.

Nearby attractions: Adventureland, an amusement park; Living History Farms, a 600-acre agricultural farming village museum; White Water University, a water ride park; and the Des Moines Botanical Center, with more than 1,500 species of plants.

GREATER IOWA AQUARIUM

501 East 30th Street
Des Moines, IA (515) 263–0612

When people think of the great state of Iowa, it's probably a pretty safe bet that most would think of just about everything else before they would think of piranhas and moray eels. But this aquarium, located on the Iowa State Fairgrounds, not far from the cattle and hog barns, houses just such exotic, and far-from-home marine specimens.

In fact, it houses more than 300 species of aquatic life, including sharks, lion fish, grouper, fancy goldfish, turtles, frogs, shrimp, and sea horses. In addition, videos depicting all types of aquatic life are available by request at all times, and are shown full-time on weekends.

The most popular exhibits of the sixty displayed are the one featuring an electric eel from South America and the one showcasing a colorful lion fish, which is 12 inches long and has a 14-inch mane of fins.

Fauna Fun Facts

There are more than 350 kinds of sharks known today but only a few, such as the great white shark, are dangerous to people.

Open daily, 10:00 A.M. to 5:00 P.M., except holidays. Admission: under $1.50 for ages 10–65; ages 5–10, under $1; 5 and under and seniors, free.

Take the East University exit (Route 163) off I–235, go east to East 30th, where fairgrounds begins and turn right. Go south 3 blocks to Grand Avenue; aquarium is just inside the fairgrounds' main gate.

Kansas

EMPORIA ZOO

In Soden's Grove Park
Commercial Street
Emporia, KS (316) 342–7306

A nice selection of animals, beautiful landscaping, and some picturesque stone buildings from the mid-1930s make this small zoo, which nestles on the northern bank of the Cottonwood River, a popular attraction in this part of the state.

Located in the city-owned Soden's Grove Park, the eight-acre facility is considered a good stopover point for those traveling between Topeka and Wichita. It's about halfway between those two cities along the Kansas Turnpike.

Season: Year-round, holidays too.

Hours: 10:00 A.M. to 4:30 P.M. most days of the year. During June, July, and August, the zoo remains open until 8:00 P.M. on Wednesdays and Sundays.

Admission: Free.

The animals: More than 400 animals, nearly 100 species. The two most popular exhibits are the prairie dogs and the lemurs, and there are about 60 species of birds on display.

Entertainment: During occasional special events, zoo docents will conduct tours and programs at the various exhibits.

Special events: The only regularly scheduled event is a holiday lighting ceremony in early December.

Food service: 1 concession stand sells a variety of fast food, snacks, and beverages on Wednesdays, Saturdays, and Sundays only. A picnic area is also provided.

Plan to stay: 1 hour.

Directions: Take I–35 to 6th Street exit. Go east on 6th to Commercial Street. Turn right on Commercial, traveling away from the center of town. Soden's Grove Park is the last park on the right before you go over the bridge.

Nearby attractions: Lyon County Historical Museum, in Emporia, features exhibits on pioneer life and other phases of Kansas history. From El Dorado, you can take a 2-day wagon-train trek fashioned after those of the 1870s, with pioneer-style meals and evening campfires; Flint Hills National Wildlife Preserve.

LEE RICHARDSON ZOO

In Finnup Park
(at the end of South Fourth Street)
Garden City, KS (316) 276–1250

You can see most of this zoo from your car, but if you really want to get up close to the animals and get a good feeling of the offerings, it's best to do a little walking.

Located on forty-seven acres in Finnup Park, the zoo is one of the largest in the state and contains animals from five continents. It was opened in 1929 and provides a wonderful area of green trees and lawn in the middle of the surrounding Plains terrain.

Season: Year-round, closed Thanksgiving, Christmas Day, and New Year's Day.

Hours: 8:00 A.M. to a half-hour before sunset, March through November; 8:00 A.M. to 4:30 P.M. the remainder of the year.

Admission: Free to pedestrians, under $1.50 per car for access to drive-through area.

The animals: More than 300 animals, more than 90 species, in naturalistic settings according to continent of origin. Mixed-species exhibits feature North America, South America, Asia, Africa, and Australia. Highlights include South American Pampas; North American Plains; and a walk-through, free-flight aviary.

Entertainment: During the summer there is an African elephant training demonstration held twice daily.

Extras: In other areas of the park are a playground, a historic museum, and what is believed to be the world's largest concrete municipal swimming pool with free admission.

Special events: Zoobilee, on July Fourth. Other events are held periodically.

Food service: The Safari Shop snack bar has a complete line of fast-food and snack items, as well as ice cream and beverages. Picnics are also permitted.

Plan to stay: 2 hours. Less if you only drive through.

Directions: Located in the southwestern part of the state, northwest of Dodge City. U.S. Route 50 (Main Street) runs east-west through town. Take Highway 50 to 4th Street. Go south on 4th directly into the park/zoo.

Nearby attractions: Old Fort Dodge, Boot Hill Museum, and historic Front Street are about 50 miles away, in Dodge City.

SEDGWICK COUNTY ZOO AND BOTANICAL GARDEN

5555 Zoo Boulevard
Wichita, KS (316) 942–2213

One of the earliest master-planned zoos in the country, Sedgwick opened in 1971 and has become the largest tourist attraction in the state. Located on the western edge of Wichita, the zoo covers 212 acres, eighty of which are accessible to the public.

Bring your walking shoes if you plan to see all of the thousands of species of animals and plants that occupy the five major exhibit areas. During the warmer weather you can also enjoy a boat ride along a canal, which is part of the Wichita Valley Flood Control System.

Season: Year-round, holidays too.

Hours: 10:00 A.M. to 6:00 P.M. during daylight saving time; 10:00 A.M. to 5:00 P.M. the rest of the year.

Admission: Adults, under $6; ages 5–11, under $2; under age 5, free. Additional fees: boat ride, under $3; horse rides, under $2.

The animals: More than 1,000 animals, more than 250 species, in both indoor and outdoor exhibits arranged in settings corresponding to the five major continents. Included are the African Veldt, South American Pampas, Australian Outback, Asian Jungle, and North American Prairie.

Entertainment: Provided by staff employees during seasonal special events, including Zoobilee Day, in the fall; at Halloween; and at Easter. Tours are available upon request.

Extras: During the summer a boat ride in the canal adjoining the zoo provides visitors with a close-up look at an island occupied by spider monkeys. Horse rides are given at the children's zoo, which is in an American farm setting. There is also a fragrant herb garden in the farm area, and a nature trail in the Prairie exhibit.

Food service: 1 year-round restaurant, with additional concessions open during the summer months.

Plan to stay: 3 hours.

Directions: I–235 to exit 10. At end of exit ramp, turn left. Zoo entrance is a quarter-mile on your left.

Nearby attractions: Old Cow Town Museum, a forty-four–building restored village; Omnisphere and Science Center, planetarium and science museum; Botanica, a self-guiding botanical garden; Joyland amusement park.

SUNSET ZOOLOGICAL PARK

2333 Oak Street
Manhattan, KS (913) 587–2737

Built in 1933 as a WPA project, the zoo is set on fifty-two acres in the beautiful Flint Hills and is surrounded by an expanse of parkland. Through the years, the exhibits have been upgraded to naturalistic habitats, leaving the original barred cages a thing of the past. As you stroll down the hillside toward the back of the zoo, make a point of stopping and enjoying the view of Wildcat Creek.

Season: Year-round, closed Thanksgiving, Christmas Day, and New Year's Day.

Hours: 10:00 A.M. to 6:00 P.M., daily, March through November; noon to 4:00 P.M., weekdays, and noon to 6:00 P.M., weekends, December through February. In June, July, and August, open until 9:00 P.M. on Thursdays.

Admission: Adults, under $2.50; ages 5–12, under $1.50; under age 5, free.

The animals: More than 180 animals, more than 60 species, in indoor and outdoor naturalistic habitats. Highlights include the Asian Forest Preserve, with cranes and red pandas; Australian Outback; and the Snow Leopards of Tibet, which visitors pass through by means of a glassed-in walkway. In the spring of 1993, the new Primate Conservation Center, which will contain a 3-acre outdoor loop, is expected to premiere.

Entertainment: During the summer months there is a live animal show on Thursday evenings; Meet the Keeper demonstrations are held on weekends.

Extras: Children's zoo, with animal contact area; playground.

Special events: Zoobilation, a carnival held every Memorial Day weekend; Cool Cats Jazz Festival, in September; and Zpooktacular, a 3-day Halloween event held at the end of October.

Food service: The Watering Hole serves snack food items. Picnicking is encouraged.

Plan to stay: 2 hours.

Directions: Located about 1 hour west of Topeka. Take I–70 to State Route 18 (Fort Riley Boulevard). Go west on Route 18 through town to Westwood Road. Go west on Westwood to Oak Street. Turn left on Oak and zoo will be 1 block down.

Nearby attractions: Riley County Historical Museum; Hartford House, a prefabricated house brought to Manhattan by steamboat in 1855. The Eisenhower family home and presidential library is in Abilene, about an hour away, as is the Museum of Independent Telephony, which depicts the history of the telephone.

TOPEKA ZOO

In Gage Park
635 Southwest Gage Boulevard
Topeka, KS (913) 272–5821

Intimate and friendly is a good way to describe the Topeka Zoo. Located in a city park, this thirty-acre facility is full of docents, keepers, and other staff people who do their best to help the public get the most out of their visits.

Originally constructed during the 1930s, the exhibits have been updated to modern zoological standards. Well-established trees, shrubbery, and lawns, in addition to the ornate Depression-era buildings, rose garden, carousel, and miniature train (in the adjoining park) provide a great potential for a family outing.

Season: Year-round, closed Christmas Day.

Hours: 9:00 A.M. to 4:30 P.M., daily.

Admission: Adults, under $4; ages 3–12 and seniors, under $3; under age 3, free. Additional fees: carousel and miniature train ride in Gage Park, each under $2.

The animals: More than 300 animals, more than 125 species in both indoor and outdoor settings. Most outstanding exhibits include a walk-through Tropical Rain Forest under a geodesic dome; a Discovering Apes exhibit, where visitors walk in a glass tunnel only inches from orangutans and gorillas; and the Lion's Pride, a natural setting inhabited by a pride of lions.

Extras: Children's zoo, where youngsters can jump like kangaroos, hang from trees like sloths, and pet domestic animals. Outside the zoo itself, in Gage Park, there is a restored 1908 carousel and a miniature train ride.

Special events: Monthly and annual special events include Who's Who in the Zoo, the first Sunday of each month; Earth Day, in June; Teddy Bear Fair, in June; Boo at the Zoo, the end of October; and Zoo-luminations, in December.

Food service: 2 concessions offer a variety of fast foods, snacks, and beverages. Picnics are permitted.

Plan to stay: 2 hours.

Directions: From I–70 get off at the Gage Boulevard exit. Go south on Gage to 6th Street, about a quarter-mile. Turn right on 6th Street and travel approximately one block to Zoo Boulevard. Turn left. Entrance to zoo is half a block down.

Nearby attractions: Reinisch Memorial Rose and Rock Garden, across from zoo entrance; Combat Air Museum, with examples of aircraft used in combat since the Spanish-American War; Ward-Meade Park and House, containing a Victorian-era house; log cabin; Santa Fe Railroad depot; and botanical gardens. Also, the zoo operates an off-premises Conservation Center, where rare and endangered animals, such as Asian wild horses, are bred. Ask for directions at the zoo entrance gate.

Kentucky

LAND BETWEEN THE LAKES

Woodlands Nature Center
Golden Pond, KY (502) 924–5602

Located in the heart of this 170,000-acre peninsula between Kentucky Lake and Lake Barkley, which are located in Kentucky and Tennessee, is the Woodlands Nature Center. A group of native animals, including the coyote, bald eagle, golden eagle, and white-tailed deer, as well as many reptiles and amphibians, are housed here.

Also on exhibit are fallow deer, which were brought to the area by settlers, and red wolves, brought to Woodlands as a part of the breeding program for that endangered species. Different demonstrations and exhibits are held at the center throughout the season.

Down the road, about 16 miles on The Trace, the road that runs the length of Land Between the Lakes, a herd of American buffalo roams on some 200 acres of land. The best time to see the herd is early morning or late evening. During the hot days, they will migrate to the woods a great distance from the road.

But that's not all the animals you'll find here. While driving The Trace, or any of the side roads, it's quite likely you'll also see coyotes, deer, great blue herons, a variety of ducks, raccoons, foxes, turkeys, and other wildlife in their natural setting.

Tim's Trivia

An annual "Winter Carnival" is held each August at the Mesker Park and Zoo in Evansville, Indiana. Snowball fights, ice sliding, ice carving demonstrations and an iceberg in the lake are all made possible by modern technology.

Woodlands Nature Center is open daily March through November, and weekends only December through February. Hours are 9:00 A.M. to 5:00 P.M. Admission is $2 for adults; $1 for children 6–17; under 6 free when accompanied by family. Viewing of buffalo at the Buffalo Range is free.

To get to Woodlands Nature Center from the North Welcome Station off

I–24 at Lake City, go east on The Trace to Silver Trail Road, turn left, and follow the signs. From the South Welcome Center off Highway 79 (in Dover, TN), go west to Silver Trail Road, turn right, and follow the signs. The Buffalo Range is just a few miles west on The Trace from the South Welcome Station, and approximately 20 miles east on The Trace from the North Welcome Station.

LOUISVILLE ZOO

1100 Trevilian Way
Louisville, KY (502) 459–2181

The downtown is on one side and a residential community is on the other, but you can't see either of them from the zoo. Nestled among gently rolling hills and shaded by hundreds of mature trees, this seventy-four-acre zoo is virtually hidden from the outside world.

A large lake in the center acts as a hub for exhibits and educational facilities. The innovative MetaZoo Education Center offers some of the best interactive exhibits of any zoo in the country. It also houses a "pond room," in which a pond functions as home to turtles, birds, and fish.

The HerpAquarium facility is a 14,000-square-foot structure divided into three distinct biomes: water, rain forest, and desert. Each area has a wide selection of appropriate flora and fauna.

Season: Year-round, closed Christmas Day, New Year's Day, and Mondays during the winter.

Hours: Daily, April through Labor Day, 10:00 A.M. to 5:00 P.M.; Tuesday through Sunday, Labor Day through March, 10:00 A.M. to 4:00 P.M. Times are the latest a ticket is sold; zoo stays open an hour past the posted closing time.

Admission: Adults, under $5; ages 3–11 and seniors, under $3; 2 and under, free. Additional fees: parking; miniature train; zoo tram.

The animals: More than 1,600 animals, more than 412 species, displayed in naturalistic settings, with most exhibits free from bars and screens. Outstanding exhibits include: the HerpAquarium; polar bears, with a seating area in front of an underwater viewing window; and mixed animal settings representing six land types—African Veldt, Asian Plains, North and South American Panorama, Aquatics, and the Australian Outback.

Entertainment: The seals are fed individually twice a day, with trainers "health checking" each one as it is fed. Also, the public gets to watch most of what is going on, such as elephant foot trimming, etc.

Extras: Miniature train ride and the zoo tram (in-park transportation), both for additional costs.

Special events: There's an extra charge for the 5-night summer concert series featuring the Louisville Orchestra. Other events include: zoo's birthday party, late April, held in conjunction with the Kentucky Derby Festival; The World's Largest Halloween Party, late October; Winter Light Safari, December.

Food service: A central area near the lake, housed in thatched-roof buildings, features Kentucky Fried Chicken, Pizza Hut, and Taco Bell. Additional snack concessions are located throughout. Picnicking is also permitted in the zoo.

Plan to stay: 3 hours

Directions: Take Poplar Level exit (exit 14) off I–264 (Watterson Expressway). Go north on Poplar Level and turn right onto Trevilian at second light. Zoo is 1½ blocks on the right.

Nearby attractions: Kentucky Kingdom, amusement park; Freedom Hall Arena and the Kentucky State Fairgrounds; Kentucky Center for the Arts; the birthplace of Abraham Lincoln.

Louisiana

ALEXANDRIA ZOOLOGICAL PARK

In Bringhurst Park
City Park Boulevard
Alexandria, LA (318) 473–1385

Comfortably nestled between the past and the future, this cozy zoo takes up only part of its twenty-two acres in Bringhurst Park. Almost completely shaded, it provides visitors a scenic setting for animal watching. Opened in 1926 as a menagerie elsewhere in the park, it was consolidated in its present location during the 1930s.

Traces of the past can be found in some of the architecture on the grounds. The buildings are a blend of the old and the new—the turtle and waterfowl exhibit makes good use of what used to be the park's old fish pool.

Season: Year-round, closed Christmas Day and New Year's Day.

Hours: Daily, 9:00 A.M. to 5:00 P.M.

Admission: Adults, under $3; ages 5–12, under $2; under 5 and over 64, free.

The animals: More than 450 animals, more than 150 species, displayed in both indoor and outdoor habitats. Highlights include the tiger complex and the Sumatran gibbon exhibit, which opened in 1992. A new Louisiana Habitat exhibit, showing natural flora, fauna, and land formations, is expected to open within the next few years.

Extras: In other areas of the park there are athletic fields, a playground, a par-3 golf course, and a nature trail.

Special events: Conservation Day activities, in the spring or summer, coordinated with Central Louisiana (CENLA) Earth Fair; Zoo Day, in May; Safari Night, in October, for adults; Zoo Boo, October 30 and 31; Christmas with the Animals, and 12 Days of Christmas, a local promotional event, in December. An additional fee may be charged for some of the events, and the dates vary from year to year.

Food service: 1 small fast-food concession and vending machines. Picnics are not permitted in the zoo, but there is a large picnic area in the park.

Plan to stay: 1 hour.

Directions: I–71 to Masonic Drive; then pick up Cotton Wright Drive. Zoo is located behind the Bringhurst Park ballfield.

Nearby attractions: There are national forest recreation areas to the north, west, and south of Alexandria, where outdoor activities are offered. In Alexandria is the Kent House State Commemorative Area, featuring a restored plantation from the early 1800s; and the Alexandria Museum/Visual Arts Center, with changing exhibits of fine arts.

AQUARIUM OF THE AMERICAS

111 Iberville Street
New Orleans, LA (504) 595-3474

On the banks of the Mississippi River, just a few blocks from the French Quarter, this high-tech marvel of an aquarium overlooks the river's famed crescent curve that provided the city with its nickname, the Crescent City.

Opened in 1990, the aquarium and its adjacent sixteen-acre park are part of the city's project to revitalize its waterfront that began in the early 1980s with construction for the Louisiana World Exposition (1984). Both of these facilities, as well as the Audubon Zoo, are operated by the Audubon Institute.

Inside, technology provides guests with unique ways of getting closer to the fish, and the action. At several of the exhibits, you'll be able to control underwater video cameras that will allow some up-close-and-personal shots of what truly interests you. Also unique, are several windows that allow you to look behind the scenes at some of the aquarium's technical activities, including an overview of the facility's filtration system.

The aquarium shares a family of the world's only white alligators with the Audubon Zoo.

Season: Year-round, closed Christmas Day and Mardi Gras.

Hours: Daily, 9:30 A.M. to 9:00 P.M., during summer months of June, July, and August. Closing times vary the rest of the year.

Admission: Adults, under $9; ages 2–12, under $5; 2 and under, free.

The animals: More than 7,000 animals in 4 major exhibits areas: Caribbean Reef, a simulation reef through which visitors pass in an acrylic tunnel 20 feet below the surface; Amazon Rain Forest, complete with Indian huts, a 20-foot waterfall, piranhas, butterflies, and birds; Mississippi River Delta, a re-creation of life along the river, with underwater displays of sturgeon, catfish, paddlefish, and more; Gulf of Mexico, a 500,000-gallon tank featuring creatures of the gulf, including lemon sharks, sand tiger sharks, and sawfish.

Extras: Penguin encounters; Microlab, where you can get a microscopic look at undersea life; Touch Tank for a hands-on experience.

Food service: The Aqua Cafe overlooks the Mississippi River and serves a full menu for breakfast, lunch, and dinner. A full bar is in operation.

Plan to stay: 2 hours

Directions: Located at the foot of Canal Street, on the banks of the river.

Nearby attractions: The sights, sounds, food, and attractions of the French Quarter and historic New Orleans, including: the Jax Brewery; the Riverfront Streetcar; Moonwalk observation deck; Spanish Plaza; and the Riverwalk, with more than 200 shops, restaurants, and bars.

AUDUBON PARK AND ZOOLOGICAL GARDEN

6500 Magazine Avenue
New Orleans, LA (504) 861–5108

If you like history, beautiful gardens, and lots of animals, you're going to love this place! Overlooking the Mississippi River, the fifty-eight-acre zoo is located on a portion of the property that was once the plantation of Pierre Foucher, the son-in-law of Jean Etienne de Bore, the first mayor of New Orleans and the man who was the first to successfully granulate sugar.

In 1884–85 this location was the scene of the World's Industrial and Cotton Exposition, the first ever with both indoor and outdoor electric lighting.

The zoo opened in 1914 and contains many rare and endangered species, including part of the world's only family of white alligators (the rest of the family is housed at the Aquarium of the Americas), and lush tropical gardens.

Season: Year-round, closed New Year's Day, Mardi Gras, Thanksgiving, and Christmas Day.

Hours: 9:30 A.M. to 5:00 P.M., daily, except during daylight saving time, when it stays open till 6:00 P.M. on weekends.

Admission: Adults, under $9; ages 2–12 and seniors, under $6, under 2, free. Additional fees: trams, under $3; elephant and camel rides, under $3 each.

The animals: More than 1,500 animals, more than 400 species, exhibited in natural habitats. Outstanding exhibits include Louisiana Swamp, Tropical Bird House, Grasslands of the World, Reptile World, and World of Primates.

Entertainment: Reptile and birds-of-prey shows at Wendy's Wildlife Theater; also elephant shows.

Extras: Mombasa Tram, provides visitors with a guided tour of the zoo;

Pathways to the Past, an interactive natural history museum with a life-size moving dinosaur replica; children's zoo.

Food service: 5 fast-food concessions, featuring hot dogs, hamburgers, pizza, fried chicken, and cajun dishes. Also a picnic area.

Plan to stay: 3 hours.

Directions: I-10 to Carrollton Avenue. Go west on Carrollton to its end, at River Road. Turn left on River. Entrance to zoo is about 1 mile ahead, on the right.

Nearby attractions: French Quarter of New Orleans; Musee Conti Wax Museum; Louisiana State Museum.

GREATER BATON ROUGE ZOO

In Greenwood Park
3601 Thomas Road
Baker, LA (504) 775-3877

Surrounded by large trees and a lot of lush, natural foliage, this facility, which was built in the 1970s, was literally carved out of the woods. Located in a northern suburb of Baton Rouge, the 130-acre zoo has wide sidewalks to accommodate both walking visitors and the tour trams that pass by the exhibits. There is also a train ride for those who want to explore the big woods without all the walking.

Season: Year-round, closed Christmas Eve, Christmas Day, New Year's Eve, and New Year's Day.

Hours: Daily, 10:00 A.M. to 5:00 P.M. On weekends in June, July, and August, closes an hour later.

Admission: Adults, under $3; ages 5–17, under $2; under age 5, free. Additional fees: sidewalk tram, under $2; train ride, under $2; elephant ride, under $2; photo with elephant, under $3 per shot.

Fauna Fun Facts

A kangaroo is only about an inch long when it's born. It then crawls into its mother's pouch and stays there to nurse as it grows.

The animals: More than 900 animals, more than 200 species, most of which are displayed in natural outdoor settings. Highlights include the elephant exhibit, the chimps, and the giraffes.

Entertainment: No regular shows or demonstrations, but keepers will occasionally bring an animal or bird out to meet the public.

Extras: Children's zoo, with farm, petting area, and climb-through prairie dog exhibit; sidewalk tram, a 25-minute guided tour of the zoo; train ride around perimeter of property; elephant rides; nature walk; and playground.

Food service: 2 concessions and a snack bar, which offer hot dogs, hamburgers, nachos, Blue Bell ice cream, Sno-Cones, and animal crackers.

Plan to stay: 2 hours.

Directions: I–10 to exit 8 (Scotlandville-Baker exit). After you get off the ramp, go east to the second traffic light. Make a right on Thomas Road. Travel south on Thomas for 1 mile to zoo entrance, on the left.

Nearby attractions: Louisiana Naval War Memorial, museum complex and World War II destroyer; Old State Capitol, a Gothic Revival castle; Mount Hope Plantation; Old Governor's Mansion and Louisiana Arts and Science Center Planetarium.

Maine

MOUNT DESERT OCEANARIUM

Mount Desert Island
Bar Harbor, ME (207) 244–7330

Two creatures closely associated with the state of Maine are seals and lobsters. Here you can see them both, up close, in their natural settings on an island shared with Acadia National Park.

The Oceanarium is actually divided into three separate sites on Mount Desert Island, with two attractions in Bar Harbor and one in a small fishing village called Southwest Harbor. In Bar Harbor you'll find the Oceanographic Learning Center, a marine aquarium with twenty-two tanks of native New England sea life, a touch tank and several marine-related exhibits, and a small lobster hatchery and fishing museum with exhibits on aquaculture history and techniques.

In Southwest Harbor you can take a guided tour through a lobster museum and salt marsh, which leads to a live harbor seal display and demonstrations.

All three sites are open mid-May through mid- or late October, depending on the weather, Monday through Saturday, 9:00 A.M. to 5:00 P.M. Admission: Oceanographic Learning Center, adults, under $6, ages 4–12, under $5; Salt Marsh Tour, adults, under $6; ages 4–12, under $5; Lobster Hatchery, adults, under $4; ages 4–12, under $3. Children under 4 are admitted free, and a combination ticket for reduced admissions can be purchased at all three sites.

To reach the Mount Desert Oceanarium, take I–95 (Maine Turnpike) north to Bangor. At Bangor, pick up Route 395, heading for Ellsworth. Stay on 395 through Ellsworth and across the causeway onto Mount Desert Island. Follow signs to Bar Harbor and the Oceanarium. There's only one main road on the island, so it'll be hard to miss.

OLDE ORCHARD BEACH AQUARIUM

End of Pier
Old Orchard Beach, ME (207) 934–2344

Out at the end of the pier, on the second floor of a two-story building, you'll find this small, forty-tank aquarium exhibit. There's a nice selection of marine life here, ranging from Maine lobsters and groupers to tropical angelfish, small crocodiles, and piranhas.

Many of the exhibits provide an audiotape description of their inhabitants as well as the traditional signage. Just walk up, push the button, and enjoy the message.

Open daily, 11:00 A.M. to 11:00 P.M., Memorial Day through Labor Day. Admission: adults, under $5; ages 3–12, under $3; under 3, free. As you walk out to the pier's end, you'll pass a lot of retail shops, bars, and restaurants, many of which open earlier and close later than the aquarium.

Take Route 112 off I–95 and go east to Route 1. At the Route 5 intersection, go north to Old Orchard. The pier is the only one in town and is located in the downtown section of the village.

RACHEL CARSON NATIONAL WILDLIFE RESERVE

Route 9
Wells, ME (207) 646-9226

Thousands of shorebirds and migratory waterfowl flock here during spring and fall migrations, joining the hundreds of native species of herons, egrets, and other birds and wildlife that make this reserve their year-round home.

The best time to visit is in October, when you can see not only the ducks and geese on their way from Canada to warmer waters, but also the colorful views of fall foliage. A self-guided mile-long trail through the 4,600 acres of salt marsh and woodlands has eleven stops where wildlife can be observed in natural settings.

Open daily, year-round, from dawn to dusk, the Reserve has no admission charge. Pamphlets for the self-guided tour are available at the park office, open Monday through Friday, from 8:00 A.M. to 4:30 P.M., or in a small kiosk outside the office.

Take U.S. Route 1 into Wells. Once in town, go east on Route 9, toward Kennebunkport. Entrance to Reserve will be on the right, less than a mile out of Wells. Look for the big brown sign.

YORK'S WILD KINGDOM ZOO AND AMUSEMENT PARK

Route 1
York Beach, ME (800) 456-4911

There's a lot to do here for every member of the family. From wild and hairy animals to wild and scary rides, this complex links the state's largest zoo with a great little ride area.

Situated among gently rolling hills, there are a lot of large pine trees and a nice pond on the thirty acres. The walk-through Australian exhibit is shaped like the country itself, and has an Australian-looking guide that gives people a "walkabout" tour of the area. The South American exhibit, set to open in the spring of 1993, will feature a riverboat ride.

Season: May through Columbus Day weekend.

Hours: Daily, 10:00 A.M. to 7:00 P.M.

Admission: Zoo only: adults, under $10; ages 3–12, under $8. Admission to the amusement park is free, with rides on a pay-as-you-go basis. A combination unlimited ride ticket and zoo admission ticket is also available: adults, under $13; ages 3–12, under $12.

The animals: More than 400 animals representing 60 species. Exhibits include: deer, in a five-acre walk-through where you can pet and feed the herd; Australia, with emus, kangaroos, and wallabies; reptile house, a cave-theme exhibit, complete with sound effects; rabbits, a walk-through. Other animals include camels, bear, lions, tigers, giraffes, elephants, and monkeys. The newest exhibit features a white Bengal tiger.

Entertainment: Various animal presentations including a bear show and the popular Talk to the Animals show, where zookeepers speak about various baby animals and then allow children in the audience to hold and pet them. Also clown and magic shows.

Extras: Storyland, a storybook village with walk-in structures depicting popular children's stories; Fort Wild Kingdom, a Wild West village, with free-roaming chickens, cows, and horses. The amusement park has 15 rides, with 9 just for the children.

> **Tim's Trivia**
>
> Kalina, the first killer whale born and raised in captivity, made worldwide headlines when her life began at Sea World of Florida in Orlando on Sept. 26, 1985. Since then, four additional births have taken place in Sea World parks.

Special events: Every weekday, a special promotion takes place: Monday, a television is given away; Tuesday, unlimited rides for $5; Wednesday, kiddies' day, all kids get half-off on combination ticket; Thursday, a 10-speed bicycle is given away; and Friday, seniors get into zoo for half-price.

Food service: 2 food stands in zoo, plus 3 in amusement park. Public picnic grounds are adjacent to parking lot, under the willow trees.

Plan to stay: 3 hours to visit zoo and amusement park.

Directions: Take York exit off I–95; go east on exit road to Route 1 and proceed 2½ miles to park.

Maryland

ASSATEAGUE ISLAND STATE PARK

Route 611
7307 Stephen Decatur Highway
Berlin, MD (301) 641–2120

Paralleling the coasts of Maryland and Virginia, the 37-mile long Assateague Island offers a variety of activities, combining a national seashore and wildlife refuge with camping, fishing, boating, hiking, and bicycling. There are also ample opportunities for birding, viewing wild ponies, and naturalist activities throughout the year.

Perhaps best known for its wild ponies, the park service offers guided walks, talks, children's programs, and seashore recreation demonstrations daily in summer and on weekends in the fall and spring months. Guided walks include explorations of Assateague's bird life, the beach, the salt marshes, the bay, and the dunes.

The herd of ponies you'll see on this side of the island, in the state park, is owned by the National Park Service. They are descended from domesticated stock that was grazed on the island in the seventeenth century by Eastern Shore planters to avoid mainland taxes and fencing requirements. The world-famous pony-penning activity takes place on the Virginia side of the island in late July. (See Chincoteague National Wildlife Refuge in the Virginia section of this book.)

The ponies run wild and can often be seen from the road or around campsites. The park service warns that although the ponies appear docile, they are prone to unpredictable behavior and visitors should not pet or feed them.

Open daily, with no closing hours posted on the Maryland side of the park. There is a $3 vehicle-use fee that is good for seven days. Various permits and requirements must be met to participate in the activities on the island.

The state park is located at the northern end of the island, off the Maryland coast, within the Assateague National Seashore.

BALTIMORE ZOO

In Druid Hill Park
Baltimore, MD (301) 396–7102

In the 1850s, this zoo was no more than a small collection of animals on a private estate. The highlight of the menagerie at that time was a group of llamas that grazed on the front lawn.

Through the years, the 700-acre estate, which included Druid Lake, was deeded to the city and dedicated as a public park. The 158-acre zoo was formally opened in 1876, which makes it the third oldest in the United States.

Acres of huge old oaks shade the gently sloping grounds and the old mansion house, on top of the hill, now serves as the park's administration building. Another old building, the Conservatory, dates back to 1888 and contains an impressive collection of tropical plants, earning it the nickname "The Palm House."

Season: Year-round, closed Christmas Day and one Friday in June to allow the staff to prepare for Zoomerang, the zoo's annual evening fund raiser.

Hours: Daily, 10:00 A.M. to 4:20 P.M., with extended summer hours.

Admission: Adults, under $9; ages 2–15, and seniors, under $6; under age 2, free. Additional fee: tram ride, under $1 for unlimited day pass.

The animals: More than 1,000 animals, more than 200 species, including lots of birds. Most animals are in outdoor naturalistic settings. Highlights include one of the largest breeding colonies of African black-footed penguins; African Watering Hole; and Maryland Wilderness, a walk-through display of the area's marshes, mountains, caves, and farms.

Entertainment: Elephant training sessions, once a day; Kodiak bear feeding, with explanation, once a day; penguin feeding, with explanation, once a day.

Extras: Tram ride around zoo grounds; children's zoo, with interactive play area, kiddie rides, and antique carousel. In other parts of the park are a conservatory, swimming pool, walking trails, and tennis courts.

Special events: From May through September, there are special events nearly every weekend, including autograph-signing sessions with some of the Baltimore Orioles baseball players. Annually, there are observances of Mother's Day, in May; Father's Day, in June; Zoo Zoom, the second largest running (and walking) race in Baltimore, in late September; and the Halloween Spooktacular, held the weekend before Halloween.

Food service: Food concessions in the Village Green area offer vegetable platters, salads, and grilled chicken sandwiches, as well as standard fast-food fare, snacks, ice cream, and beverages. At the Oasis Stand, you can get pit beef, elephant ears (fried dough), and animal-shaped french fries. Picnics are also permitted.

Plan to stay: 6 hours.

Directions: I–83 to exit 7. At the end of the exit ramp, turn right and get on Druid Park Lake Drive. Follows signs to zoo entrance.

Nearby attractions: Cylburn Mansion and Arboretum; Pimlico Racetrack; B&O Railroad Museum; Edgar Allan Poe Home; Babe Ruth Birthplace/ Baltimore Orioles Museum; Baltimore Museum of Industry, with hands-on displays of old machinery; Star-Spangled Banner Flag House, which has a map of the United States made with stones from each state; National Aquarium in Baltimore; Kirk Stieff Silversmiths, with guided tours; quaint shopping areas; harbor boat rides; and walking tours.

CATOCTIN MOUNTAIN ZOOLOGICAL PARK

Route 15
Thurmont, MD (301) 271–7488 (recording); (301) 662–2579

Animals from six continents can be seen here, including rare Ugandan silver monkeys, a giant tortoise, a 1,000-pound grizzly bear, and one of the few white hamadryas baboons in the Western Hemisphere.

You'll also find a prairie dog village and a display of Australian dingos, which are bred here. All animals are in outdoor enclosures except the reptiles, which have their own building.

Two ponds on the twenty-six wooded acres attract a variety of waterfowl, including Mandarin ducks, swans, and geese, who wander the grounds among the visitors and can be hand-fed. There is also a petting zoo.

Closed in January and February, the zoo is open weekends in the spring and fall, and daily from May 26 through Labor Day. Hours are generally 10:00 A.M. to 5:00 P.M., but are extended during the summer. Admission is under $8 for adults and under $6 for ages 2–12.

Easy to reach, the zoo is located on Route 15, about 12 miles north of Frederick, and 20 miles south of Gettysburg, Pa. The entrance is directly across from Cunningham Falls State Park.

NATIONAL AQUARIUM IN BALTIMORE

Pier 3
501 East Pratt Street
Baltimore, MD (301) 576–3800

Amid the architecture and color of the city's festive Harborplace, it's not hard to locate the aquarium, the state's most popular paid attraction. Its pyramidal glass roof juts 157 feet into the air and its colored panels shimmer in the sun's bright light.

As one of the largest facilities of its kind in the world, more than 5,000 aquatic animals call its two million gallons of fresh and saltwater home.

From the Mountains to the Sea exhibit, where visitors learn of the diversity of Maryland's aquatic habitats, to the dolphin and whale presentations in the Marine Mammal Pavilion, the facility provides lots of fun and educational opportunities for the entire family. The facility covers two areas, the original aquarium on Pier 3 and the new Marine Mammal Pavilion (1990) on Pier 4. The two are connected by an enclosed footbridge.

Season: Open daily, year-round.

Hours: Mid-May through mid-September, daily, 9:00 A.M. to 5:00 P.M., with closing extended to 8:00 P.M. Friday through Sunday; mid-September through mid-May, Monday through Thursday, 10:00 A.M. to 5:00 P.M., Fridays, 10:00 A.M. to 8:00 P.M., and Saturday and Sunday, 9:00 A.M. to 5:00 P.M.

Admission: Adults, under $13; ages 12–17, under $10; ages 3–11, under $8; 3 and under, free. Additional fee: parking in nearby lots.

The animals: More than 450 species, more than 5,000 animals. Major exhibits include: Wings Under Water, 50 rays in a 260,000-gallon pool; Atlantic Coral Reef, re-creation of reef with fish in a 335,000-gallon tank; Open Ocean, several species of shark in an oval tank; South American Rain Forest, reproduction of a jungle, located in the pyramid at the top of the building, features 700 species of tropical plants, 25 species of fish, and 30 tropical birds; whale and dolphin habitat, in a 1.2-million-gallon pool.

Entertainment: Whale and dolphin presentations are scheduled several times each day. Most exhibits have posted times for feeding demonstrations.

Extras: Scylla, a life-size sculpture of a 42-foot Atlantic humpback whale with interactive exhibits; educational arcade with hands-on exhibits; Discovery Room, informal marine mammal study room, with authentic artifacts, from shark teeth to whale vertebrae.

Food service: Cafe for fast food and snacks.

Plan to stay: 3 hours

Directions: Take the Inner Harbor exit off I–95. Make a right onto Conway Street, then left onto Light Street, and bear right onto Pratt Street. Follow signs to the aquarium.

Nearby attractions: Harborplace has shops, restaurants, and attractions.

SALISBURY ZOOLOGICAL PARK

In City Park
750 South Park Drive
Salisbury, MD (301) 548-3188

Situated in the heart of the Delmarva Peninsula, along the banks of the Wicomico River, this fifteen-acre zoo is a stopover point for thousands of migrating birds who follow the Atlantic Flyway south for the winter and return in the spring.

A stand of pines more than 100 feet high forms a natural canopy for visitors who walk along the paved and planked path leading to the exhibits.

If you're interested in the Flyway phenomenon, October is the month when you'll see the heaviest concentrations of migrating birds, especially North American waterfowl on their way to points south.

Season: Year-round, closed Easter and Christmas Day.

Hours: Memorial Day to Labor Day, 8:00 A.M. to 7:30 P.M.; remainder of year, 8:00 A.M. to 4:30 P.M.

Fauna Fun Facts

Antlers fall off every year, but horns are permanently attached.

Admission: Free, though there is a donation box at the entrance.

The animals: More than 460 animals, more than 80 species, primarily waterfowl and animals from North, Central, and South America, exhibited in naturalistic outdoor habitats. Highlights include the guanaco exhibit and the spectacled bears. This is only the second zoo in the country where these bears have produced offspring.

Entertainment: No regularly scheduled entertainment, but there are talks, demonstrations, and tours for the general public during special events.

Extras: In other areas of the park there is a children's playground, a bandstand for seasonal concerts, horseshoe pits, and fishing spots.

Special events: Zoobilee, first Saturday in May, in conjunction with Salisbury Spring Festival; Zoo Appreciation Day, first Saturday after Labor Day.

Food service: No food concessions, but visitors are welcome to bring their own.

Plan to stay: 2 hours.

Directions: From Washington, D.C., take U.S. Route 50 over the Chesapeake Bay Bridge. Follow Route 50 all the way into Salisbury. Zoo entrance is on Route 50, on the right side, just as you enter town. From Wilmington, Delaware, take U.S. Route 13 South into Salisbury. Make a right on Route 50 and zoo entrance will be on the left. Follow green signs for Salisbury Zoo/Civic Center/City Park.

Nearby attractions: Ward Museum of Wildfowl Art, on the grounds of Salisbury State University; Maryland Lady excursions on Wicomico River, with a 90-minute narration; Newtown Historic District, a cluster of 19th-century houses.

Massachusetts

CAPE COD AQUARIUM

281 Route 6A
Brewster, MA (508) 385–9252

Education is the key word here. Sure, you can have a lot of fun too, but the exhibits and shows are set up with the goal of getting people more involved and more aware of the marine environment. "No circus acts here," say officials.

Native marine life makes up most of the 100 species on display at any one time, but you'll also find seals, sea lions, and sea turtles.

Three buildings house numerous tanks, while the small outside park area has a large tank, a touch pool, and the sea lion and seal exhibition area, where these marine mammals are fed and trained several times each day for the enjoyment of the guests.

A Sea Life Discovery program is a part of every admission. The tour takes you through the facility and gives you an in-depth view of animals and their place in the marine environment. Tours start throughout the day, depending on demand.

Open year-round, closed Thanksgiving and Christmas Day. Hours: Memorial Day through Labor Day, 9:00 A.M. to 5:00 P.M.; off-season, 10:00 A.M. to 4:00 P.M. Admission: Adults, under $6; ages 3–12, under $5. Rates are lower during off-season.

FRANKLIN PARK ZOO

Franklin Park Road, Dorchester
Boston, MA (617) 442–0991

No visit to one of America's most historic cities would be complete without stopping at the Franklin Park Zoo.

The formal entrance to the zoo, on Peabody Circle, is most impressive, with eight fluted granite columns that were moved here from the old Custom House in 1917. At the Pierpont Road entrance are two Daniel Chester French statues, representing Commerce and Industry, which until 1929 stood before the post office building in Post Office Square.

Franklin Park and the zoo are considered by many to be the brightest gem in landscape architect Frederick Law Olmsted's "Emerald Necklace," a string of green areas in the Dorchester section of Boston.

Season: Year-round, closed Christmas Day and New Year's Day.

Hours: April through October, weekdays 9:00 A.M. to 4:00 P.M., and weekends 10:00 A.M. to 5:00 P.M. Remainder of the year, 9:00 A.M. to 3:30 P.M., daily.

Admission: Adults, under $7; ages 5–17, under $4.50; under age 5, free. Every Tuesday, from noon to 4:00 P.M., everyone gets in free.

The animals: More than 900 animals, more than 230 species, in both indoor and outdoor naturalistic habitats. Highlights include a 3-acre domed Tropical Rain Forest, considered to be one of the largest free-standing zoo exhibits in the United States; Birds World, with a variety of indoor exhibits, free-flight cage, and waterfowl pond; Hooves and Horns, featuring exotic hoofstock; and the children's zoo, which features rare breeds of farm animals.

Entertainment: Animal Interviews, conducted with the help of various zoo animals; Keeper of the Day talks, at the children's zoo.

Extras: Children's zoo. In other areas of the park are a playground, tennis courts, and golf course.

Special events: Black Scientists Festival, during school vacation week in February; Animal Olympics, in April; Fleece Festival, in May; What a Wonderful World, celebration of Zoo and Aquarium Month, throughout June; Zoo Snooze, in June; The Enchanted Forest, evening hayride with scenes from children's stories, in October.

Food service: Concessions area offers a variety of fast foods, snacks, and beverages. Picnic tables are scattered throughout the grounds.

Plan to stay: 2 hours.

Directions: Located in southern part of Boston. Take the Massachusetts Turnpike (Route 90) east to Route 93 (Southeast Expressway). Go south on Route 93 to exit 15 (Columbia Road). Go left from the exit to the third traffic light, where Columbia Road turns to the left (Kentucky Fried Chicken and Store 24 will be on the left). Follow Columbia Road to the ninth traffic light, where Columbia ends at Blue Hill Avenue. Go straight across Blue Hill onto Franklin Park Road and follow zoo signs to the parking area.

Nearby attractions: New England Aquarium; Faneuil Hall; Quincy Market; Paul Revere House; Old North Church; Freedom Trail, a self-guided walking tour of the historic sights; Prudential Tower Skywalk, provides a panorama of the city from the fiftieth floor; USS *Constitution*.

NEW ENGLAND AQUARIUM

Central Wharf
Boston, MA (617) 973–5200

On the banks of Boston Harbor, this popular facility houses seventy exhibits, including a giant ocean tank and a tidal pool that provides you with a chance to touch several sea critters. Inside, most of the lighting comes from the tanks themselves, making it feel like you're really underwater with the animals you're watching.

Species from all over the world—from Boston Harbor to the Amazon River—are on exhibit in the various tanks. The *Voyager II* whale-watch boat, tied up next to the aquarium building, offers you the wonderful opportunity to take a sea trek in search of the huge mammals. There is an extra charge for this adventure, and reservations are usually a must.

Season: Year-round, closed Thanksgiving and Christmas Day. Opens at noon on New Year's Day.

Hours: July 1 through Labor Day, daily from 9:00 A.M. till 6:00, 7:00, or 8:00 P.M., depending on night of week; the day after Labor Day through June, daily from 9:00 A.M. till 5:00, 6:00, or 8:00 P.M.

Admission: Adults, under $8; ages 3–12, under $4; under 3, free; seniors, under $7. There is a separate charge for the *Voyager II* whale-watch boat.

The animals: More than 610 species, almost 10,000 specimens, including seals, sea lions, sharks, and other marine life. Included is a 3-story circular tank in the middle of the complex and a sea lion pavilion adjacent to the aquarium.

Entertainment: The Lowell Lecture Series is offered in the fall and spring. It features special guest speakers, and admission is free.

Extras: The *Voyager II* is a 100-foot whale-watch boat equipped with hands-on work stations. There is a pilot house where visitors can plot changes and read radar screens, a wet lab, a microscope station, and other information centers. Each station is manned by folks who can explain its function and answer your questions. Besides whales, guides point out birds and other sea creatures and discuss marine life in general. Whale watch season runs April through October.

Food service: Snack bar with fast foods and beverages.

Plan to stay: 2 hours (or longer if taking whale watch cruise).

Directions: Located on the wharf, along Boston Harbor. From Southeast Expressway (Route 3) heading north, exit at Atlantic Avenue, turn right and follow signs to harbor. Traveling south, exit at Dock Square/Callahan Tunnel. Turn east and cross under the expressway and follow the fish logo signs to the aquarium.

Nearby attractions: John F. Kennedy Library and Museum; Blue Hills Observatory; Museum Wharf and Children's Museum; Boston Common; USS *Constitution;* Bunker Hill Monument.

SOUTHWICK'S WILD ANIMAL FARM

Southwick Street (off Route 16)
Mendon, MA (508) 883–9182

Situated atop one of the higher elevations in the state, this zoo is the largest in New England and is still growing. To date, only seventy of its 300 acres have been developed.

Tall oak trees shade the property, and a steady light breeze keeps you comfortable even on the hottest summer day as you stroll the paths connecting the various exhibits. Don't miss a stop at Quail Pond, where you can see a bevy of brightly colored wood ducks.

Season: Mid-May through Columbus Day.

Hours: Daily, 10:00 A.M. to 5:00 P.M.

Admission: Adults, under $8; ages 3–12, under $6; under age 3, free. Additional fees: tickets are sold at the gate for pony, elephant, and kiddie rides; no ride costs more than $2.

The animals: More than 600 animals, more than 120 species, in both indoor and outdoor naturalistic habitats. Highlights include big cats, hoofstock, primates, a small aviary, a 35-acre fallow deer forest, and the South American exhibit.

Entertainment: From the second Sunday in May through Labor Day, there are circus shows twice a day, featuring white dogs, llamas, Arabian horses, elephants, and ponies. Animal demonstrations are given in the Education Building 7 times a day.

Extras: Kiddie rides (Rodeo, Boat, and Rocket); pony rides, elephant rides, playground; and a museum.

Special events: Family Day, in the spring; Animal Awareness Day, second Sunday in August.

Food service: 3 small food concessions offer a limited variety of quality food, including chicken breast sandwiches, seafood, salads, meatballs, snacks, and drinks. Picnics are also permitted.

Plan to stay: 2½ hours.

Directions: Located halfway between Worcester, Massachusetts, and Providence, Rhode Island. Take I–495 northbound to exit 140 North. Go west on Route 16 into Mendon, about 10 miles. At the top of the hill, turn south onto Millville Road, at the Citgo Gas Station. Travel about 4 miles to the entrance.

Nearby attractions: In Worcester, the Higgins Armory Museum, a Gothic castle containing displays of weapons and armor from feudal Japan, ancient Greece and Rome, and Renaissance Europe, with scheduled sound-and-light shows. Also, the New England Science Center, in Worcester, houses natural science exhibits; the Alden Omnisphere; UNICO Primate Center, miniature train ride and small zoo.

Michigan

BELLE ISLE AQUARIUM

On Belle Isle
Middle of the Detroit River
Detroit, MI (313) 267–7159

Officials here call their facility the oldest continually operated, municipally owned aquarium in America still in its original location and building.

Tim's Trivia

You can take boat-building classes at the Maritime Center, the aquarium complex in the historic oystering community of Norwalk, Connecticut.

Opened in August 1904, this facility is housed in a classic old building, and some of its fish inhabitants date back to a remodeling in the mid-1950s.

With 153 species of fish, amphibians, reptiles, and invertebrates, the aquarium is home to nearly 1,300 animals. The focus is on freshwater fish, with sixty exhibits divided into four major sections: Asia, Africa, South America, and North America.

The aquarium building is connected to a beautiful Victorian conservatory and located in a lush park setting. There are no homes on the 985-acre Belle Isle, just recreational facilities owned by the city of Detroit.

Open year-round, weekdays and Saturdays from 10:00 A.M. to 5:00 P.M.; remains open an hour later on Sundays and holidays. Free admission. Access to the island is over the Douglas MacArthur Bridge, 3 miles east of downtown Detroit.

BELLE ISLE ZOO

On Belle Isle
Middle of the Detroit River
Detroit, MI (313) 267–7160

Take a five-minute walk east from the aquarium and you'll find this nice little thirteen-acre zoo. Featured are approximately 100 animals, including California sea lions, spectacled bears and maned wolves from South America, giant red kangeroos, and siamang primates.

One of the interesting things about this lazy little island retreat is that a three-quarter-mile elevated boardwalk takes you over every exhibit in the facility, making viewing extremely easy.

Open May through October, 10:00 A.M. to 5:00 P.M. daily. Admission: adults, under $3; ages 5–12, under $1. Concession stands offer light meals and snacks, and picnics are permitted. For directions, see Belle Isle Aquarium listing, above.

BINDER PARK ZOO

7400 Division Drive
Battle Creek, MI (616) 979–1351

Shaded brick paths and wooden boardwalks make this one of the prettiest facilities in this part of the state. It's set in the woods around a pond inhabited by trumpeter swans, geese, and ducks.

Opened in 1977, the facility has grown from a children's petting zoo to a 170-acre, modern zoological park with eighteen animal exhibits, nature trail, and a miniature railroad. The present Miller Children's Zoo contains one of the world's largest accurate dinosaur replicas, a 5-story branchiosaurus. Don't miss it.

Season: Mid-April to mid-October.

Hours: Weekdays, 9:00 A.M. to 5:00 P.M.; weekends and holidays, 9:00 A.M. to 6:00 P.M.

Admission: Adults, under $6; ages 3–12, under $4; seniors, under $5; under age 3, free. Additional fee: train ride, under $1.50.

The animals: Approximately 300 animals representing 70 species, in naturalistic habitat settings. Highlights include the Northern Forest; Australian area; red pandas; gibbons; and zebras.

Entertainment: "What's Up?" carts, with small animals and animal artifacts, are located throughout the zoo.

Extras: Z.O.& O. Railroad, makes a 15-minute loop around the zoo; children's zoo, with dinosaur replica, contact area, interactive displays, and animal-oriented playground; nature trail.

Special events: The Great Zoo Boo, last two weeks in October; Christmas at the Zoo, most of December. Other events are held on a changing schedule throughout the regular season.

Food service: Beulah's Restaurant, named for donor Beulah Kendall, is located in the middle of the zoo. It features indoor and outdoor shaded seating and has a cozy fieldstone fireplace. The menu covers breakfast, lunch, and dinner. Picnics are not permitted in the zoo, but there is a picnic area in the adjoining park.

Plan to stay: 2 hours.

Directions: I–94 to exit 100 (Beadle Lake Drive). Follow Beadle Lake Drive south for 3 miles to the entrance.

Nearby attractions: Kellogg Bird Sanctuary, a Michigan State University experimental facility at Wintergreen Lake; Leila Arboretum; the grave of Sojourner Truth, a famous ex-slave; the week-long Battle Creek International Balloon Championship, held here every July, featuring hot air balloons, air shows, crafts exhibits, and sales.

CLINCH PARK ZOO

Cass Street and Grandview Parkway
Traverse City, MI (616) 922–4904

You don't need to go on a wildlife hunt for native species if you're in this area of the state. All you have to do is visit Clinch Park and you'll see the wilds of Michigan in this nicely kept little zoo complex.

Overlooking beautiful Traverse Bay, the facility houses thirty indigenous species in natural exhibits. In addition, two large aquarium tanks are divided into six sections, representing the area's fish. In the park, you'll also find a miniature steam engine ride, a museum, and a sandy swimming beach.

Open mid-April through October. Spring and fall hours, 9:30 A.M. to 4:30 P.M.; summer, 9:30 A.M. to 7:30 P.M. Admission charge: adults, under $2; ages 5–12, under $1; under 5, free. Free admission to all during spring operation until Memorial Day. Located in downtown Traverse City, off Grandview Parkway (U.S. 31/33), at Cass.

DETROIT ZOOLOGICAL PARK

8450 West Ten Mile Road
Royal Oak, MI (313) 398–0903

It's hard to believe, when you enter the grounds, that you're only a few minutes away from downtown Detroit. Situated on 122 lushly landscaped acres in a residential northern suburb of the Motor City, this is a Michigan paradise.

Lawns, wildflowers, formal gardens, fountains, reflecting pools, and a minimum of concrete beneath your feet make up the setting of one of the largest and most modern zoos in the country. There's a lot of walking here, but if you get tired you can always hop the miniature railroad that runs the length of the grounds.

Season: Year-round, closed Thanksgiving, Christmas Day, and New Year's Day.

Hours: May through October, weekdays 10:00 A.M. to 5:00 P.M., open till 6:00 P.M. on weekends and holidays; November through April, open Wednesday through Sunday only, 10:00 A.M. to 4:00 P.M.

Admission: Adults, under $8; seniors, under $6; ages 2–12, under $5; under age 2, free. Additional fee: train tour, under $4.

The animals: More than 1,200 animals, about 300 species, set in spacious cageless exhibits grouped by continent and simulated natural habitats. Outstanding exhibits include Chimps of Harm Bay, a most advanced chimp exhibit with a one-way mirror that allows you to view chimps without them seeing you; penguinarium; and bear exhibit.

Entertainment: You won't find any animal shows here. Officials have a strong policy against coercing animals to perform, preferring to display them only in natural settings.

Extras: Zoofari Train Tour, guided tour of the park; miniature railroad; Log Cabin learning center.

Special events: There are lots of them here, including a Model Boat Regatta, Canadian Day, Father's Day, and Sunset at the Zoo, in the late spring; Family Day, in September; and Zoo Boo, near Halloween. In fact, there's something special going on almost every weekend during warm weather.

Food service: 1 concession stand offers a variety of fast foods, beverages, ice cream, and snacks. Picnic facilities are provided.

Plan to stay: 2 hours.

Directions: Located at intersection of I–696, Woodward Avenue, and Ten Mile Road. Signs on all 3 roads direct you to the zoo entrance.

Nearby attractions: Henry Ford Museum and Deerfield Village restoration; Historic Fort Wayne; Motown Historical Museum; Belle Isle Zoo and Aquarium; and Boblo Island, amusement park.

DOMINO'S FARMS PETTING ZOO

44 Frank Lloyd Wright Drive
Ann Arbor, MI (313) 995–4258

This 300-acre facility is the World Headquarters of Domino's Pizza. Although the standout attraction here is the magnificent building designed by Frank Lloyd Wright, there are also many other interesting things to do. And yes, there is a Domino's Pizza restaurant inside where you can order and then dine.

Hands-on participation is urged at the facility, where more than 100 farm animals live—from chickens to pigs to cows to horses. Hayrides around the farm are available on weekends, and animal shows are held three times a day, weekends only. Make sure you meet the two Newfoundlands, Duchess and Domino, while you're here. They're a riot!

Elsewhere on the grounds, you'll find a collection of more than seventy-five classic and specialty cars, the Detroit Tiger's Museum, the Artifacts gift shop, and the Domino's Center for Architecture and Design. Guided tours are given of the headquarters building, including a view of the executive offices.

Although the petting zoo is closed during winter, the rest of the facility is open year-round. The zoo is open April through the fall. Admission to the petting zoo only: adults, under $2; ages 3–12, under $1. A passport is available that gives you access to all three museums and the petting zoo and offers a $1 discount on a pizza. Passport prices: adult, under $6; ages 3–12, under $4; a family pass, for up to five members, is available for $15.

Hours: Summer, Monday through Saturday, 10:00 A.M. to 5:00 P.M.; opens at noon on Sundays. Winter hours are the same, except that the facility is closed on Mondays and Tuesdays. Located northeast of Ann Arbor. Take exit 41 (Plymouth Road) off U.S. Highway 23. Go east a quarter of a mile to Earhart Road. Turn left at the light, and you'll head right into the complex.

JOHN BALL ZOOLOGICAL GARDEN

In John Ball Park
1300 West Fulton Street Northwest
Grand Rapids, MI (616) 776–2591

Encompassing fourteen acres, this is Michigan's second largest zoo, and it came about through the generosity of the local businessman for whom the park and zoo are named. In 1884, Ball donated forty acres in downtown Grand Rapids that was to be used strictly for recreational purposes by children and their families. Today that donation forms the core of the 140-acre county-operated facility.

Ball's legacy is marked by the bronze statue of him with two children on his lap, which stands at the entrance. Because the emphasis here is on children, the children's zoo has some special attractions, including a two-level waterfall and some potbellied pigs.

Season: Year-round, holidays too.

Hours: First Saturday after Mother's Day through the second weekend in September, daily from 10:00 A.M. to 6:00 P.M. The rest of the year, from 10:00 A.M. to 4:00 P.M.

Admission: Adults, under $4; ages 5–15 and seniors, under $2, under age 5, free. Additional fee: camel rides in summer, under $2.50.

The animals: During the summer there are hands-on "Parts Carts" stationed around the zoo, and a variety of animal demonstrations are held twice each day.

Extras: Camel rides in the summer; Conservatory, containing a display of tropical plants; children's zoo, with red barn, petting corral, waterfall, learning center, and some unusual, exotic animals. In other areas of the park are a wading pool, a playground, and athletic fields.

Special events: Conservation Day, first Saturday in June; 4 or 5 free admission days during the summer; Fright Fest, in late October; Nocturnal Tours, weekend evenings in October; Christmas for the Animals, first weekend in December.

Food service: 1 main concession stand offers standard fast-food fare, while 2 smaller stands offer snack items. Picnics are permitted.

Plan to stay: 2 hours.

Directions: Located on the west side of the city. Take I–131 to I–196 West, to Lane street exit. Go south on Lane to Fulton Street. Go west on Fulton for 6 blocks. Park entrance is at intersection of Fulton and Valley Stream.

Nearby attractions: Splash Family Water Park; Gerald R. Ford Museum, displays of the former president's public and private life; Grand Rapids Public Museum, includes a planetarium and Gaslight Village Restoration.

POTTER PARK ZOOLOGICAL GARDENS

1301 South Pennsylvania Avenue
Lansing, MI (517) 483-4221

On the banks of the Red Cedar River, this neat little zoo is in downtown Lansing, near the capitol and all the state buildings. A long, winding drive leads you from the bustle of the city through Potter Park to the zoo, which is in the rear of the park.

You might want to bring some good walking shoes, because from the zoo you can cross a foot bridge to the river walk, an 11-mile hiking trail that connects Lansing and East Lansing.

Season: Year-round, holidays too.

Hours: Open daily from 10:00 A.M. to 7:00 P.M., Memorial Day through Labor Day; to 6:00 P.M. the rest of the year.

Admission: Adults, under $5; ages 3–14, under $3; under age 3, free. Additional fees: parking, under $2.50. There are also fees for pony and camel rides.

The animals: More than 400 animals, displayed in both indoor and outdoor naturalistic habitats. Highlights include the Bird and Reptile Building; Aviary; African black rhino; pandas; and snow leopards.

Entertainment: On summer weekends, depending on weather and attendance, there are Creature Features, docent-led presentations that feature some of the smaller animals at the zoo.

Extras: Camel and pony rides in summer; children's zoo. In other areas of the park are playgrounds, a nature trail, and canoe rentals (in summer).

Special events: Teddy Bear Repair, in April; Conservation Weekend, in June; Clown Weekend, first weekend in August; Kids Olympics, in August; Boo at the Zoo, the weekend before Halloween; Holidays with the Animals, first weekend in December.

▼▼▼▼▼▼▼▼▼▼▼▼▼▼▼▼▼▼▼▼▼▼▼▼▼▼▼▼▼▼▼▼▼▼

Fauna Fun Facts

All monkeys have tails, but apes do not.

Food service: There are a couple of concessions in the park that offer a variety of fast foods, salads, snacks, and beverages. Picnics are permitted until dusk.

Plan to stay: 2 hours.

Directions: I–496 to Pennsylvania Avenue exit. Go south on Pennsylvania for about one-fifth of a mile to the zoo/park entrance.

Nearby attractions: Michigan State University has a planetarium, museums and TV studio tours; R. E. Olds Transportation Museum, with historic cars; State Capital Building, offers free tours; Carl G. Fenner Arboretum, site of Maple Syrup Festival, in March, and Apple Butter Festival, in October.

SENSEY NATIONAL WILDLIFE REFUGE

State Route 77
Germfask, MI (906) 586–9851

You'll find more than 200 species of animals on this huge, 95,455-acre refuge. Along with the beavers, muskrats, coyotes, white-tailed deer, otters, minks, and black bears, the refuge has one of the state's highest concentrations of nesting loons.

There are also large nesting populations of Canada geese, sandhill cranes, bald eagles, trumpeter swans, and osprey. Several portable observation platforms are moved by the rangers to where the nesting is taking place, so you won't have to walk the entire refuge in search of action. Telescopes are mounted on each platform for better viewing.

The visitor's center has several exhibits on wildlife and natural history, including one on loons. The "touch table" features a variety of items, from skulls to pelts. Wildlife movies are shown throughout the day, and guided walking tours are scheduled two or three times a week, evenings and mornings.

A 7-mile, self-guided auto route is open from May 15 through October

15, and a 1½-mile walking trail is open every day year-round; both can be used from dawn to dusk. Rangers suggest you visit in early morning or evening for optimum viewing of animals.

The visitor's center is located 2 miles north of Germfask on State Route 77. The scheduled guided tours are free, as is admission.

Minnesota

COMO ZOO

In Como Park
Midway Parkway and Kaufman Drive
St. Paul, MN (612) 488-4041

A glass-domed Victorian conservatory housing some of the most impressive floral displays in the country sits like a crown jewel amid the eleven wooded acres of Como Zoo. Designed by world-renowned landscape architect Frederick Law Olmsted in the late 1890s, the zoo is located adjacent to Como Lake in the 450 acres that make up Como Park, owned and operated by the city of St. Paul.

Visitors can stroll the shaded walkways among nine outdoor naturalistic habitats, which contain a modest variety of birds, mammals, reptiles and fish. Inside the seventy-five-year-old conservatory you can visit the Palm Room, referred to here as "the poor man's trip to the tropics."

Season: Year-round, holidays too.

Hours: April through September: grounds, 8:00 A.M. to 8:00 P.M.; buildings, 10:00 A.M. to 6:00 P.M.; October through March: grounds, 8:00 A.M. to 5:00 P.M.; buildings, 10:00 A.M. to 4:00 P.M.

Admission: Free.

The animals: More than 300 animals, more than 100 species. Outstanding exhibits include the Aquatic Animals Building, which contains many species native to Minnesota in an indoor trout stream. Other popular exhibits include: polar bears; penguins, sea lions and alligators; Wolf Woods, with its resident pack of timber wolves; Great Ape exhibit, featuring four endangered primate species; and the African Hoofed Stock exhibit, which includes the first giraffes to take up residence in a Minnesota zoo.

Entertainment: No visit to Como Zoo is complete without watching at least one Sparky the Sea Lion show. For more than 40 years Sparky has been entertaining guests, both in St. Paul and across the country at boat and sports shows. Daily shows are held in the Aquatic Building from May 15 through the end of September.

Extras: Lectures and demonstrations are presented by docents on weekends, and tours are given by appointment.

Special events: Zoobilee, in June; Zoo Boo, in late October; Holiday Kingdom Festival of Lights, in mid-December.

Food service: A handful of year-round fast-food snack stands, with additional small concessions open during the summer season.

Plan to stay: 2 hours.

Directions: Located northwest of downtown St. Paul. Take I–94 to Snelling Avenue (Route 51) exit. Go north on Snelling for 2 miles, to Midway Parkway. Turn right on Midway and travel three-quarters of a mile to the zoo entrance, on your left.

Nearby attractions: In Como Park are kiddie rides, pony rides, miniature golf, a full-size golf course, and a Japanese garden. In St. Paul, there is the Science Museum of Minnesota; Indian Mounds Park, containing Sioux burial places and Minnesota State Fish Hatchery; Landmark Center, a cultural center; Gibbs Farm Museum; and the Children's Museum.

LAKE SUPERIOR ZOOLOGICAL GARDENS

In Fairmont Park
7210 Fremont Street
Duluth, MN (218) 624–1502

The hillside where Kingsbury Creek joins the St. Louis River has to be one of the prettiest settings of any zoo in the country. Located in a city park and opened to the public in 1923, this facility is built around several lakes and ponds, in the generous shade of mature trees.

Just above the park is a wilderness area filled with birch and pine trees, giving the air an aroma that belies the fact that you are so close to a major downtown area.

Season: Year-round, closed Thanksgiving, Christmas Day, and New Year's Day.

Hours: April through September, 9:00 A.M. to 6:00 P.M.; remainder of year, 9:00 A.M. to 4:00 P.M.

Admission: Varies according to season. From April through September, rates are under $5 for adults, ages 4–11, under $2.50; under age 4, free. The remainder of the year, rates are less than $2 for adults; ages 4–11, under $1.50; under age 4, free.

The animals: More than 400 animals, more than 100 species, displayed in both indoor and outdoor naturalistic settings. Highlights include a two-level polar exhibit; and the Australian Connection, which includes onshore and offshore habitats of the land down under.

Entertainment: During the summer there are a variety of shows, speakers, and demonstrations, but the schedule is not available until the beginning of each summer season.

Extras: Children's zoo, with contact area. In other areas of Fairmont Park you will find a playground, a camping area, and nature trails.

Special events: Winter Picnic, one weekend in February; Spring Carnival, first Sunday in May; Zoo Year's Eve celebration, on December 31.

Food service: The Safari Cafe and several small food stands offer a variety of fast foods, snacks, ice cream, and beverages. Picnics are not permitted in the zoo, but there is a large picnic area in the park.

Plan to stay: 2 hours.

Directions: Located at the western end of Lake Superior. From downtown Duluth, take I–35 south to Grand Avenue (exit to the left). Take Grand to 72nd Street and turn right. The zoo is at the corner.

Nearby attractions: The Depot, a museum in a renovated 1892 railroad depot; Depot Square, adjacent to the Depot, is a re-created village and display of railroad cars and locomotives from the turn of the century; Aerial Lift Bridge, at canal entrance to harbor; Canal Park Marine Museum, depicts history of Lake Superior shipping. Across the street from the park, you can catch the Port Town Trolley, which circles around Duluth and along the harborfront every half-hour.

MINNESOTA ZOOLOGICAL GARDEN

13000 Zoo Boulevard
Apple Valley, MN (612) 431-9200

If ever a zoo was made for walking—or cross-country skiing—this one is it. Only twenty minutes from the downtown areas of the twin cities of Minneapolis and St. Paul, the zoo is a haven for those who love the great outdoors in all its natural splendor.

All exhibits in this 485-acre facility, which is nestled in the Minnesota woods of Dakota County, are arranged in trail systems, making visitors feel as if they have entered the forest primeval. While the surroundings are beautiful and peaceful at all times of the year, the autumn foliage and winter snows are particularly inviting.

Season: Year-round, closed Christmas Day.

Hours: April through September, weekdays 9:00 A.M. to 6:00 P.M., and weekends 9:00 A.M. to 8:00 P.M. Remainder of the year, 10:00 A.M. to 4:00 P.M., daily.

Admission: Adults, under $7; ages 3–12, under $4; 65 and older, under $5; under age 2, free. On the second and third Tuesdays of each month, everyone gets in free. Additional fee: monorail, under $4.

The animals: More than 1,800 animals, more than 300 species, all in natural habitats along 5 trails. The Minnesota Trail features wildlife native to the state; the Northern Trail exhibits contain animals from northern climes around the world; the Asian Tropics Trail is the largest indoor habitat of its kind, and one of only 6 locations in this country where koalas are on display; the Ocean Trail; and the Discovery Trail, provide hands-on animal experiences.

Entertainment: Steve Martin's World of Birds Show, 30 minutes long, is presented 3 times daily. Dolphin training sessions, held 4 times a day, except Tuesdays, are open for public viewing. In the summer there are Sunday-evening musical concerts.

Extras: Skytrail, a monorail ride, takes visitors for a 20-minute guided trip around the Northern Trail and through sections inaccessible by foot. There is also a children's zoo, and in the winter cross-country skiing is permitted. If you can't bring your own, ski gear can be rented from a private concession on the grounds during the winter.

Special events: There is usually a special event scheduled every month, most often geared to holidays and celebrations.

Food service: During the summer season, 3 Dairy Queen restaurants are in full operation. At other times of the year, only 1 is open. A shaded picnic area is always available.

Plan to stay: 4 hours.

Directions: I–35 East to Cedar Avenue exit (County Road 77). Go south on Cedar about 5 miles. Zoo entrance road will be on the left.

Nearby attractions: Normandale Japanese Garden; Historic Fort Snelling, an 1825 limestone fort containing 17 restored buildings; and Eloise Butler Wildflower and Bird Sanctuary.

ˈlississippi

GULF ISLANDS NATIONAL SEASHORE
3500 Park Road
Ocean Springs, MS (601) 875–0821

Primarily used as a recreation area, this national seashore also contains two islands, Horn and Petit Bois, both designated as wildlife sanctuaries. They are located about 10 miles offshore, and can be reached only by large private or charter boats.

Horn and Petit Bois islands lie in the chain of barrier islands that separate the Gulf of Mexico and Mississippi Sound and remain in a natural state. They are inhabited primarily by snakes, alligators, turtles, raccoons, mice, hogs, and rabbits, which is not to mention the migrating terns, snowy plovers, osprey, eagles, herons, egrets, and ducks that nest here in winter.

Tim's Trivia

You'll find the state fish of Hawaii, the humuhumunukunukuapuaa, on display both at the Sea Life Park and the Waikiki Aquarium, both in Hawaii.

At the Gulf Islands headquarters in Ocean Springs, there are nature trails, campgrounds, and a visitor's center where films about the seashore and local wildlife are shown. Information on how to get to the islands may also be obtained here. Open daily year-round, 9:00 A.M. to 6:00 P.M. in the summer, 8:00 A.M. to 4:30 P.M. the remainder of the year. Admission is free.

To reach the headquarters, located east of Biloxi, take U.S. Route 90 to Hanley Road, in the Davis Bayou area. Follow Hanley south into the park and follow signs to the parking area.

JACKSON ZOOLOGICAL PARK

2918 West Capitol Street
Jackson, MS (601) 352–2585

Downtown Jackson can boast the state's only accredited zoo. Opened in 1921 in what used to be known as Livingston Park, the 110-acre, city-owned facility is upgrading and expanding as funds become available.

Although most of the zoo proper is concentrated in its original location, it includes a lot of open land across the street. This acreage, which includes Cooks Lake, is undeveloped except for a train ride around the lake and some picnic areas. In the future, park officials plan to expand the waterside area by adding a carousel, paddleboats, a restaurant with outdoor deck, a fishing area, and, of course, more animal exhibits.

Season: Year-round, closed Christmas Day and New Year's Day.

Hours: Memorial Day to Labor Day, 9:00 A.M. to 6:00 P.M., Sunday through Friday, and until 7:00 P.M. on Saturday. Remainder of the year, 9:00 A.M. to 5:00 P.M. daily.

Admission: Adults, under $4; ages 3–12, under $3; seniors, under $2.50; under age 3 and handicapped, free. Additional fee: train ride, under $2.

The animals: More than 450 animals, more than 140 species, from around the world, displayed in geographical environments. Outstanding exhibits include an outdoor African Rain Forest, Chimp Island, and an Asian area with lions, tigers, and bears.

Entertainment: There are elephant shows, but not on a fixed schedule.

Extras: 3½-mile train ride around Cooks Lake; Children's Discovery Zoo, which includes an animal contact area and a playground containing huge simulated eggshells, spider webs, and other larger-than-life items.

Special events: Halloween celebration, in October; Christmas events, in December. During the warmer weather, special events take place nearly every weekend.

Food service: There is 1 food concession that sells fast food, candy, ice cream, beverages, and snacks. Picnics are permitted.

Plan to stay: 1 hour.

Directions: I–20 to Ellis Avenue exit. Go north on Ellis to West Capitol Street. Make a right on West Capitol and zoo entrance is a half-mile on the left. Signs are posted all along the route.

Nearby attractions: Mynelle Gardens, containing azaleas, camellias, magnolias, and water plantings; the Old Capitol, built in 1833, is now a museum; Governor's Mansion, built in 1842, offers guided tours; Mississippi Museum of Natural Science.

Missouri

DICKERSON PARK ZOO

Norton Road
Springfield, MO (417) 833–1570

Take a few steps through the front gates here and then just stop—the impressive panoramic view will astound you. From this hillside site, you're able to see practically all of the seventy acres on which the zoo is located.

A good part of the grounds remains undeveloped, so the exhibit area is relatively easy to maneuver. Most of the seventy-year-old zoo's animals are in naturalistic habitats, and there are several lakes incorporated into the exhibits that attract migratory waterfowl, including ducks, geese, and swans. These winged visitors roam the grounds freely and like to mingle with guests, as does the resident peacock population.

Season: Year-round, closed Thanksgiving, Christmas Day, and New Year's Day.

Hours: April through September, 10:00 A.M. to 6:00 P.M.; October through March, 10:00 A.M. to 4:30 P.M. Closed during inclement winter weather.

Admission: Adults, under $5; ages 3–12, under $3; under age 3, free. Additional fee: elephant rides, under $2.50.

The animals: More than 400 animals, more than 125 species, in naturalistic displays. Highlights include Cheetah Country in the African Plains, where visitors walk on a ramp above the exhibit; Missouri Habitats, with black bears and bobcats.

Extras: Elephant rides, Wednesdays through Sundays, during the summer, weather permitting. In the adjoining park, there is also a playground.

Food service: There are no food concessions here, and picnics are not permitted, but there is a picnic area in the adjoining park.

Plan to stay: 1 hour.

Directions: Located on the northwest corner of the intersection of U.S. 44 and State Route 13, to the north of the downtown area. Signs direct you from both roads.

Nearby attractions: Fantastic Caverns, one of Missouri's largest caves, which was used as a speakeasy during Prohibition; Museum of Ozarks History, in an 18-room Victorian mansion; Buena Vista's Exotic Animal Paradise.

GRANT'S FARM

10501 Gravois Road
St. Louis, MO   (314) 843–1700

Named for Ulysses S. Grant, who lived here in the mid-1850s, the farm is the 281-acre ancestral home of the Busch family—of Busch Beer fame—and is now open to the public. Attractions include the famous Budweiser Clydesdale horses; a 160-acre game preserve with thirty species, including bison, elk, and antelope; elephant and bird shows; a coach and carriage collection; the log cabin Grant built in 1856; and a trackless train tour that takes you through the game preserve.

The complex is open April 15 through October 15: April 15 through May and September through October 15, Thursday through Sunday; June through August, Tuesday through Sunday. Tour times are 9:00, 10:00, and 11:00 A.M., and 1:00, 2:00, and 3:00 P.M. Admission is free. Reservations are recommended but not required.

Located off I–70 at the Gravois Road exit, just south of the arch. Go west on Gravois to Grant Road; turn right into Grant's Farm.

KANSAS CITY ZOOLOGICAL GARDENS

In Swope Park
6700 Zoo Drive
Kansas City, MO (816) 333-7406

Now in the middle of a major renovation program that will more than double its size, this zoo provides an excellent contrast between the old and the new, as the old cages and buildings are giving way to natural habitats and less obtrusive architecture. A ride on the narrow-gauge railroad provides a nice overview of the zoo, not to mention a welcome rest for weary feet.

Season: Year-round, closed Christmas Day and New Year's Day.

Hours: Mid-April through mid-October, daily 9:00 A.M. to 5:00 P.M. Closes at 4:00 P.M. the remainder of the year.

Admission: Adults, under $5; under 12, free. Additional fees: train ride, under $2.50; pony ride, under $2; camel ride, under $3.

The animals: Growing to more than 1,000 animals, more than 200 species, in enclosures and naturalistic habitats. Highlights include 2 large free-flight aviaries, and the Australia exhibit.

Entertainment: Sea lion demonstrations and feedings, twice a day; occasional educational programs given at different exhibits, depending on attendance and weather.

Extras: Narrated train ride; camel and pony rides (daily in summer, weekends only after Labor Day); children's zoo; Touch Town, an animal contact area.

Food service: 1 concession offers a variety of fast food, snacks, and beverages. Picnics are permitted, but glass containers are not.

Plan to stay: 2 hours.

Directions: I-435 to either the 63rd Street or Gregory Street exit. Both lead directly to zoo. Follow brown-and-white signs.

Nearby attractions: In other areas of the park are nature trails, a swimming pool, athletic fields, and a lagoon with fishing and boating. Elsewhere in the city are Oceans of Fun, water park; Worlds of Fun, theme park; and the Hallmark Visitor Center, which offers tours of the world-famous greeting card manufacturer.

ST. LOUIS ZOOLOGICAL PARK

In Forest Park
Government Drive
St. Louis, MO (314) 781–0900

Remember Marlin Perkins? Well, the former host of TV's "Zoo Parade" and "Wild Kingdom" was once the director of this eighty-year-old facility and provided its development with a great deal of foresight.

On the north side of the zoo, just inside the Government Drive entrance, you will pass through a modern, two-story building topped with a white hexagonal dome. Plan on visiting the Living World exhibit in this building before viewing the outdoor animal displays. It offers visitors a fascinating introduction to the animals and ecology, and even has a lifelike Charles Darwin robot to explain the process of evolution.

Throughout the park you will be able to walk next to, through, or over the many naturalistic animal habitats that are spread out over the zoo's eighty-three acres. And don't miss the aviary, which is actually the flight cage that housed the bird exhibit at the 1904 St. Louis World's Fair.

It's a pleasant stroll along the 1½-mile landscaped walkway, but if you'd rather ride, there's a miniature railroad that loops around the grounds. It's a twenty-minute guided rail tour with stops at four convenient locations.

Admission is free, a policy in existence since the zoo's inception.

Season: Year-round, closed Christmas Day and New Year's Day.

Hours: Daily, 9:00 A.M. to 5:00 P.M. Stays open a half-hour longer during the summer, and until 8:00 P.M. on Tuesdays.

Admission: Free. Additional fees: parking, under $4; train ride, under $2; children's zoo, under $1; animal shows, under $1 each.

The animals: More than 700 species, more than 3,400 animals, including nearly 1,000 birds. Animals are displayed in both indoor and outdoor naturalistic habitats. Highlights include Jungle of the Apes rain forest; the walk-through 1904 Flight Cage; the Primate House; and Big Cat Country.

Entertainment: Elephant demonstrations and sea lion shows, daily during the summer; also daily (except Thursdays) feedings of penguins, bears, and sea lions.

Extras: Zooline train ride; children's zoo, with contact area and playground; Living World Education Center, with film presentations, computers, and living ecology exhibits. In other areas of Forest Park you'll find roller and ice skating rinks, jogging trail, golf course, history museum, and seasonal flower exhibits.

Special events: Winter and spring exhibits in the children's zoo; Celebrate Spring party for children, in March; Zoo and Aquarium Conservation Day, in June; Camera Day, Zoo Run, and Wildlife Art Walk, all during the summer; Halloween exhibit in the children's zoo; Holiday Party for children, in December.

Plan to stay: 5 hours.

Directions: I–44 to Hampton Avenue exit. Go north on Hampton for 2 miles, to Wells Drive. Turn left on Wells, parking area will be on your left.

WILDERNESS SAFARI

Safari Road
Branson, MO (417) 334–7884

A few miles outside the hustle and bustle of Branson, a peaceful setting awaits. Featuring more than 900 animals, representing 250 different species, this 365-acre wildlife park offers quite a treat for the entire family.

As you enter, you can begin the 4-mile scenic drive immediately, or take a stroll through the walk-through zoo where you'll find lions, tigers, bears, primates, and more. There's also a well-stocked petting zoo in this part of the park.

Along the drive-through, you'll see exotic animals from Africa and India, including giraffes, zebras, emus, ostrich, and water buffalo. Once you pay your fee, you can drive through the facility as often as you like. You just might see something the second time around that you didn't the first time. The entire area is quite beautiful, with several ponds, hilly inclines, and lots of trees and flowers.

Open year round, closed on Christmas Day. Hours: 8:00 A.M. to an hour before dusk. Admission: adults, under $9; ages 4–12, under $5. During the winter months, when several of the larger animals are put into warm shelters and out of sight, admission is less.

Head west out of Branson on Highway 76, take a left on Highway 165, at the traffic light. Go 2 miles and take a right on Safari Road. The park is located a mile down Safari Road.

Montana

BOWDOIN NATIONAL WILDLIFE REFUGE

Old Highway 2
Malta, MT (406) 654–2863

Bring your binoculars and bird book, because you'll get the chance to spot more than 200 species of shorebirds and waterfowl here, including white pelicans. There are also white-tailed deer, pronghorn antelope, and other wildlife native to the area.

A self-guided tour along a 17-mile gravel road, with designated viewing areas, is open to automobiles, and there are several foot trails that can be followed. The best time to visit is in the spring and summer. The birds return in April and are nesting in May, June, and July. In August and September the young birds are learning their survival skills.

Trails are open year-round, from dawn to dusk, except during inclement weather. The refuge headquarters is open Monday to Friday, from 8:00 A.M. to 4:30 P.M. Admission is free.

Located in the north-central part of the state, between Havre and Glasgow. Take U.S. Route 2 into Malta. About 1 mile east of town, turn right on Old Highway 2, and follow the road for 6½ miles, at which point you will see signs directing you to the refuge entrance.

NATIONAL BISON RANGE

State Highway 212
Moiese, MT (406) 644–2211

Nearly 500 buffalo roam while deer, elk, sheep, and antelope play on the 18,540 acres that make up this animal park in Montana's Flathead Valley. You can see the animals from the comfort of your car by taking one or all of the self-guided tours on specially designated trails.

The Red Sleep Mountain tour, a rugged 19-mile excursion, is the longest tour. Lasting about two hours, the tour follows a gravel-and-dirt road that has some rather steep hills and downgrades. A second tour, along the Buf-

▼▼▼▼▼▼▼▼▼▼▼▼▼▼▼▼▼▼▼▼▼▼▼▼▼▼▼▼

Fauna Fun Facts

Hermit crabs don't have their own shells. They use whatever discarded shells they can find and "trade up" as they grow in size.

falo Prairie Drive, is between thirty and forty-five minutes in length. During the winter, when the other tour roads are closed, there is a shorter, 10-mile route open. All tours are shut down during the buffalo roundup, in late September and early October.

Although the range is open from dawn to dusk year-round, the Red Sleep Mountain tour is open only from mid-May to mid-October. A visitor's center, which offers displays and presentations on the history of the range and its animal residents, is open daily, June through Labor Day, from 8:00 A.M. to 8:00 P.M. The rest of the year the center is open Monday through Friday, except holidays, from 8:00 A.M. to 4:30 P.M.

Located in the western part of the state. Take U.S. Route 93 North from Missoula into the town of Ravalli. Make a left on State Route 200, and travel about 4 miles to Route 212. Follow Route 212 for another 4 miles to the entrance gate.

RED ROCK LAKES
NATIONAL WILDLIFE REFUGE

Red Rock Pass Road
Monida, MT (406) 276–3347

Established in 1935, this refuge is considered to be among the most important nesting and wintering spots for the rare trumpeter swan in North America. At peak times, there are between 200 and 300 of them in residence.

In addition to the trumpeter swans, there are more than 150 other species of waterfowl that come here, along with a lot of land dwellers, such as moose, pronghorn antelope, mule deer, elk, and white-tailed deer.

The refuge is open year-round, except for a few areas that are closed during the spring nesting season. The best time to visit is in mid- to late summer. That's the only time when the public is allowed access to a drive-through trail that goes past the ponds where the swans and their cygnets can be seen.

A small visitor's center with displays and brochures is located in the refuge headquarters and is open year-round, Monday through Friday, except holidays, from 7:30 A.M. to 4:00 P.M. Admission is free.

Located in the very southern part of the state, a short distance from the Idaho border. The best way to get there is from Route 15, which goes through the small town of Monida. Once in town, look for signs directing you to the refuge entrance, which is a gravel road (Red Rock Pass Road) that goes east off Route 15. Follow the road for 28 miles to the headquarters.

A word to the wise: the gravel road and drive-through trail are not paved. They have a lot of bumps, and are not plowed in the winter, so drive slowly and carefully.

Nebraska

AK-SAR-BEN AQUARIUM

Schramm Park State Recreation Area
21502 West Highway 31
Gretna, NE (402) 332–3901

Located on a scenic bluff overlooking the Platte River, this aquarium offers twelve tanks populated with native Nebraska fish, and a large terrarium with reptiles and amphibians. Wildlife movies are shown in a small theater.

Among the more popular exhibits are the paddlefish and the blue catfish. There is also an exhibit of mounted animals that are native to the state.

Open year-round except for Thanksgiving, Christmas Day, and New Years Day. Memorial Day through Labor Day, 10:00 A.M. to 4:30 P.M. daily; Labor Day through December, same hours, but closed on Tuesdays; December through April, same hours, but closed Monday, Tuesday, and all holidays. Admission: adults, under $1.50; ages 6–15, under $1.

Located near Schramm Park State Recreation area. Take exit 132 (Highway 31), off I–80, west of Omaha. Go 6 miles south on Highway 31. There are signs on the interstate to indicate the exit.

FOLSOM CHILDREN'S ZOO

1222 South 27th Street
Lincoln, NE (402) 475–6741

One of only fourteen private zoos in the nation that are open to the public, the Folsom Children's Zoo and Botanical Gardens is located on eight and a half acres of land leased from the city of Lincoln. The zoo, which opened in 1965, was conceived by Arnott Folsom, who personally recruited volunteers and donations to help build his dream.

The facility has drawn international attention to the breeding success of the golden lion tamarin and the re-release of a group of its tamarins to a reserve in Brazil. It is also one of only three zoos in the United States to house and breed the endangered Rodrigues fruit bat.

Season: Open daily from the last Sunday in April through September 30.

Hours: Monday through Saturday, 10:00 A.M. to 5:00 P.M.; remains open an hour later on Sunday. Open till 8:00 P.M. on Thursday nights in June, July, and August.

Admission: Adults, under $4; ages 2–11, under $2; seniors, under $3; ages 2 and under, free. Pony and train rides, $1 each.

The animals: More than 200 animals including harbor seals, camels, spectacled bears, red pandas, river otters, snow monkeys, alligators, llamas, Japanese macaques, pygmy goats, and redneck wallaby. A walk-through aviary features a wide variety of birds. Additional exhibits include the mute swan, emu, European white stork, flamingos, scarlet macaw, and the bald eagle.

Extras: Grandpa's Pony Rides available for children who weigh under 80 pounds. The botanical gardens have over 7,000 annuals and more than 30 types of trees. Rides can be taken on the Iron Horse Railroad, a scale replica of an 1863 C. P. Huntington locomotive. Critter Encounter Area is where visitors can go one-on-one with animals. Eagles Nest Exhibit allows children to actually climb into the nest of our national bird.

Special events: Educational demonstrations are available weekends in June, July, and August in the amphitheater.

Food services: Whistle Stop and Food Emporium concessions offer modest variety of food along with an antique popcorn wagon.

Plan to stay: 2½ hours

Directions: Take the 27th Street exit off Highway 80, go south, and follow the signs.

Nearby attractions: National Museum of Roller Skating.

GRAND ISLE HERITAGE ZOO

In Stolley Park
2103 West Stolley Park Road
Grand Island, NE (308) 382–3899

Cozy but quite interesting, this seven-acre zoo features animals from North America and northern Eurasia. Included are ostrich, binturong, sandhill cranes, cougars, macaques, gibbons, sun bears, eagles, owls, and parrots, among others. There is also a Discovery Center, a petting zoo, and Old Town Village, where you can board a miniature train for a ride around the grounds.

Grand Isle opens for the season in mid-March and remains open through the end of October. Hours are 10:00 A.M. to 6:00 P.M., weekends from mid-March through April, and daily from May through October. Admission is under $4 for adults, and under $2.50 for ages 4–12. Ages 3 and under are free. There is an additional fee of less than $2 to ride the train.

Located in south-central Nebraska. Take I–80 to U.S. Route 281. Go north on 281 into town. Turn right at the light at Stolley Park Road, and follow to park entrance, about 1½ miles, on the right.

OMAHA'S HENRY DOORLY ZOO

3701 South 10th Street
Omaha, NE (402) 733–8401

See it by train, see it by tram, or see it on foot, but make sure you see it! This 110-acre zoo lies along the west bank of the Missouri River and contains some of the finest animal displays in the country, including one of the largest outdoor free-flight aviaries of any zoo, a large cat complex, and the world's first test-tube tiger.

Nestled into the rolling hillside, the grounds are beautiful, containing many stately trees and lots of waterfalls and streams that flow into pools and lagoons, which in turn, attract a large variety of birds and waterfowl.

Season: Year-round, closed Thanksgiving, Christmas Day, and New Year's Day.

Hours: Daily, April through October, 9:30 A.M. to 5:00 P.M.; Sunday till 6:00 during summer months. November through March, 9:30 A.M. to 4:00 P.M., daily.

Admission: Adults, under $8; ages 5–11, under $5; seniors, under $6; under age 5, free. Additional fees: train ride: adults, under $3; ages 3–11, under $2.50; under age 3, free. Tram ride, under $2 per person.

The animals: More than 7,200 animals, more than 400 species, displayed in naturalistic habitats. Outstanding exhibits include the Lied Jungle; Cat Complex, with 8 different types of cats; Free-Flight Aviary, a 4-acre walk-through; Bear Canyon; and a large saltwater aquarium.

Entertainment: Animal demonstrations are offered on a changing basis in the Wild Kingdom Pavilion Theater. During special events, there is also a variety of shows, animal rides, and other entertainment.

Extras: Miniature steam-powered train ride around the perimeter of the grounds, and a tram ride that loops around the inner area. Both rides operate every day between Memorial Day and Labor Day, and only on weekends the remainder of the year. Aksarben (Nebraska spelled backward) Nature Kingdom, contains a petting zoo and Dairy World, where visitors can milk a mechanical cow, see films, and play games.

Special events: Spring Fling, in April; Breakfast with the Animals, in May; Zoo and Aquarium Month activities, in June; Zoolympics, in July; weekly evening Safaris, in August; Grandparents' Day, in September; Zoo Run and Halloween Party, in October; holiday activities in December.

Food service: Several food concessions scattered throughout the zoo offer a complete variety of fast food, snacks, beverages, and sweets. Don't miss the Ice Cream Parlor in Sea Lion Plaza.

Plan to stay: 5 hours.

Directions: I–80 to the 13th Street exit. Go south on 13th street for about a mile, then make a left onto 10th Street, by Rosenblatt Stadium. Signs will direct you to the zoo entrance.

Nearby attractions: Old Market Area, which includes galleries, boutiques, restaurants, and Ollie the Trolley; Peony Park amusement park; Mormon Pioneer Cemetery and Information Center; Western Heritage Museum; USS *Hazard,* a World War II minesweeper and the USS *Marlin,* a training submarine, both moored at Freedom Park in the Missouri River.

RIVERSIDE ZOO

In Riverside Park
1600 South Beltline West
Scottsbluff, NE (308) 630–6236

Riverside is a fitting name for this zoo, which is located in the beautiful North Platte River valley. It sits directly below the Scotts Bluff National Monument, an 800-foot-high escarpment that once served as a prominent landmark for pioneers traveling the Oregon Trail.

The seventeen-acre zoo adjoins a popular park and camping area and offers a nice variety of indoor and outdoor animal exhibits, some of them on small islands in a series of artificial lakes.

Season: Year-round, closed Christmas Day.

Hours: October through April, daily 10:30 A.M. to 4:30 P.M. Remainder of year, weekdays 9:30 A.M. to 5:00 P.M., and until 6:00 P.M. on weekends and holidays.

Admission: Adults, under $3; ages 5–12, under $2; over 65, under $2.50; under age 5, free.

The animals: More than 100 animals, more than 50 species, exhibited in naturalistic habitats. Most of the animals are native to the Nebraska Plains, but there are also African Plains and Australian exhibits. Highlights include the North American otter exhibit, Persian leopards, and the white tiger. Scheduled to open in 1993 are new exhibits featuring chimpanzees, grizzly bears, moose, and musk oxen.

Entertainment: No regularly scheduled entertainment, but guided tours and animal demonstrations can be arranged in advance.

Extras: Children's zoo; playground. In the adjoining park there's a playground, a picnic area, and an RV campground.

Special events: Teddy Bear Rally, in September, with free admission for all visitors accompanied by a teddy bear; Spooktacular, 5

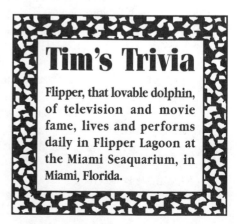

Tim's Trivia

Flipper, that lovable dolphin, of television and movie fame, lives and performs daily in Flipper Lagoon at the Miami Seaquarium, in Miami, Florida.

days at the end of October; Christmas Lights event, in December.

Food service: During the summer, 1 food stand sells fast foods, snacks and beverages. At other times, there is a beverage vending machine in operation. Picnics are not permitted in the zoo, only in the adjoining park.

Plan to stay: 1 hour.

Directions: I–80 to State Route 71. Go north on Route 71 for about an hour. After crossing the river, go left on South Beltline Highway for about a half-mile. Zoo/park entrance will be on the left.

Nearby attractions: Scotts Bluff National Monument; Agate Fossil Beds; Chimney Rock; Fort Laramie.

Nevada

ANAHOE ISLAND NATIONAL WILDLIFE REFUGE

At Pyramid Lake
Reno, NV (702) 574–0140

Designated as a sanctuary for the white pelicans that nest here, Anahoe Island is located in the middle of Pyramid Lake, on the Paiute Indian Reservation. Since the island can be reached only by boat, and there are no rentals in the area, you'll either have to bring your own or settle for viewing the pelicans through binoculars from the shoreline.

There is an unpaved road that loops around the lake, which is best traveled in a four-wheel-drive vehicle. The birds can best be seen from the east side of the lake, although you might have to share your viewing area with some of the 10,000 head of cattle that graze there. Permits for fishing and boating are available from the ranger station.

Pyramid Lake can be reached by taking Route 455 North out of Reno, for about 36 miles. When you arrive at the reservation, stop and ask for directions to the road around the lake. It is open year-round, weather permitting, and there is no charge.

BONNIE SPRINGS RANCH/ OLD NEVADA

In Red Rock Canyon
Blue Diamond Road
Las Vegas, NV (702) 875–4191

Providing a refreshing change of pace in this, the gambling capital of the United States, the Bonnie Springs Ranch's petting zoo has everything from guinea pigs to buffalo. Although the zoo is not the main attraction here, it does give visitors an opportunity to see a nice collection of animals, primarily those native to the area, including armadillos, prairie dogs, and buffalo, among others, on a gently winding walking trail.

Also on the ranch are guided horseback tours and Old Nevada, a re-created Wild West town that features staged gunfights and hangings, "old" buildings, and an 1890 melodrama. Once a working ranch, Bonnie Springs is part of the Red Rock Canyon Recreation Area.

Another attraction here is the restaurant, which offers juicy Bonnie Burgers, steaks, chicken, and ribs.

Bonnie Springs is open every day of the year, including holidays. Hours: 10:30 A.M. to 5:00 P.M. in the winter; 10:30 A.M. until dark during daylight saving time. Admission to the ranch and zoo are free, but there is a fee to enter Old Nevada. Adults, under $6; ages 5–11, under $4, seniors, under $5; 5 and under, free. Additional charge of $15 per person for the hour-long horseback tour.

Located about a half-hour drive out of the city, up in the mountains. Take U.S. 15 to exit 41 (Charleston Boulevard), westbound. Follow Charleston for about 20 miles, until you see a large sign on the right that says Old Nevada. Turn right and follow the long entrance road into the parking area.

▼▼▼▼▼▼▼▼▼▼▼▼▼▼▼▼▼▼▼▼▼▼▼▼▼▼▼▼▼▼▼▼▼▼▼

Fauna Fun Facts

A group of kangaroos is called a "mob."

New Hampshire

ANHEUSER-BUSCH, INC.

221 Daniel Webster Highway
Merrimack, NH (603) 889–6631

One of the teams of the well-known Budweiser Clydesdales is stabled here, in the heart of New England. The stable area on the grounds of the Anheuser-Busch brewery has been built to resemble an old German village.

After touring the brewery and visitor's sampling room, you can take a pleasant stroll to the Clydesdale Hamlet stable area, where twenty-minute guided tours explain the history and care of the famous horses. There are usually about fifteen horses in residence at any given time.

Open year-round, the facility is closed on New Year's Day, Easter Sunday, Veterans Day, Thanksgiving (and the day before and the day after Thanksgiving), December 24, 25, and 31. Between November 1 and April 30, it is closed on Mondays and Tuesdays. Hours: 9:30 A.M. to 3:30 P.M. Admission is free.

Located in the southern part of the state, just north of Nashua. Take I–93, northbound, to exit 8 (Merrimack). Make a right on Route 3 and follow signs to brewery.

CLARK'S TRADING POST

Route 3
Lincoln, NH (603) 745–8913

Established in 1928, this wonderful piece of Americana is a combination of museums, rides, and a bear show. The complex offers museums of antique auto and motoring memorabilia, antique advertising art, early music machines, electrical and mechanical items, an 1880s fire station with horse-drawn equipment, and other fire-department items.

Other museums offer a look at antique hotel china, cameras, railroad items, guns, swords, games, and other memorabilia.

The trademark item here, a trained bear show, is offered beginning in July, with three shows daily, noon, 2:00, and 4:00 P.M. When the ten bears are not in the ring, they are on exhibit at the facility.

A 2-mile steam train ride is available six times daily, every half-hour from 11:30 A.M. until 4:30 P.M. A bumper-boat ride is also available.

Clark's is open weekends, Memorial Day through July 1, then daily, July through Labor Day. Labor Day through mid-October, it's open on weekends. Closed, mid-October to Memorial Day.

Admission: adults, under $7; ages 6–11, under $6; ages 3–5, $1; under 3, free. Price includes admission to all museums, the bear show, and train ride, but not the bumper boats. There are fast-food concessions and two souvenir shops, the larger one accessible without having to pay to enter the grounds.

Considered one of the top attractions in the White Mountain area, Clark's is easy to find. Take exit 33 off I–93, turn left on Route 3 and go south 1 mile.

THE FRIENDLY FARM

Route 101
Dublin, NH (603) 563–8444

Clean, green, and friendly is the impression you'll get as you walk through the front gates here. Although it's not a true working farm, you'll find just about every farm animal you could ever think of. This busy barnyard contains cows, horses, pigs, donkeys, goats, sheep, turkeys, and rabbits, as well as hundreds of chickens, ducks, and geese that roam the grounds freely.

There is also a petting area where you can feed many of the smaller animals, including the calves that are born and raised here.

Open from late April through mid-October. Hours are 10:00 A.M. to 5:00 P.M. daily, from opening day through Labor Day; after that, open only on weekends through the fall foliage season, with approximately the same hours of operation. Since all the animals are outdoors, the farm is closed on rainy days. Admission is under $5 for adults and under $4 for ages 1–12.

Located about halfway between Keene and Peterborough. You can reach the farm by taking Route 101 East out of Keene. The entrance is about 10 miles out of the city on Route 101.

NEW HAMPSHIRE SCIENCE CENTER

State Route 113
Holderness, NH (603) 968–7194

Literally carved out of the wilderness, this nature center is devoted exclusively to native New Hampshire wildlife. Visitors follow a three-quarter-mile trail that winds among exhibit buildings and outdoor enclosures.

Among the wildlife on display here are bears, owls, deer, bobcats, raccoons, and others, as well as a nice collection of raptors that includes hawks, owls, kestrels, turkey vultures, and eagles.

Although it is open year-round for school groups, the exhibit trail is open to the general public only between May and October 31, daily from 9:30 A.M. to 4:30 P.M.

During July and August there are two live animal presentations every day that last about forty-five minutes each. There are also mini-talks at different locations along the trail.

Located in the center of the state. Take I–93 to exit 24. Get onto Route 3, eastbound. About 4 miles down the road, make a left onto Route 113 and the Nature Center will be on your left.

PARADISE POINT NATURE CENTER AND HEBRON MARSH SANCTUARY

North Shore Road
Hebron, NH (603) 744–3516

Run by the New Hampshire Audubon Society, these two facilities are small but cozy, and are great places to do some serious bird watching.

At the nature center, which fronts on Newfound Lake, there are a few examples of native species on display, as well as an aquarium that provides a microcosm of local lake life. Visitors can follow five trails that wind through the woods and along the lake to observe local wildlife. Here you can usually see loons, kingfishers, and lots of warblers and thrushes, as well as beaver and maybe some mink.

At the sanctuary you can either walk the trails or go up in the observation tower to see loons, snipes, wood ducks, mallards, Canada geese, and many other forms of New Hampshire wildlife.

The sanctuary and trails at the Nature Center are open year-round, while the exhibit areas at the Nature Center are only open weekends in late June, and daily from the end of June through Labor Day. Hours are 10:00 A.M. to 5:00 P.M. There is no admission charge for either facility.

Located in the center of the state. To get there, take I–93 to exit 23. Pick up Route 104 West and go into the town of Bristol. In Bristol get onto Route 3A and go north for about 2½ miles, where you will make a left onto North Shore Road. Follow signs to Paradise Point. The sanctuary is about a mile past the Nature Center, on the same road.

New Jersey

BERGEN COUNTY ZOOLOGICAL PARK

216 Forest Avenue
Paramus, NJ (201) 262–3771

Occupying only seven of its allotted eighteen acres, this compact little zoo thrives in the city known as the "Shopping Center Capital of the World."

Despite its diminutive size, there are a lot of fun things to see here. You'll realize this immediately as you're greeted by the spider monkeys in their pavilion at the zoo's entrance. The grounds are shaded and flat, and walking is easy. If you choose, you can also see the sights aboard a miniature steam train that runs the perimeter of the zoo.

Season: Year-round, holidays too.

Hours: 10:00 A.M. to 4:30 P.M., daily.

Admission: May through October, admission is charged on weekends and holidays only. Adults, (ages 19–62), under $3; ages 12–18 and over age 62, under $2; under age 12, free. The rest of the year, admission is free every day. Additional fees: train ride, under $1; pony ride, under $2.50. Both rides are available in the park adjacent to the zoo.

The animals: More than 200 animals, about 70 species, all displayed in outdoor settings. Highlights include the North American Free-Flight Aviary;

North American Plains exhibit; Spider Monkey Pavilion; and the Mountain Lion exhibit.

Extras: An 1860s farmyard, with domesticated animals and antique farm equipment. In the adjacent park are a miniature train ride, pony rides, a playground, athletic fields, tennis courts, and a lake where fishing is permitted.

Special events: Wildlife Art Show and Sale, in May; Conservation Day Weekend, in May or June; Zoolympics, in June; Zoo Boo, in late October.

Food service: No food concessions in the zoo, and picnics are not allowed. In the adjacent park, however, are food concessions and a picnic area.

Plan to stay: 1 hour.

Directions: Take the Garden State Parkway to State Route 4, eastbound. Take Route 4 to Forest Avenue exit. Go north on Forest for about 1 mile. Zoo entrance will be on the right.

Nearby attractions: Bergen Museum of Art and Science, features the Hackensack mastodon skeleton; lots of shopping malls along Route 4; Lambert Castle, in nearby Paterson; Steuben House State Historic Site, in Hackensack, served as George Washington's headquarters in 1780.

CAPE MAY COUNTY PARK ZOO

Route 9 and Pine Lane
Cape May Court House, NJ (609) 465–5271

Located in the center of the community that occupies the southern tip of New Jersey, this cozy little zoo is a great place to find some peaceful moments. Although surrounded by a 120-acre heavily-wooded public park, the zoo has a distinctive shoreline feeling to it.

Season: Year-round, closed Christmas Day.

Hours: Daily, 9:00 A.M. to 5:00 P.M.

Admission: Free. Donations are appreciated, though.

The animals: More than 170 animals, more than 70 species, primarily birds and mammals. Highlights include the bird exhibit, the giraffe, and the large cats.

Entertainment: No entertainment in the zoo, but there are Sunday afternoon band concerts in the park during the summer.

Extras: Children's playground, nature walk, and bicycle trails around the edge of the park.

Food service: One concession sells a limited variety of fast foods, snacks, and beverages. Picnics are permitted.

Plan to stay: 1 hour.

Directions: Garden State Parkway to exit 11: Go right (west) onto Crest Haven Road, which goes directly into the zoo.

Nearby attractions: Tours of the quaint Victorian homes in and around Cape May; Colonial Farm, with 27 theme gardens; the famed Jersey Shore beaches and amusement areas; and numerous waterfront recreational activities.

COHANZICK ZOO

In City Park
Mayor Aitken Drive
Bridgeton, NJ (609) 455–3230

A self-guiding tour leads you past exhibits containing black bears, leopards, African lions, bobcats, primates, hoofstock, endangered ocelots, and a variety of birds, including parrots, macaws, and bald eagles.

Occupying about fifteen acres of the 1,100-acre City Park, this country zoo is surrounded by woods, streams, and a lake on which fishing is permitted. There is also an Indian village and a Swedish village set up on the property as added attractions.

The park and zoo are open every day of the year, from 8:00 A.M. until dusk, and admission is free.

Located in the southern part of the state. From the Delaware Bridge connecting Delaware and New Jersey, take the New Jersey Turnpike to the first exit and pick up Route 49 South. Follow Route 49 all the way to Bridgeton. In the center of town, make a left on Atlantic Street and follow it into the park.

Tim's Trivia

Halloween is the most celebrated holiday at North America's zoos. Cute names for the special days abound: Zooper Pumpkin Patch; Zpooktacular; Boo at the Zoo; ZooBoo; Zoolie Ghoulies; and Hallozooween are but a few.

JENKINSON'S AQUARIUM

The Boardwalk at Parkway
Point Pleasant Beach, NJ (908) 899–1212

You certainly won't run out of things to do here. Spread out along a mile-long boardwalk, Jenkinson's offers a fifty-ride amusement park, various restaurants and clubs, miniature golf, three full games arcades, and their newest addition, the aquarium.

The centerpiece of the aquarium building is a Tahitian Village, complete with a thatched-roof hut and a two-story waterfall. In the pool below the falls, you'll find the alligators, and in the stream that flows away from the village are a wide variety of freshwater fish.

Elsewhere in the building, you'll find penguins, snakes, a display of coral reef fish, sharks, rays, and plenty of local marine life. There are also touch tanks, a wave machine, a gallery highlighting the history of the area's fishing heritage, a video viewing room where nature films are continually being shown; and several other hands-on activities.

The ship used in the movie *The Bounty* is on display, as is a great exhibit of marine artifacts.

Open year-round. Hours: Memorial Day through Labor Day, 11:00 A.M. to 11:00 P.M.; remainder of the year, 9:30 A.M. to 5:30 P.M. Admission: adults, under $6; ages 3–12, under $4; under 3, free. Free parking during off-season. The entrance is located on the boardwalk.

NEW JERSEY STATE AQUARIUM AT CAMDEN

1 Riverside Drive
Camden, NJ (609) 365–3300

Built on the east bank of the Delaware River, just across from Philadelphia, this $52 million state-of-the-art facility opened to the public in early 1992 to rave reviews.

You enter through a 1½-acre parklike setting that features lush landscaping and a 170,000-gallon open habitat where harbor and gray seals live. A special machine produces waves for the seals to play in, and a winding path and sunken amphitheater provide views from above and below the water. Also outside is a trout stream that runs between several freshwater pools.

Inside, the 760,000-gallon main tank is the nation's second-largest open ocean tank, right behind the one in the Living Seas Exhibit at Walt Disney World's Epcot Center.

Season: Year-round, closed on Easter, Thanksgiving, Christmas Day, and New Year's Day.

Hours: Daily, 9:30 A.M. to 5:30 P.M.

Admission: Adults, under $9; ages 2–11, under $6; seniors, under $8. Additional fee: parking garage across from aquarium entrance, maximum of $7 per day; or at meters along the streets. NOTE: Advance tickets are strongly recommended and can be purchased at box office or by phone: (800) 922–6572.

The animals: More than 2,000 animals, more than 180 species, housed in numerous tanks and exhibits throughout the 2 floors of the facility. Top exhibits include: Open Ocean Tank, with more than 40 species native to the North Atlantic in several areas of the 760,000-gallon tank; Ancient Mariners, Jersey shore sea turtles; Silver Schools, schooling fish; Bottom Dwellers; Under the Boardwalk, an underwater view of pilings encrusted with a community of barnacles, sponges, and tunicates.

Entertainment: Multimedia presentation on local bays, rivers, and estuaries; divers in the Open Ocean Tank feed the fish, and you can ask them questions as they do so, via the "scubaphone."

Extras: Touch tank; SeaProbe, a replica of an underwater exploratory station with true-to-life scientific equipment and video screens and audio speakers that play recordings of scientists researching sharks; each night, the dome of the building provides the next day's weather forecast—blue lights, blue skies predicted, white light signifies overcast, red lights signal that storms are brewing, and flashing red lights warn of severe weather approaching.

Food service: Riverview Cafe seats 150 indoors and 300 on an outdoor deck overlooking the Delaware River and the Philadelphia skyline.

Plan to stay: 2 hours.

Directions: Located in the Ulysses S. Wiggins Waterfront Park. From New Jersey Turnpike: take exit 4 off turnpike and pick up Route 73 North. Follow Route 73 for 1.2 miles, until you see signs for Route 38 West/Benjamin Franklin Bridge/Camden. Follow Route 38 for 5.3 miles to Camden and bear right onto overpass at sign for Camden/Philadelphia. This will take you to Admiral Wilson Boulevard. From there, follow signs to Mickle Boulevard and then to the aquarium. From Penn's Landing in downtown Philadelphia: take the Riverbus to the aquarium.

Nearby attractions: Campbell Soup Museum; Philadelphia's historic areas.

POPCORN PARK ZOO

Humane Way
Forked River, NJ (609) 693–1900

A most unusual zoo, Popcorn Park is actually a shelter run by Associated Humane Societies for animals that have been injured, abandoned, or mistreated. Most of them cannot be placed in other zoos, or are not able to survive in the wild.

Set on eight wooded acres in the New Jersey Pine Barrens, the zoo was created in 1977 as a small display of native wildlife. Its humane efforts began when a raccoon that had to have its leg amputated after being caught in a trap took up residence here. Since then, the collection has grown to include abandoned circus animals, unruly critters, and animals that were taken away from their owners because they were not permitted to be kept as pets, as is the case with the Canadian jaguar.

In addition to native wildlife, there are also farm and exotic animals, including lions, tigers, monkeys, and an elephant. Healthy domesticated animals are available for adoption at the shelter on the premises.

Popcorn Park is open year-round, including holidays. Hours are 11:00 A.M. to 5:00 P.M., May through September; and 1:00 P.M. to 5:00 P.M. the remainder of the year. If there is warm weather into the fall months, the zoo may open earlier in the day. Call first to be sure. Admission is under $4 for adults, and under $3 for those under age 11 or over 61.

To reach Popcorn Park, take the Garden State Parkway to exit 74. Turn right and follow Route 9 South for about 7 miles. A large sign marks the entrance, on the right.

New Mexico

LIVING DESERT STATE PARK

Skyline Drive
Carlsbad, NM (505) 887–5516

As the name suggests, this park of primarily native animals and plants is in the (Chihuahuan) desert. While the entire park encompasses 1,200 acres, the animal viewing area is confined to forty-five acres.

Here you can see birds of prey in the aviary, reptiles, mountain lions, bobcats, Mexican wolves, bears, prairie dogs, and nocturnal desert creatures. Hoofstock, including bison, elk, and mule deer, roam freely in a large enclosed canyon.

There's a 1.3-mile guided walking trail that loops around the animal exhibit area, which is situated atop a mesa. Other trails wind through sand dunes, gypsum hills, arroyos, chaparrals, and grassland. There is also a greenhouse and many displays of desert plants.

Open year-round, daily, except Christmas. Hours: May 15 through Labor Day, 8:00 A.M. to 8:00 P.M.; remainder of the year, 9:00 A.M. to 5:00 P.M. Admission is under $5 for everyone age 7 or older; under age 7, free.

The park entrance is located on Route 285, about 4 miles northwest of the city of Carlsbad.

RIO GRANDE ZOOLOGICAL PARK

903 10th Street SW
Albuquerque, NM (505) 843–7413

Built into a grove of cottonwood trees in a residential neighborhood bordering the Rio Grande, this well-kept sixty-two-acre facility is the pride of Albuquerque's residents and city officials alike.

A statue of a crane stands at the front gate to greet you, as do several other sculptures throughout the zoo, including a buffalo, in the prairie exhibit, and a lioness with her cub, in the Cat Walk exhibit. A large lake provides a nice touch to the landscaping, since it attracts a great variety of waterfowl.

Season: Year-round, closed Thanksgiving, Christmas Day, and New Year's Day.

Hours: Daily, 9:00 A.M. to 5:00 P.M.

Admission: Adults, under $6; ages 3–15 and seniors, under $4; under age 3, free. Additional fee: camel ride, under $2.50.

The animals: More than 1,200 animals, more than 300 species, including lots of birds. Most of the animals are in open-moated, naturalistic habitats. Highlights include the Rain Forest exhibit; Sea Lion Pool; Prairie exhibit; and Cat Walk exhibit.

Entertainment: Exotic Bird Shows are given twice daily, except on Mondays.

Extras: Camel rides during the summer; children's zoo, with contact area.

Special events: Mother's Day, in May; Zoo Run, in June; Zoo Boo, in late October.

Food service: 2 stands serve a limited variety of fast food, snacks, ice cream, and soft drinks.

Plan to stay: 2 hours.

Directions: I–25 to Lead Avenue exit. Go west on Lead (a one-way street) to 10th Street. Make a left on 10th Street and go south for about 2 blocks to zoo entrance, on the right. Brown-and-white zoo signs will direct you.

Nearby attractions: National Atomic Museum, traces development of nuclear weapons; Mission of San Agustin de Isleta, built in 1621; Tinkertown Museum, a miniature western town and circus display; a cable car ride up the Rocky Mountains; Cliff's Amusement Park; Indian Pueblo Cultural Center; Old Town Plaza, shopping area.

SPRING RIVER PARK AND ZOO

1306 East College Boulevard
Roswell, NM (505) 624–6760

More than twenty-five species of native New Mexican animals reside here in natural settings. And to add to the fun and the popularity of this park, there's also an antique wooden carousel, a miniature train, and a children's fishing lake.

Located on the eastern terminus of a 5-mile greenbelt trail that runs through the heart of the city, the park grounds are bisected by the Spring River, the winter home of a few hundred wild geese. Among the animals

```
▼▼▼▼▼▼▼▼▼▼▼▼▼▼▼▼▼▼▼▼▼▼▼▼▼▼▼▼▼▼▼▼▼▼
```

Fauna Fun Facts

There are more than 700,000 known species of insects.

and exhibits, you'll see a lot of hoofstock, a children's zoo, and one of the largest prairie dog towns in the Southwest.

Open daily, year-round, except Christmas. Hours: 10:00 A.M. to 7:00 P.M. in the summer; 10:00 A.M. to 5:00 P.M. in the winter. Admission to the park and zoo is free, but there's a 25-cent per person charge for both the carousel and the train rides. Fishing in the lake, which is stocked by the state, is free but restricted to those under age 11.

Take U.S. Route 380 to Atkinson Road, northbound. Stay on Atkinson for about 1 mile to College Boulevard. Entrance is on the southeast corner.

New York

ANIMAL FARM PETTING ZOO

184A Wading River Road
Manorville, NY (516) 878-1785

Geared for younger children, this ten-acre zoo is an excellent place to bring the kiddies for a day of fun and learning. There's a variety of domestic and exotic animals, including farm animals, monkeys, deer, llamas, peacocks, and talking parrots. Additionally, hands-on animal presentations, puppet shows, a playground, and kiddie rides will keep the young ones busy for a few hours.

Since everything is outdoors, the facility is open from April through October only, wrapping up each season with special activities geared to Halloween. Hours are 10:00 A.M. to 5:00 P.M., daily, and admission is under $10 for adults; under $8 for ages 2–17 and seniors. Those under age 2 get in free.

Located on eastern Long Island, the zoo can be reached by taking the Long Island Expressway (Route 495) east to exit 69 (Center Moriches). Go south on Wading River Road for 2½ miles to entrance.

AQUARIUM AT NIAGARA FALLS

701 Whirlpool Street
Niagara Falls, NY (716) 285–3575

One of the world's first inland oceanariums, this facility boasts the largest collection of native New York fish. The forty indoor exhibits feature nearly 200 different species, including Atlantic blue-nose dolphins, sea lions, harbor seals, sharks, electric eels, lobsters, horseshoe crabs, and Peruvian penguins, the last of which are on the endangered species list.

As you enter the building, you'll get a chance to watch the seals and sea lions playfully ham it up in their outdoor pool. In March, the aquarium celebrates Penguin Days.

Open daily, year-round; closed on Thanksgiving, Christmas Day, and New Year's Day. Summer hours, Memorial Day through Labor Day, 9:00 A.M. to 7:00 P.M.; remainder of the year, 9:00 A.M. to 5:00 P.M. Admission: adults, under $6; ages 5–14 and seniors, under $4; under 5, free.

Located 5 blocks from Prospect Park and the American Falls, in downtown Niagara Falls. Exit off I–190 onto the Robert Moses Parkway and follow the leaping dolphin signs to Aquarium exit.

BUFFALO ZOOLOGICAL GARDENS

In Delaware Park
Buffalo, NY (716) 837–3900

Shady Delaware Park, at the northern edge of the second-largest city in New York State, is the setting for the Buffalo Zoo. It is believed to be the third-oldest zoological garden in the country, having been established in 1875 with a herd of deer that inhabited the area. The 1901 Pan-American Exposition was held nearby.

The flat terrain of the twenty-three-acre zoo contains four ponds in a botanical garden setting with park benches liberally sprinkled in among the tall trees, dense foliage, and animal exhibit area.

Season: Year-round, closed Thanksgiving and Christmas Day.

Hours: Daily, 10:00 A.M. to 5:30 P.M. during daylight saving time; closes an hour earlier the rest of the year.

Admission: Adults, under $5; ages 11–16, under $2; ages 4–10, under $1; under age 4 and seniors, free. Additional fees: parking, under $3 in

June, July, and August only; carousel, kiddie train, and camel, pony, and elephant rides, all under $2 each.

The animals: 1,500 animals, more than 200 species, displayed in both indoor and outdoor settings. Most outstanding exhibits include Habicats, a collection of Siberian tigers and African lions; Lowland Gorilla African Rain Forest; and a prairie dog display.

Entertainment: In summer, there are puppet shows and magic shows; also, Birds of Prey flight demonstrations twice a day, Monday through Thursday. The education department runs tours upon request and stations docents at each exhibit to talk about the animals.

Extras: Rides on camels, elephants, and ponies; old-fashioned carousel rides; kiddie train; children's zoo; and a gallery of Boehm porcelain sculptures.

Special events: Zooper Pumpkin Patch on the weekend nearest Halloween each year.

Food service: One concession stand sells fast food, snacks, and beverages. There are picnic tables throughout the park.

Plan to stay: 2 hours.

Directions: I-190 (Niagara section of New York State Thruway) to Route 198 (Scajaquada Expressway), eastbound. Get off at the Parkside/Buffalo Zoo exit and go north 1 long block to zoo entrance, on left.

Nearby attractions: Theodore Roosevelt Inaugural National Historical Site; Buffalo and Erie County Botanical Gardens; Naval and Servicemen's Park, where visitors can board several warships; Fantasy Island amusement park; and Darien Lake amusement park.

BURNET PARK ZOO

500 Burnet Park Drive
Syracuse, NY (315) 435–8511

This sixty-acre zoo is something of an oasis in downtown Syracuse. Built into the side of a gentle, rolling hillside, and bordered by a forested area, about the only worldly sounds you'll hear around here are a few growls from the animals and a lot of laughter and happy talk from other visitors.

Opened in 1912, and remodeled during the 1980s, the popular facility has modernized its exhibits and zoological philosophies without destroying the charm of its heritage.

Season: Year-round, closed Christmas Day and New Year's Day.

Hours: Daily, 8:30 A.M. to 4:30 P.M.

Admission: Adults, under $5; ages 5–14 and seniors, under $3; under age 5, free.

The animals: More the 900 animals, more than 200 species, displayed in both indoor and outdoor naturalistic settings. Highlights include the elephant exhibit, which is part of a nationwide zoological breeding program; the aviary; the Wild North Forest.

Entertainment: No regularly scheduled entertainment, but during the summer, zookeepers will occasionally bring animals out of their habitats for demonstrations.

Extras: Contact Barn, children's zoo area where there are unscheduled animal demonstrations; veterinary clinic and animal food kitchen, which can be viewed through windows. In other areas of the adjoining park, there is a playground and park facilities.

Special events: ZooBoo, near Halloween; Elephant Celebration, one weekend during the summer, when visitors can paint an elephant.

Food service: There is a Burger King Restaurant on the property. Picnicking is permitted in other areas of Burnet Park, but not in the zoo.

Plan to stay: 2 hours.

Directions: I–90 (New York State Thruway) to I–690 East, to exit 5 (Bear Street). Go south on Bear to Spencer Street. Turn right onto Spencer and then right at Geddes. Travel on Geddes for approximately 1 mile to zoo entrance, on right.

Nearby attractions: Erie Canal Museum; Onondaga Lake Park, with tram tours and salt museum; New York State Fair, from late August through Labor Day.

CATSKILL GAME FARM

Game Farm Road
Cairo, NY (518) 678–9595

More than 2,000 animals and birds from around the world can be found here, in the only animal farm in New York's Catskill Mountains. Be prepared to spend a couple of hours here strolling through the shaded and lush landscape, watching the three daily animal shows (Memorial Day through Labor Day only), and petting and feeding the smaller residents of the petting zoo.

The Game Farm opens each year on April 15 and closes October 31. Hours: 9:00 A.M. to 6:00 P.M. Admission: under $13 for adults; ages 4–11, under $8; under 4, free.

Take the New York State Thruway to exit 20 (Route 32). Take Route 32 North. After crossing Route 23A, continue on Route 32 for a few more miles. Signs will direct you to Game Farm Road, on the left, which leads into the parking area.

CENTRAL PARK ZOO

830 Fifth Avenue
New York, NY (212) 861–6030

It's a tradition! There has been a small zoo on Fifth Avenue at Sixty-fourth Street in Manhattan since 1864. The facility was incorporated into the original design of Central Park by noted landscape architect Frederick Law Olmsted around the turn of the century. Former New York City Parks Commissioner Robert Moses was responsible for expanding the facility in the 1930s, and some of the landmark architecture he created still remains, despite a major renovation that began about ten years ago.

The 5½-acre zoo, set in the heart of midtown Manhattan, looks a lot different than it did a decade ago. Most of the old brick buildings have been replaced by a formal central garden, which is flanked on three sides by a colonnade of octagonal brick-and-granite posts and glass-roofed walkways.

These lead to the three major ecological areas displayed in the present buildings, which were first opened to the public in 1988.

Season: Year-round, holidays too.

Hours: May through October, 10:00 A.M. to 5:00 P.M. on weekdays; 10:00 A.M. to 5:30 P.M. on weekends and holidays. On Tuesday evenings, May through September, the zoo remains open until 8:00 P.M. From November through March, gates close a half-hour earlier every day.

Admission: Adults, under $3; seniors, under $2; ages 3–12, under $1; under age 3, free.

The animals: Approximately 450 animals, 100 species, displayed in naturalistic habitats representing the Tropic Zone, Temperate Territory, and Polar Circle. Highlights include the open aviary at the center of the Tropic Zone building, which contains brightly colored tropical birds, an aquarium filled with piranha, an ant nest with more than 100,000 leaf-cutter ants, and an enormous buttress-root tree that grows from floor to ceiling.

Entertainment: Sea lion feedings, 3 times daily.

Extras: Carved stone and animal friezes, bronze animal sculptures, and the Delacorte clock, all of which have been preserved from the original buildings; the Chinese Intelligence Garden; and the Wildlife Conservation Center.

Special events: Events are scheduled throughout the year.

Food service: One indoor-outdoor cafeteria, which serves a variety of fast foods, sandwiches, snacks, ice cream, and beverages. Picnics are permitted.

Plan to stay: 2 hours.

Directions: Parking is very limited near the zoo, but there are several parking garages in the area. Midtown buses and subways have convenient stops near the zoo. By Bus: take an M1, M2, or M3 bus to 65th Street and Fifth Avenue. By Subway: on the BMT line, take the R or N train to Fifth Avenue and 59th Street and walk to zoo entrance at 64th Street; or, on the IRT Lexington Avenue line, take the Number 6 train to 68th Street and walk to entrance.

Nearby attractions: F.A.O. Schwarz, the world-famous toy store; Trump Tower; Sak's Fifth Avenue; Wollman Memorial Skating Rink, also in Central Park; Radio City Music Hall; St. Patrick's Cathedral; Rockefeller Center; Lincoln Center for the Performing Arts.

CLYDE PEELING'S REPTILAND

Route 32
Catskill, NY (518) 678–3557

Snuggled in the beautiful Catskill Mountains, this is a compact version of the original Reptiland still in operation in Allenwood, Pennsylvania. The wooded surroundings provide a cool, natural setting where visitors can see an extensive variety of reptiles, ranging from common snakes found in home gardens to the most exotic cobras and tortoises.

It's a place where you can learn to lose your fear of reptiles and, if you like, handle a live python or boa constrictor. It's a unique experience.

Season: Memorial Day through Labor Day.

Hours: Daily, 10:00 A.M. to 5:00 P.M.

Admission: Adults, under $8; ages 4–11, under $5; under age 4, free.

The animals: More than 100 animals, more than 50 species, all reptiles, displayed in both indoor and outdoor settings. Highlights include a tropical solarium with green iguanas, tortoises, and crocodiles; African puff adder; Asian cobra; and a gila monster from the American Southwest.

Entertainment: There are no live shows, but there is a continuously running video program that gives an interesting overview of the reptile kingdom.

Extras: Hands-on experience with a python or boa constrictor.

Food service: No food concessions, but picnics are permitted.

Plan to stay: 1 hour.

Directions: I–87 (New York State Thruway) to exit 20 (Route 32). Take Route 32 North. Reptiland will be on your right, about 2 miles past the Catskill Game Farm.

Nearby attractions: Catskill Game Farm; Ponderosa Ranch Fun Park, with go-karts, bumper boats, and other amusements; Carson City and Indian Village, a Wild West town; Zoom Flume Water Park (in East Durham); Freehold Airport, which offers scenic air tours; and the Hunter Mountain Sky Ride.

LAKE GEORGE ZOOLOGICAL PARK

Route 9
Lake George, NY (518) 793–3393

Each year this little zoo gets better, as owner David Osborne adds to the collection of animals and expands the schedule of demonstrations. Located near the heart of busy downtown Lake George, it's a nice way to spend an hour or two in the morning or afternoon with the children during a family vacation.

The exhibit area is easy to walk through, and tall trees provide shade to keep you cool while you feed the animals, watch a chimp show, or see the lions being fed.

The facility is open from the end of June through Labor Day, daily from 9:30 A.M. to 6:00 P.M.

The zoo is located 45 minutes north of Albany. To get there, take the New York State Thruway to the Adirondack Northway (Route 87). Get off the Northway at exit 19. At the end of the exit ramp, turn left onto Route 9 and the park will be a short distance down the road, on the right. It's diagonally across from the Great Escape Fun Park.

LONG ISLAND GAME FARM
Chapman Boulevard
Manorville, NY (516) 878–6644

Located toward the eastern end of Long Island, this is one of the busiest, and most fun facilities of its type around. You can see wild Bengal tiger shows, attend animal science lectures, and observe feedings. You can even bottle-feed some of the younger animals yourself. There is also a petting zoo, an antique carousel, an 1860s-era Animal Express Train, and a sky slide.

Open from mid-April through November, when Santa makes his annual visit to the animals and their guests. Hours: 10:00 A.M. to 5:00 P.M. during the week, with closing an hour later on weekends. Admission: adults, under $13; ages 2–11 and seniors, under $10; under 2, free.

Take the Long Island Expressway (Route 495) to exit 70. Prominently posted signs will direct you from the exit ramp to the entrance.

NEW YORK AQUARIUM
West Eighth Street and Surf Avenue
Coney Island (Brooklyn) NY (718) 265–FISH

Considered the oldest continuously operating aquarium in the United States, this one is located on a fourteen-acre site adjacent to the historic Coney Island Boardwalk. It opened in 1896 in Battery Park, in lower Manhattan, and moved to its present site in 1957.

In addition to its long history, it has also had a couple of firsts. In 1897, this was the first facility in the world to exhibit beluga whales, and in 1981, the first beluga ever bred in captivity was born here.

Popular among tourists as well as locals, the aquarium features a varied array of exhibits, ranging from the 90,000-gallon shark tank, to Sea Cliffs, a 300-foot-long rocky coast habitat featuring walruses, seals, sea lions, sea otters, and penguins.

Season: Open year-round, Christmas too.

Hours: Daily, 10:00 A.M. to 4:45 P.M. Closing hours extended on summer weekends and holidays to 7:00 P.M.

Admission: Adults, under $7; ages 2–12, under $3; 2 and under, free. Additional fees: parking, fees vary with season.

The animals: More than 300 species, more than 10,000 animals. Exhibits include: Sea Cliffs; Cold Marine Gallery; Oceanic Tank, with above-and-below viewing of beluga whales; Main Gallery, fishes from Florida to the Red Sea; Penguin Rookery, featuring black-footed penguins; Bermuda Triangle, fish, sea turtles, and moray eels; and Native Sea Life, the fish commonly caught by local anglers, including bass, sea robins, and fluke.

Entertainment: Marine mammal shows scheduled several times daily. Animal feedings throughout the day.

Extras: The 20,000-square-foot Discovery Cove education center with 65 exhibits, including a 400-gallon crashing wave, a salt marsh, and a seaside village; Bathysphere, the one used by Otis Barton and William Beebe during their historic dive of 1934; Oceanic Deck, overlooking boardwalk, beach, and Atlantic Ocean.

Food service: An outside snack bar and an indoor cafeteria. Picnics are permitted in the designated picnic area.

Plan to stay: 3 hours

Directions: Take exit 6 (Cropsey Avenue) or exit 7S (Ocean Parkway South) off Belt Parkway, then follow the blue beluga whale road signs to the aquarium.

Nearby attractions: Astroland Amusement Park, home of the world-renowned Cyclone wooden roller coaster; Coney Island beaches; and a myriad of other rides and attractions scattered throughout the immediate area; the original Nathan's hot-dog stand, which still serves the most fantastic hot dogs in the world; Nellie Bly amusement park.

Tim's Trivia

First chartered in the 1850s, the Philadelphia Zoo is considered the oldest zoo in the United States. It has been in its current location since 1874.

NEW YORK ZOOLOGICAL PARK

(The Bronx Zoo)
Fordham Road and Bronx River Parkway
Bronx, NY (212) 367–1010

Plan a whole day if you want to see and enjoy this zoo to its fullest! There's plenty to keep the entire family busy.

Built in 1899, this 265-acre zoological park borders the Bronx River and is one of the most scenic places within the metropolitan New York area. It's the largest urban zoo in the United States and attracts more than two million visitors each year.

Turn-of-the-century stone buildings stand amid the more modern exhibit areas, providing a pleasing contrast between old and new, and the gently sloping grounds are well-manicured.

Season: Year-round, holidays too.

Hours: February through October, weekdays 10:00 A.M. to 5:00 P.M.; weekends and holidays 10:00 A.M. to 5:30 P.M.; November through January, gates close at 4:30 P.M., daily.

Admission: Adults, under $7; ages 2–12, under $5; under age 2 and over 65, free at all times. On Tuesdays, Wednesdays, and Thursdays, year-round, admission is by donation. Children under 16 must be accompanied by an adult. Additional fees: parking, under $7; aerial tram, under $4; animal rides, under $3; zoo shuttle, under $3; Bengali Express, under $3; children's zoo, under $2; JungleWorld, under $2.

The animals: More than 4,000 animals, more than 600 species, displayed in indoor and outdoor naturalistic habitats. Outstanding exhibits include JungleWorld, an indoor Asian rain forest; Himalayan Highlands; Wild Asia; The World of Darkness; and Birds World, with daily indoor thunderstorms.

Entertainment: Daily animal shows in the children's zoo Wildlife Theater, except in winter.

Extras: Skyfari aerial tramway; camel rides; zoo shuttle; Bengali Express, a guided monorail tour. (All rides shut down during winter.)

Food service: Zoobar, and Flamingo Pub with cafeteria. Also, snack bars and picnic areas are scattered around the property.

Plan to stay: All day.

Directions: I–95 (Cross Bronx Expressway or New England Thruway) to

Bronx River Parkway. Get off at Bronx Zoo exit, which leads right into parking area.

Nearby attractions: New York Botanical Garden (across street from zoo); Yankee Stadium; Van Cortlandt Mansion, built in 1748; Poe Cottage, where Edgar Allan Poe lived from 1846 until his death.

QUEENS ZOO

In Flushing Meadow Park
53-51 111th Street
Flushing, NY (212) 861–6030

In the shadow of the tower built for the 1964 World's Fair, this zoological facility reopened in mid-1992 under the aegis of the New York Zoological Society. Closed in 1988 for renovation, the eleven acre zoo is now a totally natural habitat with up-to-date educational graphics that enhance the viewing as well as the learning opportunities.

Devoted to North American fauna, there are approximately 250 animals here, representing forty species. Twelve major exhibit areas highlight the American bison, black bear, puma, bobcat, Roosevelt elk, prairie dog, coyote, California sea lion, and sandhill crane.

The geodesic dome houses a spectacular aviary, and is home to a variety of birds, including the snowy egret, the northern cardinal, the black-billed magpie, and Stellar's jay. Plenty of waterfowl live in the marsh pond exhibit area.

Modern techniques help bring animals and people closer together. For example, at the puma exhibit, electrically warmed rocks draw the animals out of hiding and closer to the public.

Admission: adults, under $3; seniors, under $1.50; ages 3–12, under $1; under 3, free. A sit-down cafeteria serves a full line of meals and snacks. Opens daily, year-round, at 10:00 A.M. During the summer, closes at 5:00 P.M. during the week, 5:30 on weekends. During the winter, closes daily at 4:30 P.M.

Take the Long Island Expressway to the exit for 108th Street, Turn left onto 108th Street and go to 52nd Avenue. Turn right and take 52nd Avenue to 111th Street. Stay on 52nd Avenue, bear right, and cross over 111th to the parking lot on the corner.

ROSS PARK ZOO

Morgan Road
Binghamton, NY (607) 724–5461

A woodland stream cuts through the center of this peaceful, wooded facility, which is located amid the ninety acres that make up Ross Park. It's located on a hillside outside the bustling city of Binghamton, in upstate New York. There's not a lot of paving here, either, just enough to make the pathway loop between the exhibits easily accessible.

Opened in 1875, it's the fifth-oldest zoo in the country, but exhibits have been upgraded to current zoological standards. Make sure you catch a ride on the restored antique carousel that operates just outside the zoo, and take a peek at one of the zoo's celebrity inhabitants, a female bald eagle who survived the Exxon *Valdez* oil spill in Alaska. Her name? Valdessa, of course.

Season: March through November.

Hours: April to October, daily from 10:00 A.M. to 6:00 P.M.; March and November, daily, 10:00 A.M. to 4:30 P.M.

Admission: Adults, under $5; seniors and handicapped, under $4; ages 3–12, under $4; under age 2, free. Additional fee: Discovery Center, under $4 per person.

The animals: More than 150 animals, more than 50 species, displayed in indoor and outdoor cageless settings. Outstanding exhibits include the cougar/tiger area; Wolf Woods habitat with ground-level and aerial viewing areas; spectacled bear exhibit; and bald eagle habitat, where Valdessa lives.

Entertainment: No regularly scheduled entertainment, but on occasional weekends, zookeepers will hold Animal Spotlights, bringing some of the smaller animals and birds out of their habitats.

Extras: Antique carousel ride and Carousel Museum, just outside the zoo entrance; Discovery Center, a hands-on children's museum; and a playground, just outside zoo entrance.

Special events: Zoo Do Carnival, 1 Sunday in June; Ice Cream Safaris, 1 Sunday in July and another in August.

Food service: 1 fast-food concession is on the grounds, and picnics are permitted.

Plan to stay: 2 hours.

Directions: From State Route 17, take exit 4 south to Route 363 South. Exit at Route 434 West (toward Vestal). Make a left at the first traffic light onto S. Washington Street. After passing 1 traffic light, you will come to a stop sign. Make a left at the stop sign, onto Morgan Road. Zoo entrance is a half-mile down, on the right.

Nearby attractions: Roberson Center for the Arts and Sciences, and Roberson mansion and planetarium, in Binghamton; National Soaring Museum and Mark Twain's Study and grave, in Elmira.

SENECA PARK ZOO

2222 St. Paul Street
Rochester, NY (716) 342-2744

The Genesee River gorge borders the edge of this zoo, which is located in the northern section of the city made famous by Kodak founder George Eastman. Officials say that in the years to come the river will be incorporated into the exhibits as a central theme.

Presently, the zoo is a pleasant blend of the old and the new. Opened in 1894, it is part of another park designed by landscape architect Frederick Law Olmsted. There are still some older buildings and cages on the grounds, along with more contemporary exhibits, and the landscaping offers a gentle, relaxing setting.

Season: Year-round, holidays too.

Hours: Mid-May to mid-October, opens daily at 10:00 A.M. and closes at 5:00 P.M., weekdays, and 7:00 P.M. on weekends and holidays. The remainder of the year, 10:00 A.M. to 5:00 P.M., daily.

Admission: Adults, under $3; ages 10–15, under $2.50; seniors and under 10, free. Maximum charge per family: under $6. Additional fee: children's zoo, under $1.

The animals: More than 450 animals, more than 150 species, displayed in both indoor and outdoor natural habitats, with some in cages. Highlights include free-flight bird exhibits, elephants, polar bears, sea lions, snow leopards, and lions.

Entertainment: Live animal presentations are given on a changing schedule. Animal feedings at 3:00 P.M., daily.

Extras: Children's zoo; Animal of the Month presentation, on Sundays.

Special events: Held during the summer on a changing schedule.

Food service: The Hungry Lion food stand offers a variety of fast foods, snacks, and beverages. Picnics are permitted.

Plan to stay: 2 hours.

Directions: I–490 to St. Paul Street exit. Go north on St. Paul for about 4 miles. Zoo entrance will be on the left.

Nearby attractions: Seabreeze Amusement Park and Raging Rivers water park; International Museum of Photography (Eastman House); Strong Museum, with toys and dollhouses; Susan B. Anthony House; Upper Falls Park, with 100-foot-high falls on the Genessee River.

STATEN ISLAND ZOO

In Barrett Park
614 Broadway
Staten Island, NY (718) 442–3100 (recording); (718) 442–3101

Promoted as "a great little family zoo," the Staten Island Zoo is located on eight acres of city-owned Barrett Park. Like many zoos in the country, it was built during the 1930s as a WPA project and is now updating its exhibits into more naturalistic settings.

The Depression-era main building forms the centerpiece for a cluster of more modern open exhibit areas, in which the animals enjoy a greater degree of freedom than ever before on beautifully landscaped grounds that were once part of an arboretum.

Season: Year-round, closed Thanksgiving, Christmas Day, and New Year's Day.

Hours: Daily, 10:00 A.M. to 4:45 P.M.

Admission: Adults, under $5; ages 3–11 and over 65, under $3; under 3, free. After 2:00 P.M. on Wednesdays, everyone gets in free.

The animals: More than 400 animals, more than 200 species, displayed in indoor and outdoor settings. Noteworthy exhibits include a world-renowned serpentarium with one of the most complete collections of rattlesnakes in the United States; a state-of-the-art 12-tank aquarium; and a walk-through South American Tropical Forest.

Entertainment: Provided by the animals themselves, especially during feeding times. Mammals are fed daily at 2:30 P.M., reptiles at 3:15 P.M. on

Sundays only, and fish in the early morning and late afternoon daily. Educational programs and animal demonstrations are given by the education department staff upon request.

Extras: Children's Center Petting Zoo, in farmland setting, with guanacos, pygmy goats, and ducks. Pony rides and wagon rides are offered during nice weather.

Special events: During the summer there are many special programs, including Breakfast with the Beasts, Rhino Walk, Conservation Day, and Zoo Olympics.

Food service: 1 snack bar is located on the grounds, and picnics are permitted.

Plan to stay: 1 hour.

Directions: I–278 to Slosson Avenue exit. Go north on Slosson to Martling Avenue. Turn right on Martling and follow to the end, at Clove Road. Zoo entrance will be straight ahead, with parking on the right.

Nearby attractions: Richmondtown Restoration, a restored 100-acre village that represents the appearance and lifestyles of Staten Island over the past 300 years; Snug Harbor, includes historic buildings, art gallery, concert hall, and botanical garden.

TREVOR ZOO

Millbrook School
Millbrook, NY (914) 677–3704

Deep in the woods of Dutchess County, where Revolutionary War soldiers left their mark on history, the Trevor Zoo is moving quietly into the future. On five acres of an old farm that has been occupied by a private high school for the past fifty years, the facility has evolved from a passive conservation facility to one that takes an active part in the world environmental movement.

Boarding students tend the animals during the school year, a practice initiated when the school's first biology teacher, Frank Trevor, brought his private wildlife collection to the school in 1936. Now, with recent renovations nearly complete and an interactive computer system on line, visitors have the opportunity to get personally involved with protecting the future of Planet Earth.

Season: Year-round, holidays too.

Hours: Daily, 8:00 A.M. to 5:00 P.M.

Admission: Suggested donations: Adults, under $2; ages 5–12, under $1.50, under age 5, free.

The animals: More than 150 animals, more than 60 species, displayed in natural habitats of North America, South America, Asia, and Australia. Highlights include snow monkeys, red pandas, and the Birds of Prey flight cage.

Entertainment: No animal shows, but staff members will give you a tour of the zoo upon request.

Extras: Species breeding facility; Environmental Action Center with an aquarium and interactive computers that allow visitors to participate in the environmental movement by signing petitions and letters to elected officials; landscaped sitting gardens; and a boardwalk nature trail linking the zoo property to an adjoining wetlands area owned by The Nature Conservancy.

Food service: No concessions, but picnics are permitted.

Plan to stay: 2 hours.

Directions: From the Taconic Parkway, take Route 44 East through the village of Millbrook. The Millbrook School entrance is located about 6 miles past the village, on the north side of Route 44.

Nearby attractions: Young-Morse Historic Site, in Poughkeepsie, former home of Samuel B. Morse, contains a wildlife sanctuary. In Hyde Park, there is the Vanderbilt Mansion, the Franklin D. Roosevelt home and library, and the Culinary Institute of America, whose 3 restaurants are open to the public by reservation.

Fauna Fun Facts

A cougar is also known as a puma, painter, screamer, mountain lion, silver ghost, and catamount.

UTICA ZOO

In Roscoe Conkling Park
Steele Hill Road
Utica, NY (315) 738–0472

The renowned landscape architect Frederick Law Olmsted was also busy here and left the city with another of his greenbelt gems. Situated in Roscoe Conkling Park, in downtown Utica, this eighty-acre zoo features the best of the past and present, including an animal collection that grew from a donation of fallow deer to the city by the Bronx Zoo around the turn of the century.

Most of the 1920s-style buildings, which once housed the animals, are now used for administrative purposes, while the animals roam freely in natural habitat settings. The park itself contains other public recreational facilities.

Season: Year-round, holidays too.

Hours: 10:00 A.M. to 5:00 P.M., daily.

Admission: Adults, under $4; seniors, under $3.50; ages 2–12, under $2.50; under age 2, free. Additional fee: camel rides, under $3.

The animals: Approximately 250 animals of 100 species, displayed in indoor and outdoor naturalistic habitats. Highlights include the sea lion exhibits, bald eagle exhibits, Siberian tigers and snow leopards, and red pandas.

Entertainment: Sea lion shows, twice a day.

Extras: Children's zoo; small playground; and camel rides in summer.

Special events: Easter Eggstravaganza, near Easter; Animal Fair, in May; Conservation Day, in June; Halloween Zpooktacular, in October. Other events, which are on a changing schedule, include Dinosaur Days, Teddy Bear Affair, Big Cat Day, and others.

Food service: 1 snack bar offers a limited variety of fast foods and snack items. Picnics are permitted.

Plan to stay: 2 hours.

Directions: I-90 (New York State Thruway) to exit 30. Go south on Genesee Street for 1½ miles to Memorial Parkway. Turn left on Memorial and zoo/park entrance will be on the right, just past the tennis courts.

Nearby attractions: F. X. Matt Brewing Company has tours followed by a trolley ride to the 1888 Tavern, where samples are served. In Rome, there is the Erie Canal Village, restoration of an 1840 community; and in Oriskany, the Revolutionary War battlefield.

North Carolina

NORTH CAROLINA AQUARIUM AT FORT FISHER

U.S. Highway 421
Fort Fisher, NC (919) 458–8257

River otters and sharks are among the most popular exhibits at this seaside aquarium, which features excellent nature trails along the beach. An outdoor aquaculture exhibit includes catfish, koi, and freshwater turtles.

The whale exhibit features a full-size model (49 feet long), anatomically and color correct right down to the spots, of a whale named Salt, who, directors assume, is still living somewhere off the North Carolina shore.

The shark tank has an aqua-scanner, which you can manipulate with joy sticks to get close-up looks at any of the creatures living there. Children will also enjoy the educational and fun touch tank.

Open year round; operating hours are Monday through Saturday, 9:00 A.M. to 5:00 P.M., and Sundays 1:00 to 5:00 P.M. Admission is free, but donations are accepted.

To get to the aquarium, take I–40 until it ends at Highway 421 South. The aquarium is at the end of 421 South and Kure Beach, 20 miles south of Wilmington.

NORTH CAROLINA AQUARIUM ON PINE KNOLL SHORES

Route 58
Atlantic Beach, NC (919) 247–4003

Overlooking a natural salt marsh, this facility's sixteen major tanks feature the marine life of coastal Carolina. Additional exhibits include a Turtle Room with a viewing nursery where you can watch loggerhead sea turtle hatchlings.

Precious Waters, the newest exhibit here, has three main components. The first is a 2,000-gallon salt marsh tank, the second is an alligator habitat with four gators, and the last is a video station with four different videos about water pollution along coastal North Carolina.

Close Encounters is a 700-gallon touch tank with local marine life. An observation deck has fixed binoculars that offer a nice aerial view of the salt marsh.

Outside, there's a half-mile nature walk loop that will take you through a maritime forest full of interesting vegetation and a wide variety of reptiles. Along the walk, you'll find twenty interpretive stations.

Open year-round, Monday through Saturday, 9:00 A.M. to 5:00 P.M., and Sundays, 1:00 to 5:00 P.M. Closed Thanksgiving, Christmas Day, and New Year's Day. There is no official admission charge, but a donation is requested.

Occupying a part of the 296-acre Theodore Roosevelt Natural Area, the aquarium is situated halfway between the two other coastal aquariums run by the Office of Marine Affairs.

Located on Bogue Bank (they call islands "banks" around here), 5 miles west of Atlantic Beach, on Route 58, at mile marker 7. From Route 70, in Atlantic Beach, take Route 58 West. From Route 24, at the west end of the bank, take Route 58 East. Signs marking the natural area and the aquarium are plentiful.

NORTH CAROLINA AQUARIUM ON ROANOKE ISLAND

Airport Road
Roanoke Island, NC (919) 473–3494

Freshwater and marine life, whether native to coastal North Carolina or seasonal, are featured in this 33,000-square-foot complex. Among its living displays are red drum, bluefish, trout, green and loggerhead sea turtles, and sharks. Turtles, terrapins, and alligators are featured in the freshwater exhibit.

Overlooking Croatin Sound, the facility has several beach and marsh nature trails, as well as shoreline overlooks. Marsh and estuary exploration programs are also offered aboard boats throughout the year. Special exhibits rotate regularly and might include Hurricane Awareness, Ocean Pollution, or Plight of the Sea Turtles.

Open year-round except for Thanksgiving, Christmas Day, and New Year's Day. Hours: Monday through Saturday, 9:00 A.M. to 5:00 P.M.; Sunday,

1:00 to 5:00 P.M. Admission is free, but donations are accepted. There is a charge for the boat exploration trips.

Located on Roanoke Island. Take I–64 onto the island, go through Manteo and turn left onto Airport Road; go 1 mile, the facility is located next to the airport.

NORTH CAROLINA ZOOLOGICAL PARK

Zoo Parkway
Asheboro, NC (919) 879–7000

With the breathtaking splendor of the Uwharrie Mountains and National Forest as a backdrop, this growing zoological park is surely one of the most beautiful in the country. Open since 1974, the North Carolina Zoo covers some 1,450 acres, only about one-third of which have been developed to date.

Eventually there will be exhibits reflecting the wildlife of all the major continents of the world, but for now only Africa is complete, and in such a convincing way that visitors feel they've really set foot on the "Dark Continent." Acres of lush forests and open grasslands provide the perfect habitat for the zoo's many species of mammals, birds, reptiles, and fish that live along the 2-mile path.

Season: Year-round, holidays too.

Hours: April through mid-October, 9:00 A.M. to 5:00 P.M., daily; mid-October through March, 9:00 A.M. to 4:00 P.M., daily.

Admission: Adults, Under $6; ages 2–15 and seniors, under $4; under age 2 and handicapped, free. Additional fee: tram, under $2 for unlimited use all day.

The animals: More than 850 animals, more than 130 species, displayed in indoor and outdoor natural habitats. Outstanding exhibits include the 300-acre African Plains exhibit; R. J. Reynolds Forest Aviary; and the African Pavilion.

Entertainment: During special promotional events, musical and children's shows are presented.

Extras: Tram ride around park to different exhibit areas.

Special events: Annual events include ZooFling, on weekends in April;

Valentine's Day weekend events, in February; Zoo and Aquarium Month, in June; Grandparents' Day, in September; Zoofest, and Boo at the Zoo, both in October; and Christmas at the Zoo, with free admission for everyone, on December 24, 25, and 26.

Food service: 2 restaurants, 1 in plaza area and 1 in the African Pavilion, serve a variety of fast foods, snacks, and beverages. A covered picnic area is also provided.

Plan to stay: 4 hours.

Directions: I–85 to U.S. 220 South. Take 220 for about 2 miles to U.S. 64 (Dixie Drive). Travel east on Dixie Drive about a mile to Zoo Parkway. Turn right and follow Zoo Parkway for about 6 miles to zoo entrance.

Nearby attractions: Uwharrie National Forest, with hiking trails, fishing, hunting, and camping; Potter's Museum, in Seagrove; World Golf Hall of Fame, in Pinehurst.

WESTERN NORTH CAROLINA NATURE CENTER

75 Gashes Creek Road
Asheville, NC (704) 298–5600

Formerly the Asheville Zoo, this twenty-seven-acre nature center features indoor and outdoor exhibits, and is one of the few places in the country where visitors can see red wolves in captivity. The zoo is taking part in the official breeding program for this endangered species.

Other animals on exhibit, all native to the North Carolina area, range from cougar, deer, bear, fox, and raccoon to turtles, farm stock, and fish. The petting zoo features lambs, rabbits, chickens, guineas, peacocks, pheasants, and pygmy goats.

There are self-guided nature trails, a nocturnal animals building and a touch room, where visitors can meet animals one-on-one.

Open year-round: Memorial Day to Labor Day, daily, 10:00 A.M. to 5:00 P.M.; remainder of the year, Tuesday through Saturday, 10:00 A.M. to 5:00 P.M., and Sunday 1:00 to 5:00 P.M. Admission: adults, under $3; ages 3–14, under $2; under 2, free.

Located near The Biltmore, take exit 53B off I–40 and follow the signs to the nature center, located at State Route 81 and Gashes Creek Road.

North Dakota

CHAHINKAPA ZOO AND PARK

In Chahinkapa Park
Robert Hughes Drive
Wahpeton, ND (701) 642–2811

Located in the midst of the park, which also offers camping, swimming, and an eighteen-hole golf course, this zoo offers a variety of exotic and native animals and includes a petting corral.

Tim's Trivia

Jungle Larry's Safari, in the Cedar Point Amusement Park in Sandusky, Ohio, is the longest-running animal attraction in a North American amusement park. It premiered in the early 1960s.

You'll be able to observe mountain lions, bald and golden eagles, barn and snowy owl, elk, and white-tailed deer along with llamas, snow monkeys, and zebras on the self-guided tour. There is also a nature center with stuffed animals and fish and a live bee exhibit.

Open year-round: May through August, 10:00 A.M. to 8:00 P.M.; September through April, 10:00 A.M. to noon and 1:00 to 5:00 P.M. Admission is $2 for adults, $1 for children ages 5–12, under 5 free.

Take 4th Street North exit off Highway 210 bypass and head south to 7th Avenue. Turn left onto 7th, go a short distance, then turn left onto 2nd Street North and proceed into Chahinkapa Park. Follow signs to zoo.

DAKOTA ZOO

In Sertoma Park
Riverside Park Drive
Bismarck, ND (701) 223–7543

Along with the more than 125 species of animals native to North America, officials have thrown in a few exotics, such as yaks and Bactrian camels for good measure. Two of the most outstanding displays here are the Alaskan brown bear habitat and the river otter exhibit.

The zoo, which evokes a western theme, complete with log structures, is located on the east bank of the Missouri River, surrounded by cottonwood trees and other native vegetation. A tram line and a children's petting zoo are among its other offerings.

Open May through September, 10:00 A.M. to 8:00 P.M. daily, weather permitting. Admission: adults, under $3; ages 12 and under, under $1.

To find Dakota Zoo, take exit 34 (Memorial Highway) off I–94 and head south. Stay to the left and cross the Memorial Bridge when the road splits. After crossing the bridge, take a right onto Riverside Park Road and follow signs to the zoo.

ROOSEVELT ZOO

1215 Burdick Expressway East
Minot, ND (701) 852–2751

Although it is located on twenty acres in the heart of the city, there's a lot of peace and quiet in this zoo—named for President Theodore Roosevelt—where peacocks, geese, and ducks stroll among the visitors.

The facility opened in 1920 and the education center is now housed in one of the remaining buildings from that period. Don't miss the big bronze statue of Teddy on horseback at the rear of the zoo.

Season: Year-round, holidays too.

Hours: May through September, 10:00 A.M. to 8:00 P.M., daily; remainder of the year, 8:00 A.M. to 4:30 P.M., daily.

Admission: Adults, under $3; ages 6–12, under $2; under age 6, free.

The animals: More than 200 animals, more than 40 species, displayed in both indoor and outdoor natural habitats. Highlights include the North American exhibit, the spider monkeys, and the African exhibit.

Entertainment: Shows and demonstrations scheduled only during special events or on prearranged educational tours.

Extras: Children's zoo in a North Dakota farmstead setting; education center, with hands-on learning games. In the adjacent park, there is a swimming pool with water slide, an old carousel, and the Magic Express, a scale-model replica of a Great Northern steam locomotive.

Special events: Festival of Parks, on July Fourth; Zoofari, one Friday night in the summer, for adults only; and a celebration of the summer season on the first summer Saturday.

Food service: 1 concession stand offers fast food and snacks. Picnic areas are scattered around throughout park.

Plan to stay: 2 hours.

Directions: U.S. Route 2B to Burdick Expressway S.E. The zoo/park is 15 blocks east of Broadway, on the left.

Nearby attractions: Pioneer Village and Museum; North Dakota State Fair, in late July; Norsk Hostfest, a Scandinavian festival in mid-October; and Lucy's Amusement Park, with rides, miniature golf, and go-cart track.

THEODORE ROOSEVELT NATIONAL PARK

Exits 6 and 7 from I–94
Medora, ND (701) 623–4466

Theodore Roosevelt, our twenty-sixth president, played an important role in the conservation of the nation's natural resources, and this 70,000-acre park is a tribute to his efforts. Herds of American bison, elk, and antelope roam freely throughout the park, as do mule deer, white-tailed deer, and numerous other species, ranging from coyotes to porcupines.

Roosevelt lived in and hunted this area of the country, and a part of his ranchland is now incorporated into the park. One of his cabins has been moved onto the land from his original ranch south of Medora.

A 36-mile scenic drive begins and ends here at the Medora visitor's center, while a 15-mile scenic drive begins at the North visitor's center, located on Highway 85. Rangers say the drives are the best way to see the wildlife. Although they can't guarantee you'll see anything, they say you're most likely to see deer, bison, and some elk on your drives. Numerous prairie dog towns have been built adjacent to the drives.

Also in the park is a demonstration herd of Texas longhorn steer and wild horses. In addition to the Medora and the North visitor's centers, there's the Painted Canyon visitor's center, located 7 miles east of Medora on I–94. All three have park exhibits and are free and open daily, year-round, 9:00 A.M. to 5:30 P.M. They remain open later in the summer. Park admission is $3 per car. Roosevelt's cabin is at the Medora center.

Ohio

AKRON ZOOLOGICAL PARK

50 Edgewood Avenue
Akron, OH (216) 434–8645

Cool and shady Perkins Woods is the tranquil setting for this twenty-five-acre zoo, which is located near the center of Akron on slightly hilly terrain. In 1992 a wildlife garden was added, with shrubs and flowers that make the grounds seem more like a private estate than a public park.

Be sure to check out the ponds, where you'll find all sorts of ducks, swans, and turtles.

Season: Mid-April through mid-October.

Hours: Opens daily at 10:00 A.M., closes at 5:00 P.M. on weekdays, an hour later on weekends.

Admission: Adults, under $4; ages 2–14 and seniors, under $3; under age 2, free. Additional fees: pony rides, under $2; feed packets for farm animals, under $1.

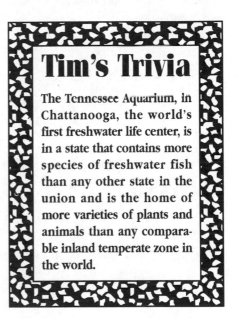

Tim's Trivia

The Tennessee Aquarium, in Chattanooga, the world's first freshwater life center, is in a state that contains more species of freshwater fish than any other state in the union and is the home of more varieties of plants and animals than any comparable inland temperate zone in the world.

The animals: More than 300 animals, more than 90 species, including a great many birds. Most animals are exhibited in habitats, although a few are still in cages. Highlights include the walk-through aviary, the South American exhibit, Monkey Island, Reptile House, and the river otter exhibit.

Entertainment: Volunteers walk around the zoo, often accompanied by one of the animals, making themselves available for questions from guests. Free-roaming peacocks are also entertaining, sometimes posing for pictures.

Extras: Ohio Farmyard, a children's zoo; pony rides. In other parts of the park there are athletic fields, tennis courts, and a playground.

Special events: Halloween activities, in October; Holiday Lights Celebration, in December. An additional fee is charged for both events.

Food service: 1 concession stand offers fast-food items, snacks, and beverages. Picnics are permitted.

Plan to stay: 2 hours.

Directions: Ohio Route 77 to Route 59 (Inner Belt). Get off Route 59 at W. Exchange Street. Travel west on Exchange, then make a right on Maple Avenue. At the third light, make a left onto Edgewood Avenue and follow to park/zoo entrance.

Nearby attractions: Goodyear World of Rubber, museum and tours; Perkins Mansion; Quaker Square shopping area, set in mills and silos of original Quaker Oats factory.

CINCINNATI ZOO AND BOTANICAL GARDEN

3400 Vine Street
Cincinnati, OH (513) 281–4701

You'll want to linger here for a while to make sure you see everything this facility has to offer. Not only is this a world-class zoo, but a colorful botanical garden as well. More than 2,500 different plants from around the world, including many exotic and endangered species, beautify the grounds.

This is one of the oldest zoos in the United States and two of its original buildings are on the National Register of Historic Places.

Season: Year-round, holidays too.

Hours: Memorial Day through Labor Day, the buildings are open from 9:00 A.M. to 6:00 P.M., while the grounds stay open until 8:00 P.M. Remainder of the year, buildings are open from 9:00 A.M. to 5:00 P.M., and grounds are closed at dusk.

Admission: Adults, under $8; ages 2–12 and seniors, under $5; under age 2, free. Additional fees: children's zoo, under $1; elephant and camel rides, under $2 each; tram and train rides, adults and children, under $2 for each ride; parking, under $5.

The animals: More than 425,000 animals (a lot of them are insects), more than 700 species. Outstanding exhibits are the Cat House, which contains one of the largest collections of big cats in the world, including white Bengal tigers that are bred here; Insect World, with lots of displays; and Gorilla World, with one of the largest gorilla families in captivity. There is also an aquarium with both freshwater and saltwater exhibits.

Entertainment: During the summer, between 11:00 A.M. and 3:00 P.M., there are cat, bird, Shetland pony, and elephant shows in the Animal Theater. At the children's zoo there are puppet shows, and in the animal recreation area you can watch the animals being trained.

Extras: Visitors have their choice of riding by tram or old-fashioned train, both of which provide excellent views of the exhibits and lush garden landscaping. The children's zoo brings youngsters in close contact with some of the smaller animals. At the Discovery Center, there is a 20-minute program explaining zoo activities. There is also a museum, which is actually a memorial to the passenger pigeon and other extinct species. The world's last passenger pigeon died at the Cincinnati Zoo in 1914. (*See* Tim's Trivia, page 217.)

Special events: Festival of Lights, begins at the end of November and runs through the holiday season. Other events are scheduled at the beginning of each season.

Food service: In addition to the cafe-style Safari Restaurant, which is open year-round, there are also several fast-food stands, including The Pizza Parlor and Marmoset Market, which are open only during the summer season. A picnic area is also provided.

Plan to stay: At least 3 hours.

Directions: Take I–75 to exit 6 (Mitchell Avenue). Follow the zoo's paw-print signs south on Mitchell for approximately 1 mile to Dury Avenue, and you'll be at the main gate.

Nearby attractions: Cincinnati Fire Museum; Cincinnati Museum of Natural History; Riverfront Stadium, home of the Cincinnati Reds baseball team; William Howard Taft Historical Site, birthplace and boyhood home of the 27th president; Kings Island, amusement park; Coney Island, amusement park; Surf Cincinnati, water park.

CLEVELAND METROPARKS ZOOLOGICAL PARK

In Brookside Park
3900 Brookside Park Drive
Cleveland, OH   (216) 661–6500

You can stroll or ride around this suburban zoo situated on 165 rolling wooded acres along Big Creek in the southwestern section of Cleveland.

Owned and managed by the Cleveland Park District, the facility is located in a city park which is maintained by an outstanding horticultural staff. In addition to the indoor and outdoor animal areas, there is also a large public greenhouse where plants for the city's other twelve parks are propagated. Established in 1882, it is the oldest zoo in Ohio and the seventh oldest in the country.

Season: Year-round, closed Christmas Day and New Year's Day.

Hours: Daily, 9:00 A.M. to 5:00 P.M. Between Memorial Day and Labor Day, closing time is extended to 7:00 P.M. on Fridays, Saturdays, Sundays, and holidays.

Admission: Adults, under $6; ages 2–11, under $4; under age 2, free. Additional fee: train ride, under $3.

The animals: More than 3,000 animals, more than 500 species, exhibited in a variety of natural habitats. Outstanding exhibits include the Birds of the World aviary; the Bactrian camel display; Bear Grotto; Rare and Beautiful Animals of China; Australian Outback; an African area, which is one of the few sites in the United States where rhinos and cheetahs are exhibited together; and a walk-through rain forest.

Entertainment: During the summer, there are Birds of Prey shows 3 times a day, and free concerts on Friday evenings.

Extras: Outback train ride around the Australia, Asia, and South America areas; free tram tours; International Children's Farm.

Fauna Fun Facts

The skin of an African elephant is from ¾ to 1½ inches thick.

Special events: Conservation Day, June 1; Zipadee Zoo Do, in June; Zoopendous Fun Day, in July; Boo at the Zoo, on Halloween; Thanksgiving Day events, animal feedings and free admission; Holiday Lights, on December evenings.

Food service: 1 sit-down restaurant in the Rain Forest area and snack bars throughout offer a variety of fast foods, snacks, and beverages. There are also sheltered and open picnic areas, some with grills.

Plan to stay: 4 hours.

Directions: Take I–71 South to Fulton Road exit. At end of exit ramp, turn left and go south on Fulton for about 1 mile. At second traffic light, turn left; zoo entrance is a short distance ahead, on the right.

Nearby attractions: Cleveland Museum of Natural History; Frederick C. Crawford Auto-Aviation Museum; NASA/Lewis Visitor Center, with aerospace displays; Geauga Lake amusement park; Sea World of Ohio; Memphis Kiddie Park.

COLUMBUS ZOO

9990 Riverside Drive
Powell, OH (614) 645–3400

More than 11,000 animals call these 404 acres their home. Located on the banks of the Scioto River, this facility is the third-largest municipally owned zoo in the United States and is one of the fastest growing and most recognized zoological parks in the world.

Founded in 1927 with a small menagerie of donated animals, the zoo made news worldwide in 1956 when the first captive-bred gorilla was born here. Today, the beautifully wooded environment houses one of the nation's largest reptile and amphibian collections and is only one of four zoos in the United States to house bonobos, also known as pygmy chimpanzees.

Since the zoo has so much success in breeding endangered species, you'll see a lot of them here, including cheetahs, bald eagles, black rhinos, Atlantic loggerhead sea turtles, lowland gorillas, Bengal tigers, and Asian elephants.

Season: Open year-round, Christmas too.

Hours: Memorial Day through Labor Day, 9:00 A.M. to 6:00 P.M., closes an hour earlier Labor Day through Memorial Day.

Admission: Adults, under $6; ages 2–11, under $4; under 2, free. Rides on the zoo tram, the *Scioto Belle* Riverboat, and the train cost extra. Parking: $2.

The animals: More than 11,000 animals, more than 700 species, housed in natural habitats. Exhibits include: North America, featuring bears, bison, wolves, bobcats, bald eagles, and Alaskan moose; Africa, Asia, and South America, highlighting white and black rhinos, Grant zebras, marabou storks, crowned cranes, and reticulated giraffes; Johnson Aquatic Complex, home to more than 250 species, including loggerhead sea turtles, sharks, Australian lungfish, and the endangered Lake Victorian cichlids.

Entertainment: Most is education-related, including lectures and demonstrations. There is a summer music series called Rhythm 'n' Zoo, and many one-day special events.

Extras: Train ride around the zoo; boat ride on the river; children's petting zoo; and an animal-theme participatory playground. Although the animals get the spotlight here, the botanical gardens should not be overlooked. There are more than 800 species represented in this $3 million collection.

Special events: Great Eggspectations, Easter celebration; Conservation Weekend; Pioneer Days, arts-and-crafts show, late September; Boo at the Zoo, late October; Wildlight Wonderland, winter holiday light celebration, month of December.

Food service: In addition to several concession stands, there's a Wendy's restaurant on the grounds. Picnics are permitted.

Plan to stay: 6 hours.

Directions: On Riverside Drive (Route 257), northwest of Columbus, off I–270. Take exit 20 (Sawmill Road) off I–270 and follow the signs.

Nearby attractions: Wyandot Lake amusement/water park is directly adjacent to the zoo; Ohio State University; historic Worthington; Ohio Historical Center/Ohio Village; and COSI, center of science and industry.

JUNGLE LARRY'S SAFARI

At Cedar Point Amusement Park
On a Lake Erie Peninsula
Sandusky, OH (419) 626–0830

Amid the people screams from the nearby thrill rides here at America's largest amusement park, you'll also be able to hear an occasional animal roar coming from Jungle Larry's, a twenty-nine-year tradition at the park.

More than sixty exotic animals live in the complex, which is the longest-running wild animal attraction at any U.S. amusement park. A large variety of species, along with close-up viewing, live shows, and educational lectures, truly makes this an animal oasis amid high-tech thrill machines.

Season: May through September.

Hours: Daily, 9:00 A.M. to 10:00 P.M.

Admission: Admission to Jungle Larry's Safari is included in the gate price to the park. Adults, under $25; children 47 inches tall and under, under $6. Additional fees: parking; miniature golf; grand prix go-karts; Soak City water park.

The animals: More than 60 animals, including Royal Bengal tigers, wolves, Indian and Chinese leopards, wolves, reptiles, alligators, ring-tailed lemurs, hedgehogs, patas monkeys, and exotic birds.

Entertainment: In Jungle Larry's Safari: 4 shows a day featuring tigers and leopards; plus wolf lectures, twice daily; educational animal encounters. In the amusement park: 5 major theaters present live musical shows throughout the day; dolphin and sea lion shows at the Oceana Marine-Life Stadium; plus an IMAX Theater.

Extras: The 364-acre park has 54 rides, including 10 roller coasters. The park's marina is one of the finest on Lake Erie with docking for boats of all sizes, just 500 feet form the park's entrance. Swimming in Lake Erie, with lifeguard supervision, bathhouse facilities, and a sandy beach are included in admission.

Food service: 14 sit-down restaurants, with 5 of them providing table service. An additional 35 food outlets offer various foods, including the famous Cedar Point french fries. Children's menus at most restaurants feature peanut-butter-and-jelly sandwiches and chicken snacks.

Plan to stay: A two-day visit is a must if you want to enjoy all of Jungle Larry's as well as the rest of the amusement park.

Tim's Trivia

When Colo was born on Dec. 22, 1956, at the Columbus (Ohio) Zoo, she became the first captive-born gorilla in the world. She still calls that zoo her home and now has more than a dozen grandchildren.

Directions: Located midway between Toledo and Cleveland. Take exit 7 off the Ohio Turnpike (I–80), go north on Route 250 into Sandusky, and then follow signs to the causeway.

Nearby attractions: Ferries to popular Lake Erie islands; Great Lakes Historical Society Museum; Follett House, an 1837 mansion; Historic Lyme Village, a restored nineteenth-century settlement; carousel museum.

SEA WORLD OF OHIO

1100 Sea World Drive
Aurora, OH (216) 995–2121

This ninety-acre marine park is one of the four Sea World facilities and is the only seasonal marine show park in the United States.

Season: Mid-May through first week of September.

Hours: Daily, 9:00 A.M. to 11:00 P.M.

Admission: Adults, under $20; ages 3–11, under $15; 2 and under, free. Free parking.

The animals: More than 415 species, almost 5,000 specimens, housed in modern facilities and open pools. Exhibits include: Penguin Encounter, an Antarctic display; and various pools of marine life, including some touch tanks.

Entertainment: 5 major shows, including the trademark Shamu the Killer Whale production, sea lion shows, and a water-skiing show. Dolphin feeding and petting, and various other pre-show presentations amuse the crowds.

Extras: Shamu's Happy Harbor, a 3-acre participatory play area for children.

Special events: Special Summer Nights series offers additional shows, laser-light productions, and fireworks during the peak summer months.

Food service: 17 eateries, serving a wide variety of foods, from fried chicken dinners to snacks.

Plan to stay: 5 hours.

Directions: Located 30 miles southeast of Cleveland on Route 43. Take exit 13 (Route 43) off the Ohio Turnpike (I–80) and go north 9 miles to Sea World Drive.

Nearby attractions: Geauga Lake amusement park; Kankorana Winery, wine tasting and touring; Aurora Farms, an outlet shopping mall complex.

TOLEDO ZOOLOGICAL GARDENS

2700 Broadway
Toledo, OH (419) 385–5721

There's truly something for everyone here, whether it's animals, plants, science, history, or music that you prefer. Located on thirty acres just outside downtown Toledo, this is one of the most comprehensive and entertaining zoos in the Midwest.

In addition to housing the world's only hippopotamus display with filtered underwater viewing, this zoo has many other displays that will catch and hold your interest. Many of the buildings date back to the Depression, when they were constructed as part of the WPA program. A great many of the big trees and shrubs also date back to that era, as do the grottoes inhabited by the polar bears just inside the entrance. If you enjoy nostalgia, don't miss taking a ride on the antique carousel located near the center of the facility.

Season: Year-round, closed Thanksgiving, Christmas Day, and New Year's Day.

Hours: April through September, 10:00 A.M. to 5:00 P.M., daily. Remainder of the year, gates close an hour earlier.

Admission: Adults, under $6; ages 2–11 and seniors, under $3; under age 2, free. Additional fees: parking, under $3; carousel, under $2; train, under $2.

The animals: More than 2,000 animals, more than 400 species, including the 1,000 fish in one of the largest aquariums in the country. Highlights include the Hippoquarium in the African Savannah exhibit; the Bird House; and the Reptile House.

Entertainment: No entertainment on a regular basis, only during special events.

Extras: Carousel; train ride with a narrated tour of the zoo; Conservatory; children's zoo; Botanical Gardens; Museum of Natural Science, which features hands-on activities; Amphitheater, used for outdoor concerts; playground.

Special events: Halloween event, in October; Lights Before Christmas, in December.

Food service: 1 concession stand offers a variety of fast-food and snack items. Picnics are permitted.

Plan to stay: 2 hours.

Directions: I–75 to exit 201A (Anthony Wayne Trail/U.S. 25). Go south on Anthony Wayne; zoo is about 3 miles south of downtown Toledo. After parking, you walk through a tunnel under the road to the zoo entrance on the other side of the street.

Nearby attractions: Toledo Botanical Gardens; Wildwood Manor House and Estate, on 460 acres of park land, with nature programs, walking trails, and visitor's center; self-guiding tours of Toledo's Old West End, a 25-block area of restored Victorian homes; Fort Meigs, a reconstructed fort.

WILD ANIMAL HABITAT

At Kings Island Amusement Park
6300 Kings Island Drive
Kings Island, OH (513) 398–5600

This is not your typical zoo or animal park, but actually one division of the 288-acre Kings Island family amusement park complex. Here you view the animals from above, inside an air-conditioned monorail that takes you on a fifteen-minute guided tour of the Habitat area. A walk-through area highlights other wildlife.

Three amusement rides found in the Habitat area, Amazon Falls, King Cobra, and Adventure Express, fit in with the "wild animal" theme.

Season: Habitat is open from Memorial Day through Labor Day, although the park is open also on weekends in April, May, and selected weekends in the fall.

Hours: Open during regular amusement park hours, 9:00 A.M. to 10:00 or 11:00 P.M., daily.

Admission: To enter the Habitat, you must buy an admission ticket to the entire complex. Single-day tickets: adults, under $25; ages 3–6 and seniors over 59, under $15; age 2 and under, free. Two-day tickets are also available at a substantial savings. Additional fees: parking, under $6; monorail, under $4.

The animals: More than 370 animals, more than 30 species of birds and mammals, displayed in a 100-acre outdoor habitat and in individual areas. Included are snow leopards, penguins, flamingos, anteaters, and others.

Entertainment: Daily dolphin shows in Saltwater Circus amphitheater on International Street area of the park; Celebrity Concerts in the Timber-wolf amphitheater (there is a small additional charge). There are other shows in the amusement park as well.

Extras: Since your admission ticket to the Habitat also covers the amuse-ment park, you may also enjoy all the offerings of the park, including its 41 rides and WaterWorks water park.

Food service: There are 40 restaurants and numerous fast-food stands throughout the park, 3 of them in the Habitat area. Kafe Kilimanjaro serves gourmet burgers, foot-long hot dogs, pork BBQ, fries, and beer. Congo Cooler serves chilled strawberry coolers. Adventure Drinks offers a variety of beverages. No picnicking is allowed inside the park, but there is a small picnic area just outside the main gate.

Plan to stay: At least 1 day to see the entire park.

Directions: Located 24 miles north of Cincinnati, 80 miles south of Columbus, off I–71. Take the Kings Island Drive exit and go east to the park entrance.

Nearby Attractions: College Football Hall of Fame; The Beach water park; Jack Nicklaus Sports Center.

Oklahoma

OKLAHOMA CITY ZOOLOGICAL PARK

2101 Northeast 50th Street
Oklahoma City, OK (405) 424–3344

Although this is the oldest zoo in this part of the country, it's one of the fa-cility's modern buildings that has become an area landmark. As you're driving down N.E. 50th Street, you'll see the pyramid-shaped, glass-and-concrete Aquaticus looming ahead long before you reach the zoo entrance.

Once inside the park, you'll want to saunter down its 3 miles of scenic walkways to the various exhibits and then rest a while on one of the benches overlooking Zoo Lake. To take in more of the beautiful landscape, you can also hop on the tram or get a bird's-eye view from the Sky Ride.

Season: Year-round, closed Christmas Day and New Year's Day.

Hours: April through September, 9:00 to 6:00 P.M., daily. Closes an hour earlier during the remainder of the year.

Admission: Adults, under $6; ages 4–12 and over 65, under $4; under age 3, free. Additional fees: tram, under $2; Sky Ride, under $2 (each way); dolphin and sea lion shows, under $2.50 each.

The animals: More than 2,000 animals, more than 500 species, displayed in both indoor and outdoor habitats. Popular exhibits include a gorilla family exhibit; hoofstock collection; bear exhibits; and Aquaticus, which houses 25 separate aquarium exhibits, a hands-on tidepool, and the dolphin and sea lion demonstration pool.

Entertainment: Weather permitting, there are daily dolphin shows, sea lion shows, and elephant behavior demonstrations.

Extras: A 20-minute tram ride provides a narrated tour of the zoo. Sky Ride goes over the core of the exhibit area.

Special events: Zoo Run, one weekend in May; Conservation Day, in June; and a Halloween celebration, last six nights in October.

Food service: 1 main restaurant, known widely for its bacon cheeseburgers, is open year-round, and several smaller fast-food stands open just for the summer. Picnics are permitted.

Plan to stay: 3 hours.

Directions: I–35 to N.E. 50th Street exit. Go west on N.E. 50th Street and drive toward the Aquaticus building. Zoo entrance is about 1 mile from I–35.

Nearby attractions: National Cowboy Hall of Fame, featuring western performers, artists, artifacts, and a simulated old-time village; Oklahoma Firefighters' Museum; National Softball Hall of Fame; White Water Bay, water park; Frontier City, amusement park; and the Oklahoma National Stockyards, one of the world's largest cattle markets.

TULSA ZOOLOGICAL PARK
AND LIVING MUSEUM

In Mohawk Park
5701 East 36th Street North
Tulsa, OK (918) 596–2400

You're going to find quite an entertainment package here—a zoo, botanical gardens, aquarium, and museum, all rolled into one and located in Mohawk Park, the sixth-largest metropolitan park in the country.

You'll especially enjoy the four-building Living Museum, which presents a fascinating look at the flora, fauna, and culture of four regions in North America: Arctic Tundra, Southern Lowlands, Southwestern Desert, and Eastern Forest, which has a cove to explore.

Season: Year-round, closed Christmas.

Hours: May through August, 10:00 A.M. to 6:00 P.M.; September and October, and March and April, 10:00 A.M. to 5:00 P.M.; November through February, 10:00 A.M. to 4:30 P.M.

Admission: Adults, under $5; ages 5–12, under $3; seniors, under $4; under age 5, free. Additional fees: train ride, under $2; parking, under $2 (fee on weekends and holidays only).

The animals: More than 1,100 animals, more than 250 species, displayed in both indoor and outdoor naturalistic habitats. Highlights include an African savannah and the 4 North American regions in the Living Museum, which houses not only native animals and plants, but artifacts and cultural displays as well.

Entertainment: Twice each day there are live presentations featuring different animals in the zoo. Sea lion feedings take place at 2:00 P.M. each day, and alligators are fed on designated days during the warmer part of the year.

Extras: Miniature train ride around zoo property; children's zoo, with con-

Fauna Fun Facts

The elephant has the largest brain of any land animal.

tact area. In other areas of the park are a nature center, polo fields, play-grounds, and bicycle rentals.

Special events: Polar Bear Days, in January and February, when admission is reduced if the temperature falls below freezing. The Tulsa Philhar-monic puts on a special performance on the first Monday in May. On Tuesdays and Fridays during the summer, there are Sunset Safaris, which feature animal demonstrations, puppet shows, and musical presenta-tions, Zoo Run is held in September. Hallozooween runs for 3 nights at the end of October; and the grounds are decorated for the holidays dur-ing the Zoolightful Festival in December.

Food service: Several concessions and a snack stand at the railroad depot offer a variety of fast-food meals, snacks, and beverages. Picnics are en-couraged.

Plan to stay: 3–4 hours.

Directions: I–244 to Sheridan Road exit. Go north on Sheridan to 36th Street North; follow it directly into Mohawk Park.

Nearby attractions: Big Splash water park; Oral Roberts University, with 200-foot-tall prayer tower; Tulsa State Fair, in mid-October; Bell's Amuse-ment Park; and the Tulsa Rose Gardens.

Oregon

METRO WASHINGTON PARK ZOO

4001 Southwest Canyon Road
Portland, OR (503) 226–1561

Like many other zoos in the country, this one began with the donation of a private animal collection to the city. Upon receiving the animals in 1887, the city moved them to Washington Park. In 1959 the facility was moved to its present location within the park.

The Coast Range forms a distant backdrop for the zoo, which overlooks the city of Portland and the Willamette River. Visitors can take the diesel or steam locomotives of the Washington Park & Zoo Railway through 4 miles of tunnels and woods. There is also a commanding view of downtown Port-land and Mount Hood from the grounds. A Japanese Garden and Rose Test

Garden add a fragrant aroma to portions of the facility.

Season: Year-round, closed Christmas.

Hours: Opens at 9:30 A.M. year-round, but closing times vary with the season. Summer, at 6:00 P.M.; spring and fall, at 5:00 P.M.; and winter, 4:00 P.M.

Admission: Adults, under $5; ages 3–11 and seniors, under $3; under age 3, free. Additional fee: train: adults, under $4; ages 3–11 and seniors, under $3; under age 3, free.

The animals: More than 650 animals, more than 150 species, displayed in geographical habitats. Highlights include Cascades Meadow, with animals native to the Oregon area; Alaska Tundra, an indoor-outdoor exhibit; the polar bear and sun bear exhibit, with 2-level viewing; African Rain Forest; elephant exhibit, featuring Packy, the zoo's mascot.

Extras: Washington Park & Zoo Railway; Animals Around Us, a hands-on education area with petting zoo.

Special events: Birthday party for Packy the elephant, in April; Pumpkin Party, in October; ZooLights Festival, in December. There are also summer concerts and days when seniors and the handicapped are admitted free.

Food service: AfriCafe, a year-round restaurant; a summer-only deli-style restaurant serves sandwiches and Mexican food; and several other summer-only food stands are open as needed. There are also picnic areas.

Plan to stay: 2 hours.

Directions: From I–5, take U.S. Route 26 West. Washington Park and Zoo are on the right, less than 5 miles from I–5.

Nearby attractions: Mount Hood Recreation Area; Columbia Gorge Sternwheeler, with boat trip along the Columbia and Willamette rivers; Oregon Museum of Science and Industry; World Forestry Center, with a 70-foot talking tree; and Oaks amusement park.

NOAH'S ARK PETTING ZOO

27893 Redwood Highway
Cave Junction, OR (503) 592–3802

Youngsters—both from the animal kingdom and the ones you bring along on your visit—are treated like royalty here. Your children can pet and touch a large variety of baby animals while the parents of those animals can be observed in their natural habitats.

Among the 100 species of animals to be found here are wallabies, zebras, llamas, mini-horses, goats, mini-donkeys, pot-bellied pigs, monkeys, bears, and raccoons. There are daily animal-behavior presentations in the summer months, as well as pony rides, and a pig train ride.

Tim's Trivia

With an annual gate count topping 4.3 million, Chicago's Lincoln Park Zoo is North America's most attended zoological facility. Founded in 1869, this zoo has never imposed an admission charge.

The 40th Day Cafe, a gourmet eatery specializing in homemade cookies and pies, is open for breakfast on the weekends and lunches daily.

Open year-round, closed Monday and Tuesday during the winter. Hours: summer, 9:00 A.M. to 6:00 P.M.; fall, winter, and spring, 11:00 A.M. to 4:00 P.M. Admission: adults, under $5; ages 7–12 and seniors, under $4; ages 3–6, under $3; under 3, free.

Located on Highway 199, (off Highway 101 at Crescent City), 30 miles south of Grants Pass, and 1½ miles south of Cave Junction.

OTTER CREST WAYSIDE

Highway 101
Otter Rock, OR (no phone)

This entire section of beautiful Highway 101, from Florence to Lincoln City is abundant with waysides where you can pull over and observe various wildlife and environmental spectacles. There are no less than a dozen state parks along this strip of highway, southwest of Portland. And the view of the Pacific provides some marvelous sunset scenes.

The Otter Crest Wayside, located 1 mile north of Otter Rock, on Cape Foulweather, is one of the highest vantage points along the way. Rising 453 feet above the tide, the flat-topped rock provides a great view of where the sea otters (thus the name) used to live. These days the area is inhabited by large families of seals, sea lions, and birds. Gray whales can be viewed year-round.

WILDLIFE SAFARI

Safari Road
Winston, OR (503) 679–6761

Your car is your cage in this, the only drive-through wild animal park in Oregon.

Wildlife Safari is aptly named, as you can see African lions, Asian cheetahs, and North American bears up close and in their natural habitats without leaving the comfort and safety of your automobile. If you want to extend your visit, or if you prefer not to drive through the wilds of Oregon, there is also a separate walk-around area with lots more to see on these 600 heavily timbered acres between the Cascades and the Coast Range.

Wildlife Safari has another notable distinction: officials say it is the top producer of cheetah cubs of any animal park in the Western Hemisphere.

Season: Year-round, holidays too.

Hours: Summer, 8:30 A.M. to 8:00 P.M.; winter, 9:00 A.M. to 4:00 P.M.; spring and fall, 9:00 A.M. to 6:00 P.M.

Admission: Adults, under $12; ages 4–12, under $8; seniors, under $10; under age 4, free. Additional fees: parking, under $3; train ride, under $2; elephant ride, under $3.

The animals: More than 550 animals, approximately 100 species, roam freely in 3 main outdoor exhibits, divided into continental groupings for Asia and Europe, Africa, and North America. Carnivores in each grouping are separated from the other animals, but run free as well.

Entertainment: During the summer, various animal shows and demonstrations geared to children, including one featuring white Bengal tigers, are held in the air-conditioned theater.

Extras: Children's petting zoo; hands-on Discovery Area; elephant rides; miniature train ride. You can also have your picture taken with some of the smaller animals.

Special events: Most are held on weekends during spring and fall. Day of Discovery, in May, which is geared to the handicapped; Easter morning sunrise services; Safari Run, in May, in which an elephant walks along with the runners; children's parties on weekends near Halloween and Christmas.

Food service: Concessions offer a variety of fast foods, snacks, and beverages. Picnics are permitted.

Plan to stay: 3 hours.

Directions: I–5 to exit 119 (State Route 42). Follow Route 42 West for about 3 miles to Looking Glass Road. Turn right at Looking Glass and then right again on Safari Road. Zoo entrance is about 1½ miles down the road.

Nearby attractions: Crater Lake National Park; Oregon Caves National Monument.

Pennsylvania

ANIMALAND

Route 660
Wellsboro, PA   (717) 724–4546

Family-owned for three generations, this scenic wildlife park is geared for kids, but the whole family can enjoy the animal exhibits. Visitors can expect to see a very large assortment of critters in naturalistic settings, including: American bison, white-tailed deer, Indian antelope, coatimundia, North American elk, four-horn sheep, American black bear, rhesus monkeys, brown-tufted capuchin monkeys, North American cougar, llamas and guanacos, Asian spotted leopards, and smaller creatures such as squirrels, raccoons, turtles, peafowl, porcupines, quail, emu, and wild turkeys.

There is also a petting area with pygmy goats, Angora goats, Sicilian donkeys, and more.

Open daily, May through October. Hours: May through June, and September through October, 10:00 A.M. to 4:30 P.M.; July and August, 9:00 A.M. to 6:00 P.M. Admission: adults, under $5; ages 3–12, under $4; 3 and under, free.

Located near the New York State border, two and a half hours from Binghamton and three hours from Buffalo, N.Y., and Harrisburg, Pa. It's just three-quarters of a mile from Pennsylvania's Grand Canyon/Leonard Harrison State Park. Take exit 30N (Route 15) off I–80, south of Williamsport. Take Route 15N through Williamsport to Mansfield, then Route 6 West to Wellsboro. At Wellsboro, get on Route 660, and go west for 9 miles.

CLAWS 'N' PAWS WILD ANIMAL PARK

Route 590
Hamlin, PA (717) 698–6154

Claws 'n' Paws, which they bill as "The Zoo in the Woods," has the potential to bring out the kid in all of us. Set under a canopy of evergreens in the Pocono Mountains, this zoo is small but friendly, and provides an hour or two of fun and education for the entire family.

Season: May through October.

Hours: Daily, 10:00 A.M. to 6:00 P.M.

Admission: Adults, under $8; ages 3–11, under $6; seniors, under $7; under age 3, free.

The animals: More than 150 animals, more than 80 species, displayed in naturalistic outdoor enclosures. Highlights include the big cats, otters, reptiles, and monkeys.

Entertainment: 3 different animal shows are presented each day, from May 1 through Labor Day. They include Wildlife Encounters, Farmyard Talk, and Critters 'n' Creatures.

Extras: Walk-through petting zoo; hands-on exhibits; Farmyard Zany Zoo, where visitors can have their picture taken standing behind animal body cutouts.

Food service: Snack bar offers a variety of fast-food items, snacks, and drinks. Picnics are permitted.

Plan to stay: 2 hours.

Directions: Take I–84 to exit 6 (Route 507). Go north on Route 507 for a half-mile. Turn left and follow signs after crossing Ledgedale Bridge over Lake Wallenpaupack.

Nearby attractions: Delaware Water Gap; Camelback Alpine Slide and Waterslide; Quiet Valley Living Historical Farm, an 18th-century Pennsylvania Dutch farm, in Stroudsburg.

CLYDE PEELING'S REPTILAND

U.S. Route 15
Allenwood, PA (717) 538–1869

As the name indicates, you're going to see a lot of reptiles here—along with a nice selection of amphibians and birds. On four acres of tropical garden settings, there are stands of ten different varieties of bamboo and ornamental grasses in which you'll get a chance to meet some of these creatures close-up and see that they're not as creepy as you may have once thought. Don't worry, though, they keep the poisonous snakes behind glass.

A similar facility with the same name is in operation in Catskill, N.Y.

Season: Year-round, closed Thanksgiving, Christmas Day, and New Year's Day.

Hours: Daily, 9:00 A.M. to 7:00 P.M., May through September. Remainder of the year, 10:00 A.M. to 5:00 P.M.

Admission: Adults, under $7; ages 4–11, under $5; under age 4, free.

The animals: 125 reptiles, 10 birds, and 10 amphibians, in outdoor habitats. Included are lizards, alligators, crocodiles, exotic and domestic snakes, turtles, and tortoises. Tortoises are not displayed during the winter.

Entertainment: 1-hour lecture demonstrations held 4 times daily during the summer; video presentation in the spring and fall.

Extras: Visitors have the opportunity to handle some of the animals.

Food service: Snack bar serves ice cream. Picnics are permitted.

Plan to stay: 2 hours.

Directions: Located in the center of the state, north of Milton and south of Williamsport. Take I–80 to exit 30B (Route 15). Go north on Route 15 for about 6 miles to entrance.

Nearby attractions: West Shore Railroad, offers rides on a restored train; Little League (baseball) Museum; White Deer Water Slide; Hiawatha Paddle Boats.

Fauna Fun Facts

It's not uncommon for a lion to sleep up to twenty hours a day.

ELMWOOD PARK ZOO
1661 Harding Boulevard
Norristown, PA (215) 277–3825

Log-cabin buildings and split-rail fences around the fields and pastures where the animals live give this outdoor zoo a homey feeling. And the fact that it occupies less than eight acres only enhances its coziness and charm.

Although you'll enjoy strolling along the wooded path and boardwalk, make sure you go indoors long enough to visit the Sensorium. It's a one-of-a-kind, high-tech interactive exhibit (with lasers, etc.) that uniquely demonstrates survival methods and sense differences between animals and humans.

Season: Year-round, closed Tuesdays from November through April. Sensorium is open only on weekends.

Hours: Daily, 10:00 A.M. to 4:00 P.M. Sensorium, 1:00 to 4:00 P.M., Saturdays and Sundays only. Hours are extended during the summer.

Admission: Suggested donation of $2 for adults and $1 for children. Additional fees: Sensorium, under $2; pony rides, under $3.

The animals: With a few exceptions, most of the 175 animals in the collection are native to North America and are displayed in naturalistic outdoor exhibits. Highlights: the Birds of Prey exhibit, which contains golden eagles and red-tailed hawks; the bison exhibit, which includes a pueblo shelter; cougars; wolves; and primates.

Entertainment: On weekends in the summer there are shows that focus on some of the smaller mammals and reptiles.

Extras: Sensorium; pony rides (April through September only); Petting Barn. In other areas of Elmwood Park are children's playgrounds and a bandshell, where summer concerts are held.

Special events: Country Fair, third weekend in September, featuring games and hayrides; holiday programs and activities for Halloween, Thanksgiving, and Christmas. There are also educational and promotional events held about once a month.

Food service: Snack bar is in operation from April through October. Picnics are permitted all year.

Plan to stay: 1 hour.

Directions: Located northwest of Philadelphia. Take the Pennsylvania Turnpike (I–276) to State Route 202. Go north on Route 202, following green-and-white zoo signs to Harding Boulevard. Go west on Harding for less than a mile to zoo entrance.

Nearby attractions: Valley Forge National Historical Park, site of the Continental Army encampment in 1777–78.

ERIE ZOOLOGICAL GARDENS

In Glenwood Park
423 West 38th Street
Erie, PA (814) 864–4093

Down by the old Mill Creek is where you'll find this neat little zoo. Tucked away on fifteen acres in a city park, this facility is nearly seventy years old, but wears its age well.

Although located in downtown Erie, the well-established trees and lawns give the zoo a more rural ambience. As you enter the front gate, you pass by one of the original buildings, which has concrete animal sculptures adorning the brick walls.

Season: Year-round, closed Christmas Day and New Year's Day. Children's zoo is open from mid-May to Labor Day.

Hours: Daily, 10:00 A.M. to 5:00 P.M. On holidays and summer Sundays, closing is extended to 7:00 P.M.

Admission: Adults, under $4.50; ages 3–11, under $3; seniors, under $4; under age 3, free. Additional fees: train, under $2; carousel, under $1.50; camel rides, under $2.50.

The animals: More than 300 animals, more than 90 species of birds, mammals, and reptiles, displayed in indoor and outdoor naturalistic habitats. Highlights include the Savanna and the 2-level North American River Otter exhibit.

Entertainment: During the summer months there are animal shows and demonstrations every half-hour in the children's zoo.

Extras: Safariland Train, allows you to see wild deer and bison; an old-fashioned carousel; camel rides; children's zoo. In other areas of the park are a playground, golf course, and ice skating rink.

Special events: There's something going on nearly every weekend in the summer. Zoo Boo at Halloween, and Zooluminations in December, when the zoo is decorated with holiday lights.

Food service: 6 concessions offer a variety of fast foods, snacks, and beverages. Picnics are also permitted.

Plan to stay: 2 hours.

Directions: I–90 to exit 7. When you get off, go north on Route 97 (Glenwood Park Avenue) for 3 miles. Zoo entrance will be on the left.

Nearby attractions: Erie Historical Museum, in a 24-room mansion; Firefighters Historical Museum; Presque Island State Park, a small peninsula in Lake Erie, which has beaches, conservation area, and wildlife refuge; Waldameer amusement park and WaterWorld water park.

LAND OF LITTLE HORSES

125 Glenwood Drive
Gettysburg, PA (717) 334–7259

Nope, those aren't ponies you see over there on the hillside, that's the largest herd of Falabella miniature horses in the United States. The herd of fifty range in size from incredibly tiny colts to a full-grown stallion, not quite 3 feet tall.

Visitors here can see these little creatures up close in their stables and paddocks, then watch them perform in the indoor arena. The show includes jumping, displays of intelligence, and sulky racing. At various times, training sessions take place, to which visitors are welcomed.

There's a snack bar, but picnics are also allowed, and there are plenty of picnic tables. Open April to November. Spring and fall hours are 10:00 A.M. to 5:00 P.M., with summer closing extended one hour. Admission: Adults, under $7; ages 3–12, under $4; under 3, free. Located 3 miles west of Gettysburg. Take U.S. 30 to Knoxlyn Road, go south, and follow the signs.

PHILADELPHIA ZOOLOGICAL GARDEN

In Fairmount Park
34th Street and Girard Avenue
Philadelphia, PA (215) 243–1100

Billed as "America's First Zoo," the Philadelphia Zoo was first chartered in the 1850s and opened at its present location in 1874. It's situated on forty-two acres west of the downtown area, in southern Fairmount Park, along the Schuylkill River. Victorian-style buildings are set amid the mature trees and shrubbery in a botanical-garden setting.

Although the buildings may be dated, the exhibits definitely are not. The zoo is laid out in a semicircle, with interconnecting paths among the numerous exhibits.

Season: Year-round, closed Thanksgiving, Christmas Eve, Christmas Day, New Year's Eve, and New Year's Day.

Hours: Buildings: April through October weekdays, 10:00 A.M. to 4:45 P.M.; an hour later on weekends and holidays. November and March, 10:00 A.M. to 4:45 P.M., daily. December through February, weekdays, 10:00 A.M. to 4:15 P.M.; weekends and holidays, 10:00 A.M. to 4:45 P.M. Grounds remain open 1 hour after buildings close.

Admission: Adults, under $8; ages 2–11 and seniors, under $7; under age 2, free. In December, January, and February, admission is free to everyone on all Mondays, except holidays. Additional fees: parking, under $4; Tree House, under $2 for adults and children over 2; under age 2, free. During December, January, and February, admission to Tree House is free for all visitors on Mondays, except holidays. Monorail, under $5; camel rides, under $2; children's zoo, under $2.50.

The animals: More than 1,700 animals, more than 500 species, displayed in natural indoor and outdoor habitats. Outstanding exhibits include African Plains, a re-creation of the African veldt; Carnivore Kingdom, with an elevated walkway above a natural habitat of mountain cats and other carnivores; World of Primates, with tropical rain forest; Bear Country, with a 200,000-gallon bear swimming pool; and the Bird House, full of lush foliage and cascading waterfalls.

Entertainment: Birds of Prey Show and Wildlife Theater, daily during summer; keeper talks, scheduled on a daily basis; animal feedings at Small Mammal House, Rare Animal House, and Carnivora House; milk and dairy demonstrations in children's zoo daily.

Extras: Camel rides; Safari Monorail tour; elephant pictures; Penn's Woodland Trail; Tree House, activity-oriented discovery center; children's zoo.

Food service: Impala Fountain Cafe, open year-round; Tiger Terrace, open mid-March to Thanksgiving; Victorian Picnic Grove, open April through October; and several snack and food concessions that are open as needed.

Plan to stay: 5 hours.

Directions: I–76 to exit 36 (Girard Avenue). Go west on Girard to zoo entrance, about a quarter-mile, on left.

Nearby attractions: Independence Hall; Liberty Bell Pavilion; Fairmount Park Historic Houses (next to zoo); Franklin Institute Science Museum and Planetarium; Edgar Allan Poe National Historic Site; Betsy Ross House.

PITTSBURGH AVIARY

In West Park
Allegheny Commons West
Pittsburgh, PA (412) 323-7235

Situated in the heart of downtown Pittsburgh, the aviary occupies less than two acres of West Park, not far from Three Rivers Stadium and right next to the Allegheny Mall.

The outside of the building, which resembles a conservatory, only hints at the junglelike setting indoors, where hundreds of birds, particularly those from the tropical regions of the world, are flying free.

Season: Year-round, closed Thanksgiving, Christmas Day, and New Year's Day.

Hours: Daily, 9:00 A.M. to 4:30 P.M.

Admission: Adults, under $3.50; ages 2–12 and seniors, under $1.50; under age 2, free.

The animals: More than 770 birds and reptiles from over 250 species, displayed in 3 large walk-through exhibits and several smaller ones. Highlights include the Tropical American Marsh Room and the African Jungle Room.

Tim's Trivia

Martha, the last passenger pigeon in the world, died at age 29 on Sept. 1, 1914, at the Cincinnati (Ohio) Zoo. Being the last of her species, she was stuffed and mounted and is now on display at the Smithsonian, in Washington, D.C. There is also a special memorial at the zoo where she spent her last fifteen years.

Special events: Egg Week, at Easter; Hummingbird Week, in July; Bird Art Festival, on Thanksgiving weekend, an arts-and-crafts festival featuring artists who specialize in bird themes.

Food service: No food concessions in the aviary or the park, but picnics are permitted in West Park.

Plan to stay: 1 hour.

Directions: Take I–279 South to 9th Street North, which turns into Cedar Avenue. Go north on Cedar Avenue to E. North Avenue. Follow North Avenue west to Federal Street, which runs along the park. Park on the street or in the adjacent public lot.

Nearby attractions: Three Rivers Stadium, home of the Pittsburgh Pirates and Steelers; Buhl Science Center and Planetarium; Old Post Office Museum; Pittsburgh Children's Museum; Kennywood amusement park; Sandcastle water park; Pittsburgh Zoo.

PITTSBURGH ZOO

In Highland Park
Baker Street
Pittsburgh, PA (412) 665–3639

Good grief. A reef. In Pittsburgh? That's probably what you're thinking when you enter the Aqua Zoo here and see what officials say is the largest living coral reef exhibit in the world. Without taking an expensive trip to the Caribbean, you'll be able to see what a diver would see underwater in that part of the world.

Officials say this is one of only a few living reefs on display in the country. Two others are at the Smithsonian Institution, in Washington, D.C., and at the St. Louis Zoo.

As you'll notice, Pittsburgh is quite hilly, and the zoo is built on the side of a hill overlooking the Allegheny River. An escalator is in service to take visitors from the parking area to the main gate. To minimize the amount of steep climbing, head to the left after entering the gate and follow the walkway in a clockwise fashion.

Season: Year-round, closed Christmas.

Hours: Memorial Day through Labor Day, daily, 10:00 A.M. to 6:00 P.M. Remainder of the year, daily, 9:00 A.M. to 5:00 P.M.

Admission: Adults, under $7; ages 2–13 and over 60, under $3.50; under age 2, free. Additional fees: train ride, under $1.50; carousel, under $1.

The animals: More than 4,000 animals, more than 360 species, including lots of fish. Highlights include the Aqua Zoo, with living coral reef in a 5,000-gallon tank; a 5-acre indoor-outdoor, fog-enshrouded Tropical Rain Forest; African Savanna; and North America exhibit.

Entertainment: Shark-diving demonstrations on Saturdays; daily feeding of sharks, gorillas, bears, and penguins; farm demonstrations at children's farm.

Extras: Train ride, a 10-minute informative trip around the zoo; carousel; children's farm, with contact area; Discovery Center.

Special events: Easter Egg Party; Twilight Tours, 2 evenings per month, May through August; Conservation Day, in June; Senior Day, in September; Zoo Boo, last week in October; Zoolights, in December.

Food service: 3 year-round concessions—the Plaza Restaurant, Outback Cafe, and Outfitters Restaurant—which sell a complete variety of fast-food items, pizza, sandwiches, snacks, ice cream, and beverages. In the summer, there are also snack carts around the zoo. Picnics are permitted.

Plan to stay: 3 hours.

Directions: I–76 (Pennsylvania Turnpike) to exit 5 (Allegheny Valley). Make a right onto Freeport Road (Pittsburgh South exit). Go to the second traffic light and make a right. Enter the Expressway (Route 28) and head south toward Pittsburgh. Take the Highland Park Bridge exit. Go across the bridge in the right-hand lane, then take the first right turn off the bridge. Make a left turn at the second traffic light into the zoo parking lot.

Nearby attractions: Pittsburgh Aviary; Fort Pitt Museum, in Point State Park; Phipps Conservatory, in Schenley Park.; Pittsburgh Aviary (see previous listing).

POCONO SNAKE AND ANIMAL FARM

U.S. Route 209
Marshalls Creek, PA (717) 223–8653

Think you've seen big turtles before? Well, check out the 125-pound freshwater turtle here. The owners say it's one of the largest you'll find on exhibit anywhere. Another popular exhibit is the exotic African lungfish. Other animals scattered throughout the farm are Siberian tigers, bears, wolves, monkeys, alligators, and mountain lions, along with a reptile and snake exhibit that includes pythons, cobras, and rattlesnakes.

There are several feeding and petting areas where you can enjoy hands-on experiences with mini-goats and the tamer varieties of wildlife.

The farm is open April through December, daily, 10:00 A.M. to 6:00 P.M. Hours tend to vary, so calling ahead might save you a trip. Admission: adults, under $4; children, under $3. Take exit 52 (Marshalls Creek) off I–80, go 1½ miles north on Route 209, and follow the signs to the farm.

ZOOAMERICA

In Hersheypark
100 West Hersheypark Drive
Hershey, PA (800) HERSHEY

Though nestled in the back quadrant of the amusement park, this eleven-acre zoo matches the park and its surroundings for beauty. Rolling hills, naturalistic exhibits, and beautiful landscaping make this a great entertainment center as well as an educational opportunity.

Originally opened in the early 1900s by Milton Hershey as a way to share his private collection with the public, the zoo now offers a naturalistic home to more than 200 animals from five North American regions. The habitats and landscaping change dramatically as you walk from one geographic display area to another.

Season: The zoo is open year-round, the amusement park is seasonal.

Hours: September through mid-June, daily, 10:00 A.M. to 5:00 P.M.; mid-June through August, daily, till 8:00 P.M.

Admission: Admission to the zoo is included in the Hersheypark one-price admission plan during the regular park season: adults, under $20; ages 3–12, under $13. Separate admission to zoo when park is not in operation: adults, under $5; ages 3–12, under $3; 2 and under, free. No separate admissions when amusement park is open.

The animals: More than 75 native species, more than 200 animals in 5 region-themed, naturalistic settings: Big Sky Country (elk, bison, golden eagles, and prairie dogs); North Woods (wolves, black bears, peregrine falcons, snowy owls, and tundra swans); Grassy Waters (alligators and other reptiles, and wading birds); Gentle Woodlands (deer, wild turkey, bobcats, otters and raccoons, barn owls and red-tailed hawks); and Cactus Community (roadrunners, Gambel's quail, lizards, ground squirrels, and thick-billed parrots).

Entertainment: In the zoo: various lectures and special events throughout the year. In the park: 8 hours of shows daily, including several musical presentations, a children's show, a dance revue, and a dolphin and sea lion show.

Extras: Miniature golf and paddleboats (extra charge). Chocolate World, located next to the park, offers a ride-through tour of how chocolate is made (free). Make sure you check out the street lights in the town of Hershey, they're shaped like Hershey chocolate kisses.

Food service: 50 different locations, 1 of them in the zoo. The Tudor Rose Tavern is a table-service indoor restaurant.

Plan to stay: 8 hours if you want to see the zoo and the shows and also ride the rides.

Directions: Take exit 20 off the Pennsylvania Turnpike to Route 322. Follow Route 322 to Hershey and take Route 39 West to Hersheypark Drive. The separate zoo entrance, for when the park is not in operation, is located on Route 743, just beyond the park entrance.

Nearby attractions: Indian Echo Caverns; Gettysburg National Military Park; Pennsylvania Dutch country.

Rhode Island

ROGER WILLIAMS PARK ZOO

Elmwood Avenue
Providence, RI (401) 785–9450

Named after the founder of Rhode Island, this 110-year-old zoo, the only one in the state, was originally scattered throughout Roger Williams Park. In 1979 the animal exhibits were consolidated in a thirty-five-acre area that contains a free-flight aviary and tropical greenhouses among its highlights.

Two of the original stone-and-wood buildings, near the entrance, are now occupied by a restaurant and a gift shop, while the animals are housed in a variety of indoor and outdoor natural habitats.

Season: Year-round, closed Thanksgiving, Christmas Day, and New Year's Day.

Hours: April Through October, daily, 10:00 A.M. to 5:00 P.M. Remainder of the year closing time is an hour earlier.

Admission: Adults, under $5; ages 5–12 and seniors, under $3; under age 5, free. Admission is free to everyone on the first Saturday of every month.

The animals: More than 400 animals, more than 130 species, in a variety of naturalistic habitats. Highlights include an award-winning polar bear exhibit; the African exhibit; and a Tropical America building.

Entertainment: No regularly scheduled shows or demonstrations, but docents sometimes conduct informal presentations.

Extras: Children's Nature Center. In other areas of the park are playgrounds, kiddie rides, an antique carousel, a natural history museum, nature trails, and extensive flower gardens. Outdoor concerts in summer in the William E. Benedict Memorial Music Amphitheater.

Special events: Teddy Bear Rally, in September; Halloween Festival, in October; and Starlight Festival, weekends between Thanksgiving and Christmas.

Food service: There are 2 places to eat. One is a concession near the main gate, the other is Alice's Restaurant, in the African exhibit, named for one of the zoo's larger inhabitants, Alice the Elephant. Picnics are permitted.

Plan to stay: 2 hours.

Directions: Take the Elmwood Avenue exit off I–95. Go left on Elmwood, which is the first traffic light after exiting the interstate. The park entrance is on your right.

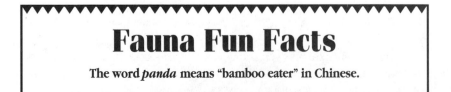

Fauna Fun Facts

The word *panda* means "bamboo eater" in Chinese.

Nearby attractions: Betsy Williams Cottage, built in 1773; Roger Williams National Memorial and Visitor Center, which offers a short slide show on local history; Museum of Art at the Rhode Island School of Design, includes sculptures, paintings, and Early American furniture.

South Carolina

BROOKGREEN GARDENS

U.S. Highway 17 South
Murrells Inlet, SC (803) 237–4218

This unique zoological park was created in 1931 by railroad heir Archer M. Huntington and his wife, the sculptor Anna Hyatt Huntington. The 9,000-acre former rice plantation is one of the most beautiful gardens in the South, boasting 230-year-old oak trees draped with Spanish moss, old boxwoods, dogwoods, azaleas, and many other exotic plants, not to mention fountains and reflecting pools.

Set within the gardens is the 100-acre zoo and sculpture garden. The zoo grounds border both forests and freshwater marshlands, and have been maintained through an endowment fund established by the Huntingtons to make sure the public could continue to enjoy the surroundings they once called home.

Season: Year-round, closed Christmas.

Hours: Daily, 9:30 A.M. to 4:45 P.M.

Admission: Adults, under $8; ages 6–12, under $4; under age 6, free. Additional fee: tour-tape rental, under $5.

The animals: More than 80 animals, more than 15 species, displayed in 6 enclosures. Exhibits contain only mammals, birds, and reptiles indigenous to the southeastern United States and are set up along a curved path less than a mile long.

Entertainment: Fine arts events, including concerts and lectures, are held, though not on a regular basis.

Extras: Self-guided-tour tapes of the property; nature trails; a 500-piece sculpture garden, featuring animals and mythological and human figures created by 19th- and 20th-century American sculptors.

Food service: Food stand serves fast food and sandwiches, open from mid-March to September. Picnic facilities are provided.

Plan to stay: 2 hours for sculpture garden, 1 hour for wildlife area.

Directions: Entrance located on the west side of U.S. Route 17, about 18 miles south of Myrtle Beach. Huntington Beach State Park is directly across the street.

Nearby attractions: Huntington Beach State Park features nature trails, a beach, and a camping area.

GREENVILLE ZOO

In Cleveland Park
150 Cleveland Park Drive
Greenville, SC (803) 240–4310

This quiet little zoo, which occupies fifteen acres of city park in downtown Greenville, has lots of trees and lush landscaping, making for a pleasant visit. The outdoor animal exhibits are arranged in a figure-8 pattern with a paved pathway connecting them. A boardwalk provides a rustic trail through the African animal area.

Season: Year-round, closed Thanksgiving, Christmas Day, and New Year's Day.

Hours: Daily, 10:00 A.M. to 4:30 P.M.

Admission: Adults, under $5; ages 3–15, under $3; under age 3, free.

The animals: More than 300 animals, more than 100 species, housed in outdoor African, Asian, and South American habitats. Exhibits contain primarily smaller species.

Entertainment: No regularly scheduled shows or demonstrations, but docents will occasionally speak about some of the animals at the various exhibit areas.

Extras: Barnyard area, where children can pet and feed goats, is located within the zoo. In other areas of the park are a playground and a picnic area.

Special events: Hot Dog Day, in mid-July; Zoo To Do, formal fund-raiser (for adults; tickets required); and Boo in the Zoo, October 28–31.

Food service: 1 concession stand sells snack food items. Picnics are not permitted in the zoo, but are allowed in other areas of the park.

Plan to stay: 1 hour.

Directions: I–85 to Route 385, into Greenville. Get off Route 385 at exit 42. At the end of the exit ramp, go left on Stone Avenue. At the second traffic light, turn left onto East Washington. Stay on East Washington past the first traffic light. Zoo entrance is a short distance ahead, on the left.

Nearby attractions: Greenville County Museum of Art, which houses one of the largest collections of Andrew Wyeth paintings; and Roper Mountain Science Center.

RIVERBANKS ZOOLOGICAL PARK

50 Wildlife Parkway
Columbia, SC (803) 779–8717

As the state's leading tourist attraction, this modern facility, which first opened its gates to the public in 1974, is located on 170 acres that straddle the Saluda River.

During a day here, you can travel from the plains of Africa to the rain forests of South America to the reefs of the Pacific Ocean. Natural habitats position such barriers as moats, lights, and water between visitors and animals.

Season: Year-round, closed Christmas.

Hours: Memorial Day through Labor Day, daily, 9:00 A.M. to 6:00 P.M. Closes one hour earlier the remainder of the year. Sale of tickets stops one hour before closing.

Admission: Adults, under $6; ages 3–12, under $3; over 62, under $4; students and military in uniform, under $4; under age 3, free.

The animals: More than 2,000 animals, more than 400 species, arranged in groupings according to species and climate of origin. Outstanding exhibits include the Aquarium-Reptile complex, consisting of 4 galleries (South Carolina, the Desert, the Tropics, and the Ocean) and the Birdhouse, with daily rainstorms in the rain forest area.

Entertainment: Sea lion and penguin feedings, twice a day; scuba diving demonstrations and fish feedings, twice a day; farm milking demonstrations, once a day; and tropical rainstorms in the Birdhouse, 3 times a day on weekdays, 4 times a day on weekends.

Extras: Nature trails; Riverbanks Farm, a children's zoo featuring domestic animals and daily farm activities. Discovery Room, a hands-on educational center, is open on weekends.

Special events: Musical concerts and children's shows on Friday nights during the summer; Conservation Day, in early June; Christmas lights in December.

Food service: The largest concession is the Kenya Cafe, an indoor fast-food restaurant. There is also a pizza station and several smaller refreshment stands. Picnic area is located at the west end of the park.

Plan to stay: 3 hours.

Directions: I–126 to Greystone Boulevard/Riverbanks exit. Go south on Greystone to the end. Zoo entrance is directly opposite.

Nearby attractions: Hampton-Preston Mansion and Garden, once the home of Confederate general Wade Hampton; Woodrow Wilson boyhood home; fairgrounds, where the South Carolina State Fair is held in October; Robert Mills Historic House, built in 1823 and designed by the man who designed the Washington Monument.

South Dakota

BEAR COUNTRY USA

Route 16
Rapid City, SD (605) 343–2290

With a name like that, you'd expect to see a lot of bears in this drive-through zoo. Well, you won't be disappointed. Nearly 250 bears, including blacks and grizzlies, serve as the main attraction here, but you'll also see many other species of North American animals, including wolves, bison, elk, deer, antelope, bighorn sheep, moose, and Rocky Mountain goats.

This park also serves as a breeding facility that supplies bear cubs to other zoos and to Hollywood moviemakers who need a bear or two for their latest picture. Born in the winter, the cubs are housed in the Babyland area of the park, which they share with other offspring of the zoo's resident animals.

After taking the hour-long car tour through the park, you can then walk around Babyland and pet and feed the young animals. The best time to visit is during June and July, while the babies are still fairly small.

Open from Memorial Day weekend until the end of October. Hours:

8:00 A.M. to 6:00 P.M., daily, from opening day through June, and in September and October. Closing time is extended to 8:00 P.M. in July and August.

Admission is under $10 for adults, under $5 for ages 6–15, free for those under 6. The maximum charge is $24 per car. Autos can be rented for a nominal fee by cyclists and visitors with soft-topped vehicles. There is also a $1-per-person charge for the park's pony ride.

Located to the south of Rapid City. Take I–90 to I–190 South. Follow I–190 to 8th Street, which becomes Route 16. Follow signs to the entrance on Route 16, about 8 miles south of the city.

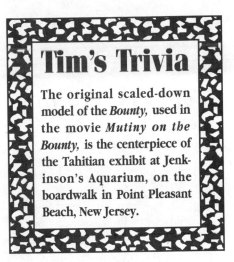

Tim's Trivia

The original scaled-down model of the *Bounty*, used in the movie *Mutiny on the Bounty*, is the centerpiece of the Tahitian exhibit at Jenkinson's Aquarium, on the boardwalk in Point Pleasant Beach, New Jersey.

GAVINS POINT AQUARIUM AND HATCHERY

State Route 52
Yankton, SD (605) 665–3352

A visit to this aquarium and fish hatchery, downstream from the Gavins Point Dam and Power House, along the Missouri River, will give you a good idea of the marine life indigenous to this area.

Near the highway, the air-conditioned aquarium building features thirteen tanks of fish, reptiles, and amphibians representing thirty different species. The aquarium building is open April through November, 10:00 A.M. to 4:00 P.M. daily. Admission to both the aquarium and the hatchery is free.

Down by the river, the hatchery features thirty-six open ponds on seventy acres, as well as other breeding and spawning tanks. Best time to visit the hatchery is in April, before the newly hatched fish are put in the ponds. They raise thirteen different species here, including channel catfish, northern pike, and muskies. The hatchery is open 8:00 A.M. to 4:00 P.M. daily, year-round.

No food is permitted on the grounds. A large state park with picnic facilities is nearby, and there are 700 campsites within a 5-mile radius of the complex. Located 3½ miles west of Yankton, along Highway 52, in the southeast portion of the state.

GREAT PLAINS ZOO

805 South Kiwanis Avenue
Sioux Falls, SD (605) 339–7059

Animals native to the Great Plains are featured here, and there are more than 300 of them on exhibit.

The Big Sioux River runs through this thirty-two-acre zoo, which keeps its animals in naturalistic outdoor enclosures. Some of the most popular exhibits include the penguin habitat, the North American Plains exhibit, the prairie dog town, and the bear exhibit.

Open daily, year-round, except for Christmas Day. Hours are 9:00 A.M. to 7:00 P.M. from Memorial Day through Labor Day. The rest of the year hours are 10:00 A.M. to 4:00 P.M. Admission is under $6 for adults, under $5 for seniors, and under $4 for ages 4–16. Ages 3 and under are admitted free.

Located in the southeastern part of the state. Take U.S. 29 to 41st Street. Go east on 41st Street to Kiwanis Avenue. Make a left on Kiwanis and go north for 2½ miles to entrance gate, on left.

REPTILE GARDENS

U.S. Highway 16 (Mt. Rushmore Road)
Rapid City, SD (605) 342–5873

The Black Hills of South Dakota provide the setting for one of the most extensive collections of reptiles in the United States.

Housed in the unique Sky Dome, reptiles are displayed on three different levels. The lower ring contains alligators, crocodiles, snakes, bats, and frogs. On the middle level is the Safari Room, where rain forest and desert reptiles are displayed in their respective settings. The upper level is a series of display cases containing what officials here claim to be the largest collection of venomous reptiles in the country, as well as some giant cockroaches.

Also on the grounds are a prairie dog town and outdoor gardens, in addition to miniature horses and Galapagos turtles, both of which smaller children are permitted to ride during nice weather.

In summer there are four different shows presented on a continuous schedule, including a snake presentation, alligator wrestling, a birds of prey demonstration, and Bewitched Village, where small domesticated animals perform tricks.

Open daily, April through October. Hours: April, May, September, and October, 9:00 A.M. to 5:00 P.M.; June through August, 7:00 A.M. to 9:00 P.M. Admission: adults, under $7; ages 6–14, under $4; ages 5 and under, free.

Located on U.S. Highway 16, about 6 miles south of Rapid City. Prominent signs direct you to the entrance.

Tennessee

DOLLYWOOD

700 Dollywood Lane
Pigeon Forge, TN (615) 428–9488

Co-owned by country music superstar Dolly Parton, this 100-acre, heavily wooded facility is much more than an amusement park with rides and musical presentations. It's also the home of the Eagle Mountain Sanctuary and the state's only butterfly atrium.

Located deep in the Smoky Mountains, the park's Eagle Mountain Sanctuary is an outdoor aviary showcase housing the largest collection of nonreleasable bald eagles in the country. The eagle complex is a cooperative effort between the park and the National Foundation to Protect America's Eagles.

The Butterfly Atrium is the focal point of the Butterfly Emporium, the park's largest merchandise shop. The butterfly has long been a symbol for Parton, and a drawing of one shows up as the "W" in Dollywood's logo. The atrium houses approximately 400 butterflies (20 species, both tropical and regional) in a controlled environment. Guests can cross a 30-foot walkway in the atrium for a close-up view.

Season: Late April through October. Opens again the day after Thanksgiving for its Christmas celebration.

Hours: Daily, 8:30 A.M. to 6:00 or 9:00 P.M.

Admission: Adults, under $20, includes animal shows as well as most other attractions and rides. Additional fees: parking; concerts in the Celebrity Theater.

The animals: Butterflies, eagles, and birds of prey.

Entertainment: Wings of America show in the eagle complex several times each day features various birds of prey. In addition, there is free musical entertainment throughout the park; and for an additional fee, there are 2 top-name country concerts each day.

Extras: A special butterfly hatching area, where you'll be able to see new butterflies emerging from their chrysalis is open to the public. Craftsmen Valley features the food, crafts, art, and customs of the Smoky Mountains. Black-powder gun shooting and gold panning activities are available for an additional charge. There are fifteen amusement park rides, including the Dollywood Express steam railroad, which takes you on a 5-mile excursion up the mountain.

Special events: American Quilt Showcase, May; National Crafts Festival, October; and the Smoky Mountain Christmas, featuring 300,000 lights, between Thanksgiving and New Year's Day.

Food service: 9 full-menu restaurants and many additional fast food outlets. After 4:00 P.M., a good-priced all-you-can-eat plan is offered at several of the restaurants. Open for breakfast.

Plan to stay: 5 hours.

Directions: Located 1 mile east of Highway 441 in Pigeon Forge, about 5 miles north of Gatlinburg. Turn at the Dollywood Information Center, located below the area's largest billboard and beside a 110-ton Dollywood Express locomotive.

Nearby attractions: Dixie Stampede Dinner; Magic World amusement park; Smoky Mountain Deer Farm and Petting Zoo; Smoky Mountain National Forest.

GRASSMERE WILDLIFE PARK

3777 Nolensville Road
Nashville, TN (615) 833-1534

As shopping centers, housing developments, and highways encroach on the green space of the city, this 200-acre wildlife park continues to provide an oasis of solitude. Located near the center of Nashville, the park features native Tennessee animals in natural settings.

A three-quarter mile paved trail takes you past the numerous animal exhibits which are nestled among the large trees and thick vegetation that were left undisturbed when the facility was built in 1990. The park is far enough from major highways that the sounds of the outside world aren't noticeable.

In addition to the outdoor exhibits, a two-story aviary in the Croft Center houses some of the state's native birds and ducks. Also in the center is a permanent exhibit concerning the history of human occupation on this specific parcel of land, from the first Native Americans to the last family who donated the land to make Grassmere possible.

Season: Open year-round, closed Thanksgiving, Christmas Day, and New Year's Day.

Hours: Opens daily at 10:00 A.M., closes at 5:00 P.M. during the summer, at 4:00 P.M. during the winter.

Admission: Adults, under $6; ages 3–12 and seniors, under $5; 2 and under, free. Free parking.

The animals: Animals native to Tennessee, including bison, elk, black bear, gray wolf, North American otter, bald eagle, cougar, white-tailed deer, and Przewalski's horse. Indoor exhibits feature snakes and the aquatic life of the Cumberland River.

Entertainment: A slide presentation about Tennessee, several times daily; fish feeding at set times; various curator talks and tours.

Extras: Changing art exhibits in gallery.

Special events: Boy Scout's Day, February; Wildflower Weekend, late April; Halloween Howl haunted trail; Teddy Bear Weekend, late November.

Food service: Overlook Cafe offers a daily luncheon special as well as a set menu. Enjoy a view of the bison and elk exhibit while dining. In the summer, additional snack stands are open on the trails.

Plan to stay: 3 hours.

Directions: Take exit 6 (Nolensville Pike) off I–440 and go south to park. Or take Harding Place exit, off I–24 (exit 56, go west) and I–65 (exit 78A, go east) to Nolensville Pike and go north to park.

Nearby attractions: Cumberland Science Museum; Opryland USA; Music Row shops and museums; and Second Avenue historic warehouse area, which offers shopping and dining.

KNOXVILLE ZOOLOGICAL GARDENS

3333 Woodbine Avenue
Knoxville, TN (615) 637–5331

If it weren't for the sounds of the animals, you'd think you were entering a botanical garden, not a zoo. Opened in 1947, the complex encompasses ninety acres of wooded hillsides, beautiful plantscapes, and shaded pathways. The gardens feature 100 flowerbeds, 70,000 annuals, and 125 varieties of trees and shrubs.

The zoo claims the largest big cat collection and the largest African elephant collection in the eastern United States. It has the distinction of having bred the first African elephant in captivity in the Western Hemisphere.

Season: Year-round, closed Christmas Day.

Hours: Daily, April through September, 9:30 A.M. to 6:00 P.M.; October through March, 10:00 A.M. to 4:30 P.M.

Admission: Adults, under $7; ages 3–12 and seniors, under $4; 3 and under, free.

The animals: More than 1,000 exotic animals, including the snow leopard, white rhinoceros, cheetah, Siberian tiger, chimpanzee, red panda, red wolf, bald eagle, gorilla, African elephant, kangaroo, and a reptile house full of snakes. A marine exhibit features polar bears, harbor seals, black-footed penguins, and many others.

Entertainment: Tropical bird and bird of prey shows; seal and sea lion show, daily.

Extras: Zoo Choo train ride, camel rides, and elephant rides, under $3 each (weather permitting for animal rides); and the Interactive Children's Zoo, under $1.

Special events: Zoo Olympics, in March; Teddy Bear Picnic, in July; Boo at the Zoo, in October; Zoo Lights, in December.

Food service: Tiger Tops Cafe and various other snack stands.

Fauna Fun Facts

The word "koala" is Aborigine for "it does not drink."

Plan to stay: 2 hours.

Directions: 2 miles east of Knoxville off I–40 from downtown, take Rutledge Pike exit 392 and follow signs to zoo.

Nearby attractions: Knoxville Museum of Art; Great Smoky Mountains National Park; Dollywood; and numerous outlet malls in Pigeon Forge.

MEMPHIS ZOO AND AQUARIUM

In Overton Park
2000 Galloway Avenue
Memphis, TN (901) 726–4787

Built in the early 1900s, the Memphis Zoo mixes the new with the old and provides visitors with a great opportunity to learn and have fun at the same time.

The thirty-six-acre complex is located in Overton Park, near the midtown section of the city. Memphis, of course, takes its name from a city of ancient Egypt, and the zoo carries that association along in its entrance gates, which are modeled after Egyptian walls. You enter onto the Avenue of Animals, which leads you to a plaza. From there, you take any number of pathways to each animal group exhibit.

Season: Year-round, closed Thanksgiving, Christmas Eve, and Christmas Day.

Hours: Daily, 9:00 A.M. to 5:00 P.M., October through April; till 6:00 P.M., May through September.

Admission: Adults, under $6; ages 2–11 and seniors (60 plus), under $4; under 2, free. Admission is for both zoo and aquarium.

The animals: More than 400 species, more than 2,800 specimens, including 13 species of cats in a new exhibit; tropical birds; hoofstock such as deer and antelope; aquariums with fresh water and marine life; African veldt; primate exhibit; children's zoo.

Entertainment: Birds of Prey shows.

Extras: Kiddie rides (additional charge); children's zoo takes on an Early American agriculture theme with domesticated pygmy animals such as pigs, sheep, and cows. Brooks Art Gallery, located in Overton Park.

Special events: Lectures, slide shows, workshops.

Food service: Concession stands with fast food.

Plan to stay: 4 hours.

Directions: From Loop 240, get off at Poplar Avenue exit, go to crossroads of Poplar Avenue and East Parkway in midtown Memphis, Overton Park is at crossroads. There are signs posted around the loop that guide visitors to the zoo.

Nearby attractions: Elvis Presley's Graceland mansion and grave; Sun Studio, where Elvis recorded his first record; Children's Museum; Pink Palace Natural History Museum; Libertyland amusement park; and the Great American Pyramid, a thirty-two–story stainless steel pyramid on the banks of the Mississippi River that houses a 20,000-seat arena.

NASHVILLE ZOO

1710 Ridge Road Circle
Joelton, TN (615) 370–3333

Out in the peaceful countryside, just north of Music City, U.S.A., you'll find this developing zoological park. Opened in 1991, the modern 135-acre facility is located in a wooded area that provides a great deal of shade for both the visitors and the animals.

Several elevated walkways provide excellent viewing of the various prairie and plain exhibits. If you're lucky, a giraffe may wander by and stare you in the eye.

Season: Year-round, Christmas too.

Hours: Daily, 9:00 A.M. to 6:00 P.M., Memorial Day through Labor Day; 10:00 A.M. to 5:00 P.M., the remainder of the year.

Admission: Adults, under $6; ages 3–12, under $4; 3 and under, free.

The animals: More than 150 species, more than 700 animals, all living in natural habitats. Animals include: oryx antelope, Bengal tigers, monkeys, lemurs and clouded leopards, the timber wolf, the Siberian Tiger, and the deer and antelope of Asia. Exhibits include: African Savannah, Wilds of India, Valley of the Cats, the Fields of North America, and the Reptile House.

Extras: Children's petting zoo; animal nursery.

Special events: Special animal-related programs and lectures are held on a regular basis during operating hours.

Food service: 2 concession stands, serving fast-food and snack items. Picnics permitted.

Plan to stay: 2 hours.

Directions: Take exit 31 (New Hope Road) off I–24, north of Nashville. Go west on New Hope Road to Highway 41A. Turn right (north) and proceed to Ridge Road; turn right and the zoo will be on your left. Once you get on Highway 41A, there are plenty of signs to direct you.

Nearby attractions: Nashville and its country music–related activities and attractions, including: Opryland USA, where the Opryland theme park, Grand Ole Opry, The Nashville Network, and the General Jackson Showboat are all located; Nashville Toy Museum; Nashville Palace, live music and country cooking; and on Music Row, near downtown Nashville, you'll find Barbara Mandrell Country, the Country Music Hall of Fame, and various other country retail stores and museums.

SMOKY MOUNTAIN DEER FARM AND PETTING ZOO

478 Happy Hollow Lane
Sevierville, TN (615) 428–DEER

You can walk with—as well as talk to and feed—the animals here. Located in the Smoky Mountains, you'll find more than 150 tame deer in a large field waiting for you to arrive with that little red cup full of food.

Although most of the deer don't like to be petted, they're all more than happy to eat out of your hand, that's a guarantee here. As the owner says, they're not looking for affection, they're convinced by the food. In addition to feeding the fallow, mule, and Sitka deer, you'll be able to feed and pet wild sheep, miniature horses, and miniature Sicilian donkeys.

African pygmy goats, hand-tamed zebras, llamas, a wallaby, and a myriad of ducks and chickens also call this place home. Visitors can choose to walk through several of the pens or observe, pet, and feed the animals through a fence. The $1 or $2 portions of feed come in souvenir plastic cups that you can take home when you leave. Pony rides are also available.

Open year-round, closed Thanksgiving, and Christmas Days. Opens at 10:00 A.M. every morning; closes at 5:00 P.M. during the off-season, 8:00 P.M. during the summer months. Admission: adults, under $5; ages 9–12, under $4; ages 3–8, under $3; ages 3 and under, free.

From Sevierville, take Route 411 (Dolly Parton Parkway) approximately 4 miles east to Walnut Grove Road. Turn left (north) and follow Happy Hollow Lane to the farm.

Fauna Fun Facts

There are more than 20,000 species of spiders.

TENNESSEE AQUARIUM

101 West Second Street
Chattanooga, TN (615) 265–0695

Billed as the "world's first major freshwater life center," this beautiful facility opened in 1992 on the banks of the Tennessee River, in the city's downtown area. Take a walk through here and you'll get an excellent understanding of the Tennessee River and its related ecosystems.

The exhibits are organized so to guide you on a journey from the river's source in the Appalachian high country, through its midstream, and finally to the Mississippi Delta. The journey takes you through living environments that re-create the habitats of the fish, birds, amphibians, reptiles, mammals, and insects that rely on the Tennessee River for sustenance.

Tennessee contains more species of freshwater fish than any other state and is the home of more varieties of plants and animals than any other comparable inland region in the temperate zone worldwide.

Season: Year-round, closed Thanksgiving and Christmas Days.

Hours: Daily, 10:00 A.M. to 6:00 P.M. Closing hours are extended till 8:00 P.M. on Fridays, Saturdays, and Sundays, May through Labor Day.

Admission: Adults, under $10; ages 3–12, under $5; 3 and under, free.

The animals: More than 350 species, more than 3,500 animals, including fish, birds, mammals, reptiles, and amphibians. There are 5 major galleries, each with multiple exhibits: Appalachian Cove Forest, the mountain source of the river; Tennessee River Gallery, the river at midstream; Discovery Falls, a look at the interdependent ecosystem and animal adaptation; Mississippi Delta, where the river slows to meet the sea; and the Rivers of the World, which compares 6 of the world's great river systems with the Tennessee.

Entertainment: Visitors may ask questions during scheduled fish feedings. You will also find various folk artists in residence, creating their wares.

Extras: Folk Art Gallery, a display and sale of artwork created by the people of the Tennessee River Valley. In what might be the largest bookstore in any aquarium facility anywhere there are more than 500 titles for sale, most of them concerned with environmental and wildlife issues.

Food service: None in the facility itself, but many in adjacent areas.

Plan to stay: 2 hours.

Directions: Located in downtown Chattanooga. Take I–24 downtown to U.S. 27 North. Take exit 1C (4th Street), turn left at second light onto Broad Street, then proceed 2 blocks to the aquarium.

Nearby attractions: Lake Winnepesaukah amusement park; Rock City; Ruby Falls; The World's Steepest Incline Railway; The Chattanooga Choo Choo, hotel, shopping, and dining complex in historic railway station.

Texas

ABILENE ZOOLOGICAL GARDENS

1800 East South 11th Street
Abilene, TX (915) 672–9771 (recording); (915) 676–6222

You don't have to be a veteran bird watcher to get up close and personal with the fine feathered friends here. More than fifty species of birds can be seen enjoying life in a large walk-through aviary.

Adjoining the thirteen-acre zoo is a large park, complete with a grassy picnic area, ballfields, playground, and a lake on which fishing is permitted.

Season: Year-round, closed Thanksgiving, Christmas Day, and New Year's Day.

Hours: Daily, 9:00 A.M. to 5:00 P.M.; open till 7:00 P.M. on summer weekends and holidays.

Admission: Adults, under $5; ages 3–12 and seniors, under $2; under age 3, free.

The animals: More than 500 animals, more than 150 species, displayed in naturalistic settings simulating those found in Africa.

Entertainment: No regularly scheduled entertainment, but once a year, in early June, Zoo Day (a day of animal lectures and demonstrations) is held in conjunction with Earth Day.

Extras: Discovery Center, contains walk-through aviary, exhibit of small mammals, and an aquarium.

Food service: A small fast-food concession is open daily during summer and weekends in the spring. Vending machines are available year-round, and picnics are permitted.

Plan to stay: 1 hour.

Directions: Located on the eastern edge of town, near the airport. Take I–20 to Loop 322 South. Get off at Highway 36 exit. Zoo entrance is less than a mile ahead, on your right.

Nearby attractions: Buffalo Gap Historical Village, a collection of 19th-century buildings reassembled on the site of the original Taylor County seat; ruins of Fort Phantom Hill, once part of a string of forts along the Texas frontier.

CALDWELL ZOO

2203 Martin Luther King Boulevard
Tyler, TX (903) 593–0121

A wooden walkway snakes through the tropical foliage and surrounds the artificial lakes of this growing facility. Currently about one-third developed, this forty-year-old zoo, owned and operated by a private elementary school, contains both indoor and outdoor exhibits of animals from three continents.

The town, named for President John Tyler, is known as the "rose capital of the world," because of the extensive variety of roses grown in the area, and the zoo grounds have a nice sampling.

Season: Year-round, closed Thanksgiving, Christmas Day, and New Year's Day.

Hours: Daily, April through September, 9:30 A.M. to 6:00 P.M.; till 4:30 P.M. the remainder of the year.

Admission: Free.

The animals: More than 1,250 animals, more than 250 species, exhibited in habitats of Texas, East Africa, and South America. There is also an interesting collection of flamingos and ducks from around the world.

Entertainment: Tours, slide shows, and demonstrations are given by docents.

Extras: Texas Farm Area, a hands-on children's zoo featuring goats, sheep, rabbits, calves, and other farm animals.

Food service: 1 year-round concession and 2 seasonal ones that offer a variety of fast-food items, snacks, and beverages. Picnics are permitted.

Plan to stay: 1 hour.

Directions: Located in the northwest quadrant of the city. Take I–20 to Highway 69 exit. Go east on Highway 69 to Martin Luther King Boulevard. Zoo entrance is 1 block from intersection.

Nearby attractions: Municipal Rose Garden, containing 38,000 rose bushes representing 500 varieties with additional camellia garden and tropical greenhouse; Brookshire's World of Wildlife, containing African and North American animals and a full-size replica of an early 1900s grocery store.

CENTRAL TEXAS ZOOLOGICAL PARK

3601 Zoo Park Road
Waco, TX (817) 750–5976

Opened in 1955, this 10-acre zoo is located next to the Waco Municipal Airport and overlooks Lake Waco. The facility is part of Airport Park, which was built on an old Army base.

As you walk through the front gate, you'll be greeted by the gibbons, whose enclosure is right under the main sign. The flat terrain makes for easy walking, while lots of shade trees keep the Texas sun from becoming too uncomfortable, and some strolling ducks help keep the grounds tidy by snapping up any edible tidbits that may have been dropped.

Season: Year-round, closed Christmas Day and New Year's Day.

Hours: Memorial Day through August, 9:00 A.M. to 6:00 P.M. on weekdays; till 7:00 P.M. on weekends. Rest of the year, 9:00 A.M. to 5:00 P.M. weekdays; till 6:00 P.M. on weekends.

Admission: Adults, under $3; ages 3–11, under $2; under age 3, free.

The animals: More than 300 animals, more than 140 species, displayed in both enclosures and cages. Highlights include the Reptile House, the elephant exhibit, and a small aquarium.

Extras: Petting zoo, playground, small nature museum.

Special events: July Fourth celebration, and observance of special animals' birthdays throughout the year.

Food service: 1 concession stand offers snacks and drinks. Picnics are permitted in the pavilion.

Plan to stay: 1 hour.

Directions: I–35 to the Lake Brazos Drive exit. Go west, following signs to airport and zoo. Stay on Lake Brazos, which becomes Old Steinbeck Bend Road. Follow Steinbeck to the end, about 8½ miles. At the end of the road, turn right and enter zoo.

Nearby attractions: Texas Ranger Hall of Fame, with films, wax figures, and exhibits; Strecker Museum of Baylor University, with fossils, minerals, live native reptiles, and a reconstructed 19th-century cabin; Fort Fisher Park, with museum on Texas Rangers; Dr. Pepper Museum, in original bottling plant, featuring displays and memorabilia.

DALLAS AQUARIUM

In Fair Park
First Avenue and Martin Luther King Boulevard
Dallas, TX (214) 670–8443 (recording); (214) 670–8453

The original building of the Dallas aquarium opened in 1936 in Fair Park to coincide with the Texas Centennial celebration; a separate marine section opened in 1964.

After a 1991 renovation, under the direction of the Dallas Zoo, the popular facility now has 300 species of various aquatic animals on display, plus reptiles and amphibians.

Included in the exhibits are a 100-pound snapping turtle, a 4-foot-long electric eel, sea horses, sharks, a 2,000-gallon tank featuring African fishes, and the first exhibition of Mexican fish in the United States.

Facilities are open daily, 10:00 A.M. to 4:30 P.M., closed on Thanksgiving

Fauna Fun Facts

A lizard can regenerate a tail that breaks off.

and Christmas Day. Admission: adults, under $1.50; ages 3–12, under $1; under 3 free. No food facilities are available, but the large park offers ample picnic space. Located southeast of downtown, off I–30 (Thornton Freeway). Going east, take First Avenue exit; going west, take Second Avenue exit. Aquarium is on corner of First Avenue and Martin Luther King Boulevard.

DALLAS ZOO
In Marsalis Park
620 East Clarendon Drive
Dallas, TX (214) 670–6825

There's a lot to see and a great deal of walking to do here, so wear comfortable shoes and cool clothing and you'll surely enjoy the eighty acres.

The zoo is divided into two sections: the zoo proper, which covers fifty-four acres; and the Wilds of Africa habitat on another thirty-five acres, all in Marsalis Park, in a southern suburb of the city.

Although the zoo opened in 1888, virtually all of the old-style enclosures and exhibit areas have been replaced with naturalistic habitats to give the animals lots of space. In fact, the gorillas alone have two acres to themselves. All exhibits are outdoors except the Bird and Reptile House, the only air-conditioned exhibit at the zoo, which also makes it one of the most popular on hot summer days.

Season: Year-round, closed Christmas Day.

Hours: Daily, 9:00 A.M. to 5:00 P.M.

Admission: Adults, under $7; ages 3–11 and seniors, under $3; under age 3, free. Additional fees: monorail, under $3 per person, age 2 and under, free.

The animals: More than 1,400 animals, more than 300 species, with lots of birds and reptiles. The outstanding exhibit here is the Wilds of Africa, which is the first in the world to replicate every major habitat of an entire continent.

Entertainment: No regularly scheduled shows or demonstrations, but there are often Touch Stops throughout the zoo, where visitors can learn more about the animals from docents who bring out animals and animal artifacts.

Extras: Children's zoo, in summer; 1-mile guided monorail tour; and self-guided 1,500-foot walking trail through the Wilds of Africa, all year.

Special events: Big Cat Week, in August; Spanish Heritage Week, in September; Birds of Prey celebration, in October.

Food service: The African Cafe, located in the African Plaza at the Wilds of Africa exhibit, offers African and Spanish food, as well as a full range of fast food, snacks, ice cream, and drinks; 2 other concessions serve fast food, and there is a picnic area for those who bring their own food.

Plan to stay: 3 hours.

Directions: I–35 South to Ewing Avenue exit. Go north on Ewing to East Clarendon Drive. Zoo entrance will be on your immediate right.

Nearby attractions: John Fitzgerald Kennedy Memorial, a tribute to the late president, who was assassinated nearby in 1963; The Sixth Floor, an exhibit and memorial to President Kennedy, on the sixth floor of the Texas School Book Depository; Old City Park, a restored village with museum; and Dallas Arboretum and Botanical Garden, with 66 acres of gardens.

ELLEN TROUT ZOO

In Ellen Trout Park
Loop 287 at Martin Luther King Jr. Drive
Lufkin, TX (409) 633–0399

What started out as a gag gift to a local businessman back in the 1960s has become one of the most popular attractions in the east Texas town of Lufkin.

Located in a city park, the zoo began as a small collection of animals native to the area that was owned by Walter Trout, who was president of Lufkin Industries at the time. One day a friend sent him a baby hippo as a joke, prompting Trout to donate it—and the land—to the city.

The zoo is in a beautifully landscaped setting, filled with palm trees and shaded walks. Some eye-catching features have been built into the animal exhibits, including fountains, a replica of a Mayan temple, and a re-creation of an abandoned gold mine.

Season: Year-round, holidays too.

Hours: During daylight saving time, hours are 9:00 A.M. to 6:00 P.M., daily. The remainder of the year, till 5:00 P.M.

Admission: Free. Officials are considering adding an admission charge, so call first if it makes a difference to you.

The animals: More than 500 animals, more than 170 species, displayed in both indoor and outdoor natural habitats. Highlights include the African savannah lion exhibit; northern temperate forest tiger exhibit; wolf exhibit; West African crowned cranes; and pine snakes.

Extras: In other areas of the park you'll find a train ride, a playground, a lake where fishing is permitted, and a nature trail along the lake and woods.

Special events: Zoo Safari, in the summer; July Fourth celebration in the park. Other events are held sporadically.

Food service: 1 concession stand sells snacks and drinks. Picnics are permitted in both the zoo and park.

Plan to stay: 1 hour.

Directions: Located in eastern portion of the state. Take U.S. 59 or U.S. 69 to Loop 287. Follow the loop around to Lake Street, but don't get off there. Across from the Expo Center there will be a sign directing you to the park entrance, 1,000 feet ahead.

Nearby attractions: Texas Forestry Museum, includes a fire lookout tower, blacksmith's forge, logging train and moonshiner's still; Angelina Woodland Trail, a nature walk; Texas Forest Festival, held at Expo Center the third week in September.

EL PASO ZOO

In Washington Park
4001 East Paisano Drive
El Paso, TX (915) 521–1850

A circular gatehouse and steeple form the main entrance here, and once you pass through it you've entered one of the most compact zoos in the country.

Since its opening in 1941 the facility has occupied five acres of this downtown city park, only a short drive from the Mexican border. The anticipated opening of the Asia exhibit in 1993 will double the size of the zoo.

Season: Year-round, closed Thanksgiving, Christmas Day, and New Year's Day.

Hours: Open weekdays year-round, 9:30 A.M. to 4:00 P.M. Weekend hours: June, July, and August, 9:30 A.M. to 6:00 P.M.; April, May, September, and

October, 9:30 A.M. to 5:00 P.M.; and November through March, 9:30 A.M. to 4:00 P.M.

Admission: Adults, under $3; ages 3–11, under $1.50; under age 3 and over 61, free. Additional fees: coin-operated kiddie rides.

The animals: More than 400 animals, more than 140 species, in both indoor and outdoor naturalistic exhibits. Highlights include: the Biome, 2 connected buildings with walk-through Tropical Forest, and Chihuahuan Desert; South American Pavilion, with saltwater tank and freshwater aquarium; Hard Pan Flats, a prairie dog town; and the Asian exhibit.

Entertainment: Sea lion feedings, twice daily; Wildlife films, on Sundays.

Extras: Coin-operated kiddie rides; costumed characters at holiday times (Easter Bunny, Santa Claus, etc.).

Special events: Easter party, in the spring; Mona the Elephant's birthday, in October.

Food service: Bear Cove concession offers hamburgers, hot dogs, nachos, personal-size pizzas, beverages, and ice cream. Picnics are permitted.

Plan to stay: 2 hours.

Directions: I–10 to Raynolds exit. Go south on Raynolds Street to Paisano Drive. Make a right on Paisano and zoo will be on the right, at Evergreen. Follow brown and tan park signs with "E Bear" silhouette.

Nearby attractions: U.S. Army Air Defense Artillery Museum; Fort Bliss Replica Museum; Border Patrol Museum and Memorial Library; bus tours of El Paso and nearby Juarez, Mexico, are available; Western Playland amusement park.

FORT WORTH ZOO

1989 Colonial Parkway
Fort Worth, TX (817) 871–7050

As the oldest continuous zoo site in the state, this facility retains much of its 1909 charm, though it has since grown into a modern zoo and aquarium facility, and work on the master plan brings more change every year.

In 1992, two major exhibits opened: the World of Primates, a 2½-acre habitat that includes an indoor tropical rain forest for housing endangered lowland gorillas in natural family groups; and the Asian Falls, a unique presentation carved out of the hillside, where you'll walk along raised paths beside a 40-foot waterfall to view endangered Asian tigers, bears, cranes, and a white tiger.

As new exhibits are created, the older ones are updated and enhanced, such as the aquarium and the herpetarium.

Season: Year round, holidays too.

Hours: Opens daily at 10:00 A.M., and closes at 5:00 P.M. most of the year. Extended hours during peak seasons. Open Noon to 5:00 P.M. on Thanksgiving, Christmas Day, and New Year's Day.

Admission: Adults, under $6; ages 3–12 and seniors, under $3; under 3, free. Everyone gets in for half-price every Wednesday.

The animals: More than 4,400 animals, more than 755 species, displayed in naturalistic indoor and outdoor habitats. Top exhibits include: African Savannah; aquarium, featuring sea lions, sharks, amphibians, invertebrates, and fresh- and saltwater fish; small animal village, featuring small mammals, tortoises, wallabies, and kangaroos, and a walk-through aviary.

Extras: "Texas!" an 11-acre turn-of-the-century pioneer town, complete with animals native to the state and a prairie dog village where kids can crawl through a tunnel and pop up in a plastic dome among the animals.

Special events: Earth Day Awareness, in late April; Big Cat Weekend, highlighting the plight of endangered big cats, in mid-August; Zoo Doo, family festival, in mid-September; Boo at the Zoo, in late October; and Santa's Zoobilee, the first two weekends in December.

Food service: Sidewalk Cafe and concession stands among the animal exhibits. The Yellow Rose Saloon, in the "Texas!" area, serves up soft drinks and traditional Texas cuisine.

Plan to stay: 4 hours.

Directions: Take University Drive exit off I–30. Go south 1 mile, take a left on Colonial Parkway and you can't miss it.

Nearby attractions: Billy Bob's Texas, the world's largest honky-tonk; Amon Carter Museum of Western Art; Cattle Raisers Museum; Six Flags over Texas, amusement park; Stockyards Historic Area.

Fauna Fun Facts

Dolphins are mammals, not fish.

FOSSIL RIM WILDLIFE CENTER

Highway 67
Glen Rose, TX (817) 897–2960

There are three ways to see the animals here: from the comfort of your car; on foot; in a personalized, behind-the-scenes tour; or on an overnight safari.

There are nearly 3,000 acres of hills, woods, and grasslands here that look remarkably like settings you'd find in Africa. Whether riding or walking, it's definitely a great way to get away from civilization for a while.

Season: Year-round, closed Thanksgiving and Christmas Day.

Hours: Daily, 9:00 A.M. to 6:00 P.M. or dusk, whichever is earlier.

Admission: Adults, under $12; ages 4–11, under $9; seniors, under $11; under age 4, free. Additional fees: $35 per person for 2-hour, personalized "Behind the Scenes" tour; horseback riding, $20 for 90 minutes.

The animals: More than 1,000 animals, more than 37 species, of rare and endangered African mammals and birds, including cheetahs, gazelles, zebras, giraffes, fallow deer, and red deer, all running free in natural outdoor habitats.

Extras: 9½-mile self-guided auto tour; Petting Pasture; Overnight Safari Camp (extra charge), where guides lead participants into the wilderness for a safari and camp-out; nature trails; horseback riding; behind-the-scenes tours.

Special events: Christmas on the Rim, in December; Owl Prowl, on a changing schedule.

Food service: 1 restaurant and 1 snack bar offer fast food, sandwiches, soup, salad, snacks, and drinks.

Plan to stay: 3 hours.

Directions: Located south of Fort Worth. Take I–35 West to exit for Glen Rose (Highway 67). Go west on Highway 67 into Glen Rose, about 30 miles. Stay on Highway 67 for another 3 miles past town, following signs to entrance.

Nearby attractions: Dinosaur Valley State Park, which has real dinosaur footprints; Museum of Time, a clock museum in Granbury; boat trips on Lake Granbury.

GLADYS PORTER ZOO

500 Ringgold Street
Brownsville, TX (512) 546–2177 (recording); (512) 546–7187

Opened in 1971, the Gladys Porter Zoo is named after the woman whose father founded the J. C. Penney department store chain. Ms. Porter traveled extensively through Africa and decided to establish the zoo with her inheritance. Right up to her death in 1981, she was involved with the day-to-day operations of the facility.

Brownsville is at the southern tip of Texas along the Mexican border and the climate is well-suited to the tropical foliage and animals that abound here. The animals are grouped according to geographic areas and separated from visitors by moats, streams, and caves that run throughout the zoo.

Season: Year-round, holidays too.

Hours: Exhibits are open daily, 9:00 A.M. to 5:30 P.M., with extended hours during the summer. Visitors are free to walk the grounds until dusk.

Admission: Adults, under $6; ages 2–13, under $4; under age 2, free. Additional fees: parking, under $2.50; train ride, under $2. Some of the special events held throughout the year involve an additional charge.

The animals: More than 1,700 animals, about 400 species, exhibited in outdoor displays according to continent of origin, or in a simulated habitat. Zoogeographic areas include Tropical America, Indo-Australia, Asia, and Africa. There is also a herpetarium, an aquatic exhibit, and a free-flight rain-forest aviary.

Entertainment: No shows or demonstrations except during special events (see below), when animal-related educational activities take place.

Extras: On Sundays, between 1:30 and 3:30 P.M., there are guided tour trains that go around the zoo; a children's zoo and an animal nursery.

Special events: Zoobilee, a children's carnival, in April; Zoofari, for adults, the first week in October; Boo at the Zoo, on Halloween night; Zoolympics, in November; and Luminaria, in early December.

Food service: Concessions include the Asian Grill, Lion's Den, and Tropical Pavilion. In addition to the standard American fast-food and snack fare, you can also enjoy salads, dieters' platters, grilled chicken, fries, and burritos.

Plan to stay: 2 hours.

Directions: U.S. Route 77 South to the 6th Street exit. Follow signs on feeder road to zoo, which is less than a mile from Route 77, on the right.

Nearby attractions: Fort Brown, the establishment of which in 1846 by General Zachary Taylor led to the start of the Mexican War; Padre Island National Seashore; Charro Days, a week-long Mardi Gras, is held here in February.

HOUSTON ZOOLOGICAL GARDENS

In Hermann Park
1513 Outer Belt Drive
Houston, TX (713) 525–3000

Located in the southwest corner of a public park, this zoo is a colorful respite within the inner city. Visitors are pleasantly surprised at how much green space they find here, surrounded by tall buildings and busy streets.

Extensive plantings of hibiscus, and ginger and banana trees, among other tropical plant varieties, give the grounds an added splash of color.

Although there are still some animals in cages, most have taken up residence in natural habitats, where the warm climate allows them to live year-round.

Season: Year-round, holidays too.

Hours: Daily, 10:00 A.M. to 6:00 P.M.

Admission: Adults, under $4; ages 3–12, under $2; seniors, under $3; under age 3, free. On all holidays observed by the municipality everyone gets in free.

The animals: More than 3,000 animals, more than 700 species, including lots of birds. Highlights include a walk-through rain-forest aviary, a gorilla habitat, an albino reptile exhibit, vampire bats, and large cats. There is also a small aquarium.

Entertainment: On a daily basis there are puppet shows, animal feedings, and docent demonstrations.

Extras: Discovery Court, an education and interpretive center, has hands-on animal learning experiences, as well as a kiddie train ride. In other areas of the park there is the Houston Museum of Natural Sciences, with a planetarium and an IMAX theater, where nature films and travelogues are shown.

Food service: Several concessions serving a variety of fast foods, including hamburgers, hot dogs, Mexican dishes, ice cream, and beverages.

Plan to stay: 1 hour.

Directions: I–610 to Bellaire Boulevard exit. Go east on Bellaire to Main Street (Route 90). Go left on Main Street; zoo/park entrance will be on your right, just after the Texas Medical Center.

Nearby attractions: Museum of Art and the American West; Lyndon B. Johnson Space Center, with NASA displays and tours of the Mission Control Center, from which space flights are monitored; AstroWorld amusement park; and WaterWorld water park.

SAN ANTONIO ZOOLOGICAL GARDENS AND AQUARIUM

In Brackenridge Park
3903 North Saint Mary's Street
San Antonio, TX (512) 734–7183 (recording); (512) 734–7184

Ranked among the area's top attractions, the San Antonio Zoo is situated at the headwaters of the San Antonio River and surrounded by the limestone cliffs of an abandoned rock quarry.

Located in Brackenridge Park, this eighty-year-old zoo is well suited for displaying a variety of animal habitats.

Right inside the gate is the new Mercado Plaza, an ambitious expansion and modernization of the gardens, reptile exhibit, aquarium, and visitor services. Beyond the plaza are a system of paths leading to an outer ring of animal exhibits.

This zoo houses one of the largest animal collections in the country. Included in its outstanding bird collection is the only endangered whooping crane now on exhibit, as well as the first white rhino born in the United States, and the first penguin born in Texas.

Season: Year-round, holidays too.

Hours: April through October, daily, 9:30 A.M. to 6:30 P.M.; remainder of the year, till 5:00 P.M.

Admission: Adults, under $7; ages 3–11, under $5; seniors, under $5.50; under age 3, free. Additional fees: boat ride, under $2; elephant and camel rides, under $3.

The animals: More than 3,000 animals, more than 700 species, including many birds, displayed in outdoor habitats, according to continent of origin. Highlights include Australian Walk-About; Amazonia; the barless bear pits; fresh- and saltwater aquariums; and several waterfowl exhibits.

Entertainment: Sea lion demonstrations twice daily; penguin feedings, twice daily; Theater of Birds, 2 or 3 times a day on Wednesdays through Sundays during the summer; fish and alligator feedings, once a day (alligators on Thursdays only); elephant show, 3 times daily.

Extras: Camel and elephant rides, various days and times; boat rides at children's zoo; Tropical Tour in children's zoo includes a playground, desert building, animal arena, Everglades exhibit, and education center with rain-forest exhibit. Other areas of Brackenridge Park feature sunken oriental gardens, outdoor theater, lagoons, horseback riding, miniature railroad, skyride, and paddleboats.

Special events: Fiesta Art Exhibit, in April; Family Picnic at the Zoo, in May; Conservation Day, in June; Zoo Run, in September; Senior Day and Zoo Boo Halloween party, in October; Zoobilation Ball, in November.

Food service: The full-service Riverview Restaurant offers a menu of fast foods, snacks, and beverages, while 7 smaller concessions sell snacks. Picnics are permitted.

Plan to stay: 3 hours.

Directions: I–37/281 to St. Mary's Street/Hildebrand Avenue exit. Go south on St. Mary's; zoo entrance will be a short distance ahead, on your left.

Nearby attractions: Fiesta Texas, theme park; Sea World of Texas; the Alamo; Hertzberg Circus Collection and Circus Museum; Buckhorn Hall of Horns Museum, a collection of animal horns on the grounds of the Lone Star Brewery, which also features the Buckhorn Bar, a city landmark, where free beer and root beer samples are offered; Natural Bridge Caverns.

Tim's Trivia

Gomek is the largest crocodile living in the Western Hemisphere. He's 17½ feet long and weighs more than 1,700 pounds. He lives at the St. Augustine (Florida) Alligator Farm.

SEA WORLD OF TEXAS

10500 Sea World Drive
San Antonio, TX (512) 523–3600

This is the largest and the newest of the Sea World parks. In fact, with 250 acres, it's the world's largest marine zoological park.

Shamu and his killer-whale buddies star in the major show here in the 4,500-seat Shamu Stadium, one of the largest facilities in the world for the presentation of marine animals. Plus, there's a lot of other action, from two amusement rides to a water ski show to a walrus and otter show.

Season: Daily, May through Labor Day; weekends only, March, April, and September through November.

Hours: 10:00 A.M. to 10:00 P.M., though hours vary during weekend operations and during peak summer periods.

Admission: Adults, under $22; each child under 12 gets in free with a paying adult. (The free-admission policy for children began in 1992, and officials weren't sure it would continue into 1993). Additional fee: parking, under $2.

The animals: More than 5,200 animals, more than 200 species, mostly fish and birds, displayed in aquariums and open pools. Exhibits include: Shark and the Coral Reef, a 4-aquarium exhibit that highlights sharks and colorful fishes; Penguins and Alcids, in a re-created sub-Antarctic environment; a seal and sea lion community, where guests are allowed to feed the animals; marine mammal pool, where guests can touch and feed dolphins.

Entertainment: 5 shows, including: the trademark Shamu the Killer Whale show; Cetacean Sensation show, featuring whales and dolphins interacting; the sea lion, walrus, and otter show; free musical concerts featuring top names in entertainment; and a water ski show.

Extras: 2 family-oriented water rides—the Texas Splashdown log flume, and Rio Loco raging-rapids raft ride; a large game center; Shamu's Happy Harbor, 3-acre participatory play area for the kids; Cypress Gardens West, a 16-acre botanical showcase.

Food service: 4 sit-down, air-conditioned restaurants and 12 snack stands. The nonalcoholic frozen drinks available at the Daiquiri Factory are fantastic, especially on a hot Texas afternoon.

Plan to stay: 7 hours.

Directions: Located 16 miles northwest of downtown San Antonio, off State Highway 151 between Loop 410 and Loop 1604, on Sea World Drive.

Nearby attractions: San Antonio Riverwalk, shopping and dining establishments along the San Antonio River; the Alamo; Fiesta Texas musical theme park.

TEXAS STATE AQUARIUM

One Shoreline Plaza
Corpus Christi, TX (800) 477–4853; (512) 881–1300

The marine wonders of the Gulf of Mexico and the Caribbean Sea are featured at this beautiful facility, first opened in 1990. Located on seven acres on Corpus Christi Beach, the aquarium is dedicated to creating a better understanding and appreciation of the Gulf. Through its exhibits and educational programs, it fulfills its mission quite nicely.

Entry to the main Gulf of Mexico Exhibit Building is through a plaza that includes intricate mosaic walkways depicting whales, rays, dolphins, sharks, and the Gulf itself. But these bursts of color are only a prelude to the colors and shapes of the marine life living inside. The progression of the exhibits gives you the feeling that you begin at the surface and work your way down to a mile below the surface of the Gulf.

Season: Year-round, closed Christmas Day.

Hours: Monday through Saturday, 10:00 A.M. to 6:00 P.M.; Sunday, noon to 6:00 P.M.

Admission: Adults, under $9; ages 4–7, under $4; seniors and active-duty military, under $5; ages 3 and under, free.

The animals: More than 250 species, representing the marine life of the Gulf of Mexico and the Caribbean Sea. Indoor exhibits include: Marsh; Dune and Bay; The Estuaries; Animals of the Texas Coast; The Barrier Islands; The Near Shore Fauna; and the Coral Reef, a recreation of the Flower Gardens Coral Reef, 115 miles offshore. The Islands of Steel exhibit shows a full-scale section of an oil platform and the life that lives around it.

Entertainment: Scheduled fish feedings and occasional lectures and demonstrations.

Extras: The Ocean Technology exhibit features interactive discoveries of deep-sea exploration and research. Outdoor exhibits include: a 1-acre re-creation of a Texas coastal marsh, complete with sea grass and shorebirds; the endangered ridley turtles are featured in the turtle display; and river otters play in a freshwater habitat. The 120-foot-high Oxychem Tower provides you with a panoramic view of the bay and the ship channel.

Food service: A concessions stand sells "convenience-oriented" foods, in-cluding sandwiches, salads, and desserts.

Plan to stay: 2 hours.

Directions: Located on Corpus Christi Beach, just over the Harbor Bridge from downtown. Take the last exit (Portland) off I–37 downtown and cross the bridge. Take the exit at the bottom of the bridge and follow the signs.

Nearby attractions: Bayfront Arts and Science Park; Convention Center and Wintergardens; Art Museum of South Texas; Corpus Christi Museum.

THE TEXAS ZOO

In Riverside Park
110 Memorial Drive
Victoria, TX (512) 573–7681

At first glance it appears that the only things they grow down in this part of Texas are oil rigs, but the Texas Zoo provides a refreshing change of scenery.

Located on six acres within Riverside Park, the grounds, which straddle the Guadalupe River, are completely wooded with stands of bamboo and other native Texas plants.

There are several endangered animal species here, but one of the more popular sights is an endangered species of another kind—an old railroad caboose, which houses a nature museum.

Season: Year-round, closed Thanksgiving, Christmas Day, and New Year's Day.

Hours: May through mid-October, daily, 10:00 A.M. to 7:00 P.M.; remainder of year, till 5:00 P.M.

Admission: Adults, under $3; ages 3–12, under $2; seniors, under $2.50; under age 3, free.

The animals: More than 250 animals, representing approximately 100 native Texas species, are exhibited in both indoor and outdoor naturalistic habitats. Highlights include red wolves, black bears, and birds of prey, especially bald eagles.

Entertainment: No regularly scheduled entertainment, but there are demonstrations given during special events.

Extras: In other areas of the park are 4 playgrounds, a nature walk, rose garden, golf course, RV park, and large duck pond where paddleboats are available.

Special events: Easter egg hunt, the Thursday before Easter; Conservation Day, on June 1; ZooFeast, in August; Halloween costume contests and trick-or-treating, on Halloween; Christmas events, in December.

Food service: Several food concessions sell a limited variety of fast foods, snacks, ice cream, and beverages. Picnics are permitted.

Plan to stay: 1 hour.

Directions: Victoria is located about 90 miles north of Corpus Christi. Take I–77 to Stayton Avenue exit. Go west on Stayton for three-quarters of a mile to the park entrance.

Nearby attractions: An old Dutch gristmill is located in Memorial Square, the city's oldest cemetery; McNamara House, built in 1876, features changing historical displays and Victorian-period rooms.

Utah

HOGLE ZOOLOGICAL GARDEN

2600 East Sunnyside Avenue
Salt Lake City, UT (801) 582–1632

What began in 1911 as a cage full of monkeys in downtown Liberty Park is now a fifty-two-acre zoological garden and home to more than 1,000 animals from all over the world, including a bunch of friendly peacocks that love to mingle with the guests.

The zoo was moved to its present location in 1931, after James Hogle donated the land for it. A natural creek that runs through the property has been incorporated into some of the exhibits, helping to create some very realistic habitats.

One must-see is the feline exhibit. There, in a glass display cage, is a large stuffed cat named Shasta. The unique thing about her, besides being stuffed, is the fact that she's a "liger," the first one born in captivity in the United States. Shasta was born here in 1948 and died in 1972. Her father, Huey, an African lion, and her mother, Daisy, a Bengal tiger, apparently grew quite fond of one another while on display in neighboring cages.

Season: Year-round, closed Christmas Day and New Year's Day.

Hours: Opens daily at 9:00 A.M. Closes at 6:00 P.M., June through August; at 5:00 P.M., September through December 20, and late February through May; and at 4:30 P.M., December 21 through late February.

Admission: Adults, under $6; ages 5–14 and seniors, under $4; under age 5 and handicapped, free. Additional fee: train ride, under $1.50 for everyone age 2 and older.

The animals: More than 1,000 animals, more than 300 species, displayed in indoor and outdoor natural habitats. Highlights include a large collection of birds, the Great Apes exhibit, the Giraffe Building, and the Animal Giants complex.

Entertainment: During the summer there are sea lion programs held 5 days a week and an elephant program once a week.

Extras: Discovery Land, includes a 10-minute ride on a miniature steam train, a farm, a children's contact zoo, and the "Knoll and Burrow" playground. The playground equipment resembles things in nature, such as a giant spider web, turtle shell, and oversized egg.

Food service: 6 concessions offer a variety of fast foods, including hamburgers, hot dogs, corn dogs, tacos, ice cream, and beverages. The

Fauna Fun Facts

One colony of prairie dogs in Texas covered 247,000 square miles and was home to about 400 million prairie dogs in the early 1800s. Colonies have become much smaller as humans have taken over the prairies.

Sweet Shop in Discovery Land is known for its funnel cakes and great milk shakes. Picnicking is permitted.

Plan to stay: 3 hours.

Directions: I–15 to 13th South exit. Go east on 13th to Foothill Drive (Route 186). Go north on Foothill to Sunnyside Avenue. Make a right on Sunnyside and travel east for less than a mile. Zoo entrance is on the right, opposite "This Is the Place" monument and Brigham Young's Farm Home and Desert Village.

Nearby attractions: Tracy Aviary, in Liberty Park (see listing); Trolley Square, an indoor shopping mall housed in an old trolley barn; Brigham Young's Farm Home and Desert Village; The Beehive House, Brigham Young's restored official residence; Fort Douglas Military Museum; Utah State Arboretum, on the grounds of the University of Utah; Mormon Tabernacle, where visitors can listen to organ recitals and practice sessions of the famed choir; and Lagoon Park, amusement and water park.

TRACY AVIARY

In Liberty Park
589 East 1300 South
Salt Lake City, UT (801) 596–5034

As its name indicates, the Tracy Aviary houses only birds, hundreds of them, from all around the world. This sixteen-acre aviary occupies a section of Liberty Park in downtown Salt Lake City and contains one of the largest collections of wild birds in the country.

Season: Year-round, closed Christmas Day.

Hours: April through October, daily, 9:00 A.M. to 6:00 P.M. Remainder of the year, till 4:30 P.M.

Admission: Adults, under $3; ages 6–12, under $1.50; seniors, under $2; under age 6, free.

The animals: More than 900 birds, more than 230 species, housed in both indoor and outdoor exhibits that duplicate their natural habitats. Highlights include the Asian Uplands exhibits and a collection of guinea fowl and peacocks that roam the grounds.

Entertainment: On weekends, March through November, there are at least 2 performances put on by some of the 100 trained birds at the aviary.

Extras: In other areas of the park there are conservatories, a swimming pool, a small amusement park, and a museum in the former home of the Chase family, who donated the land for the park.

Special events: Nature Fair, in mid-August, features arts and crafts by local artists on nature themes.

Food service: No food concessions in either the aviary or the park, but picnics are permitted.

Plan to stay: 1 hour.

Directions: I–15/80 (southbound) to 6th South Street exit. Go east on 6th South to 600 East Street. Go south on 600 East to 9th South Street. Entrance will be straight ahead. From I–15 (northbound) to 9th South Street exit. Go east on 9th South. Entrance will be on your right, at 600 East Street intersection.

Nearby attractions: Hogle Zoological Garden (see listing).

Vermont

MORGAN HORSE FARM

Pulp Mill Bridge Road
Weybridge, VT (802) 388–2011

If you like beautiful horses, this is the place to visit. Owned by the University of Vermont (UVM), the farm was established in the late 1800s by Joseph Battelle, founder of the Morgan Horse registry, which makes it one of the oldest horse farms in the country, as well as one of the largest.

Located on rolling green pastures and woods, the farm is home to some sixty-five adult horses year-round, with the population swelling to seventy-five or eighty during foaling season, in late spring. The best time to see the babies is during May and June, when they are still quite young, although a visit in October will enable you to take in the colorful New England fall foliage at the same time.

Open daily to the public, May through October, 9:00 A.M. to 5:00 P.M. Admission: adults, under $3; teens, under $1.50; ages 12 and under, free. Admission includes a slide show and twenty-minute guided tour of the facility.

▼▼▼▼▼▼▼▼▼▼▼▼▼▼▼▼▼▼▼▼▼▼▼▼▼▼▼▼▼▼▼▼▼▼▼

Fauna Fun Facts

An elephant uses its trunk to give itself dust baths and as a snorkel for breathing when it walks under water. The trunk can also hold up to 1½ gallons of water at a time.

Tours are given every hour on the hour, with the last one starting at 4:00 P.M.

Take U.S. Route 7 to Middlebury. When you get into town, follow signs to Route 23. Follow Route 23 North for about 1 mile. Turn right onto Pulp Mill Bridge Road. Entrance to the farm is about 1 mile ahead, on the right.

VERMONT RAPTOR CENTER

Vermont Institute of Natural Science
Church Hill Road
Woodstock, VT (802) 457-2779

A sanctuary for raptors that couldn't survive in the wild due to injuries or handicaps, this is home to more than two dozen species of native northern New England birds of prey. Hawks, owls, eagles, peregrine falcons, ravens, and turkey vultures are among the birds that rely on the center for their survival.

The birds are on display all year, but are less active in the winter. In the spring, the hawks may be seen mating, and if the mating is successful, nesting behavior can be observed throughout the summer.

Open year-round. Hours: 10:00 A.M. to 4:00 P.M., closed Tuesday, May through October. The remainder of the year: 11:00 A.M. to 4:00 P.M., closed Tuesday and Sunday. Admission: adults, under $5; children, under $2.

Located in the south-central part of the state. Take U.S. Route 4 West from Rutland into Woodstock. After going around the village green in the center of town, you will see a stone church. Turn left just before the church and then make an immediate right behind the church, onto Church Hill Road, which leads directly to the Vermont Institute of Natural Science. The Raptor Center is on the Institute grounds.

Virginia

CHINCOTEAGUE NATIONAL WILDLIFE REFUGE

On Assateague Island
Tom Cove Visitors Center
Chincoteague, VA (804) 336–6122

You've seen the wild pony penning on television, now here's your chance to see those ponies up close. This refuge is located on the Virginia side of Assateague Island, a 37-mile-long barrier island paralleling the coasts of Maryland and Virginia.

The Fish and Wildlife Service offers wildlife-oriented interpretive walks and audiovisual programs for visitors. Among the waterfowl you might see along the various trails are the snowy egret, dunlins, American widgeon, black-crowned night heron, and peregrine falcon. On summer weekends, holidays, and during Pony Penning Week, local artists and craftsmen exhibit their work at the Lighthouse Oil Shed.

Waterfowl Week takes place in November when visitors can learn about wintering waterfowl. The pony penning happens usually on the last Wednesday and Thursday of July on the Virginia side only. The wild ponies, descendants of domesticated stock that were grazed on the island in the seventeenth century by planters who sought to avoid mainland taxes and fencing requirements, are rounded up, and many of the foals are sold at auction.

Proceeds from the pony auction help support the Chincoteague Volunteer Fire Company, which owns the Virginia herd. Park officials stress that although the ponies appear docile, they are unpredictable and should not be fed or petted.

For best viewing of the ponies, look for them in Black Duck Marsh from the observation platforms along Beach Road and Woodland Trail. A wildlife loop road passes by various swamp and wooded areas and is open daily, 3:00 P.M. to dusk.

There is a $3 vehicle-use fee that is good for seven days, and visitors should contact the park office ahead of time to inquire about prices on any other activities. The park is open year-round; opening and closing hours varying with the season.

Chincoteague Refuge Center is located on the southern end of Assateague Island, off the Virginia coast. Access to the visitor's center is via Highway 175. Another herd of ponies can be found on the northern part of the island in Maryland, but they are not rounded up as they are here. See Assateague Island State Park listing in the Maryland section of this book.

THE GREAT DISMAL SWAMP

Route 675
Suffolk, VA (804) 986–3705

If you enjoy seeing animals in their natural habitat, there's nothing dismal at all about this 106,000-acre refuge of forested wetland that is home to a large number of plants, birds, mammals, reptiles, and amphibians.

Among the animals you might see throughout the refuge are otters, bats, raccoons, minks, gray and red foxes, gray squirrels, and white-tailed deer. Although rarely seen, black bears and bobcats also inhabit the area. Birding is best from mid-April to mid-May, the peak of the spring migration.

More than 140 miles of unpaved roads provide opportunities for hiking and biking. An interpretive boardwalk trail on Washington Ditch Road is open during daylight hours.

Refuge headquarters are open Monday through Friday, 7:30 A.M. to 4:00 P.M., closed holidays. The refuge itself is open daily from half an hour before sunrise to half an hour after sunset. Admission is free.

The headquarters are located south of Suffolk. Take Route 13 to Route 32, proceed south for 4½ miles, then follow the signs. To get to the Boardwalk Trail, from Suffolk take East Washington Street to White Marsh Road (Route 642) to Washington Ditch. Boat access is adjacent to Route 17, at Dismal Swamp Canal.

MILL MOUNTAIN ZOOLOGICAL PARK

Mill Mountain Park
Roanoke, VA (703) 343–3241

Here you can watch the animals, enjoy the country air, and keep an eye on the city, all at the same time. Located 2,000 feet above Roanoke, in the Blue Ridge Mountains, Mill Mountain must qualify as one of the highest zoos in the country. It certainly has one of the prettiest settings. Although the zoo itself is only about ten acres in size, it's set in the woods, near the Blue Ridge Parkway, so you get the feeling that it's much larger.

Make sure you meet Ruby the tiger, whose arrival at Mill Mountain was the inspiration for the tiger habitat. She had been seized by the local game warden because she was being held illegally. Other zoos weren't interested in her for their breeding programs, so she was brought to Mill Mountain.

The zoo really shines at night, literally. A huge electric star is lit up and can be seen from anywhere in Roanoke.

Season: Year-round, holidays too.

Hours: Opens at 10:00 A.M. daily. Closes at 6:00 P.M., Memorial Day through Labor Day, 4:30 P.M. the remainder of the year.

Admission: Adults, under $5; ages 3–12, under $4; under age 3, free. Additional fee: train ride, under $1.50.

The animals: More than 40 species of animals from North America, South America, Asia, and Australia are displayed in outdoor settings, each in its own enclosure. Highlights include a Siberian tiger, red panda, bald eagle, and reptiles.

Entertainment: On summer weekends, there is a rotating schedule of animal demonstration programs.

Extras: Small train takes visitors for rides around the entire zoo; small animal contact area.

Special events: Celebration of Cats, in May; Conservation Festival, in June; Mother's Day and Father's Day, special admissions; Breakfast with the Animals, visitors have breakfast while watching the animals eat.

Food service: Concession stand serves a selection of fast foods, snacks, and beverages. Picnics are permitted.

Plan to stay: 1 hour for the zoo, longer if you enjoy breathtaking panoramic views.

Directions: Take I–81 to exit 42 and pick up Route 581 South. Get off Route 581 at exit 6. At the first light, turn right onto Elm Avenue. Make a left at the second light, onto Jefferson Avenue. Follow Jefferson to the fourth light, then turn left on Walnut Avenue. Walnut becomes the Blue Ridge Parkway spur. Take the first right off the spur and follow signs to the zoo. Park at the bottom of the hill and walk up the path.

Nearby attractions: Virginia Museum of Transportation; Mill Mountain Theater; Science Museum of Western Virginia.

VIRGINIA ZOOLOGICAL PARK

350 Granby Street
Norfolk, VA (804) 441–2706 (recording); (804) 441–2374

Brightly colored, well-manicured flower beds and lawns, free-roaming peacocks, and the amusing antics of the primates, who live near the zoo's entrance all help make your initial impression of this facility a favorable one. Set on fifty-five acres in Lafayette Park and bordering the Lafayette River, this zoo is a good place to get away from it all.

You can get a good view of the river and the surroundings when you're near the Conservatory and duck pond.

Season: Year-round, closed Christmas Day and New Year's Day.

Hours: Daily, 10:00 A.M. to 5:00 P.M.

Admission: Adults, under $3; ages 2–11 and over 61, under $2; under age 2, free. On Sundays and Mondays, between 4:00 and 5:00 P.M., everyone gets in free.

The animals: More than 300 animals, more than 100 species, displayed in indoor and outdoor natural habitats. Highlights include African elephants, tapirs, and lemurs.

Entertainment: Elephant demonstrations, daily between Memorial Day and Labor Day, and on weekends the rest of the year. Sea lion demonstrations twice a day, year-round.

Extras: Barnyard petting zoo. Next door, in Lafayette Park, are athletic fields, a playground, and picnic facilities.

Special events: Conservation Day, in April; Zoo-La-La, first Saturday evening after Labor Day, a formal event for adults; Halloween costume parade, in October; Thanksgiving charity collection of canned goods; Santa Claus at the Zoo, in December.

Fauna Fun Facts

Ostriches don't really bury their head in the sand. They do, however, stretch their heads down along their bodies in defense.

Food service: 1 concession stand serves a variety of grilled items, candy, ice cream, sodas, and a delicious vegetable-filled pita. Picnics are permitted.

Plan to stay: 1 hour.

Directions: Take I–64 East and get off at the Granby Street exit. Go straight south on Granby for 2 miles. Turn left at zoo entrance, which is on 32nd Street.

Nearby attractions: Norfolk Naval Station tours, which include the Naval Air Station, submarine piers, and waterfront area; Portsmouth Naval Shipyard Museum; tours of the harbor; St. Paul's Church, built in 1739, which has had a British cannonball embedded in a wall since 1776; Norfolk Botanical Gardens.

Washington

NORTHWEST TREK WILDLIFE PARK

11610 Trek Drive
Eatonville, WA (206) 847–1901

Only flora and fauna native to the Pacific Northwest can be found on the 600 acres of this park, located at the foot of Mount Rainier, a dormant volcano and the highest peak of the Cascade Mountain Range.

The entire park is nestled under a canopy of fir and alder trees, and rough-hewn timber buildings enhance the setting.

Since the policy of the park is to exhibit animals in settings that are as close to nature as possible, you won't find any trained sea lions or dancing bears here.

Season: Year-round, holidays too.

Hours: Mid-February through October, daily, 9:30 A.M. to 6:30 P.M.; remainder of the year, 10:00 A.M. to 3:30 P.M., Fridays, Saturdays, and Sundays only.

Admission: Adults, under $8; ages 5–17, under $6; ages 3–4, under $3.50; seniors, under $7; under age 3, free.

The animals: More than 370 animals, more than 75 species, all native to the area, running free in native habitats. Exhibit areas include Cat Country, forest wetlands, and the grizzly and black bear complex.

Entertainment: Orientation slide show; naturalist programs in individual exhibit areas from time to time.

Extras: 1-hour tram ride with guided tour; Cheney Discovery Center, with touch tank, beehive, fish tank, and butterfly atrium; nature trails.

Food service: Fir Bough Restaurant features hot meals and light snacks. Picnics are permitted.

Plan to stay: 3 hours.

Directions: Located 35 miles southeast of Tacoma. Take I–5 to exit 142B (State Route 161). Take 161 southbound. After passing through town of Puyallup, you'll go another 17 miles south to the park's entrance, on left side of road.

Nearby attractions: Mount Rainier National Park.

OLYMPIC GAME FARM

Ward Road
Sequim, WA (206) 683–4295

These star-studded ninety acres offer more than your basic camera-shy animals—they offer animals who have been on television and in movies. While many of the resident creatures haven't been on the silver screen, there's a moviemaking feel to the entire complex. A driving tour of the facilities is available year-round, and a guided walking tour is available during summer months.

There are fifty-one species of animals on the farm, including wolverines, lions, tigers, bears, wolves, coyotes, and bobcats. One of the favorite family stopping-off points on the drive-through is the prairie dog town. Other animals one might expect to see are bison, rhinos, deer, zebras, bears, elk, llamas, most of which are free-roaming and will come up to the car.

On the walk-through tour, you'll have the opportunity to visit Bozo the bear, the star of the *Grizzly Adams* television series, and take in the petting area with goats, sheep, turkey, ducks, and other small farm animals.

There are also movie sets, an aquarium, and a studio-barn. You may see trainers working with various animals preparing for roles in upcoming movies or television shows.

Hours: Memorial Day through Labor Day, daily, 8:00 A.M. to 6:00 or 7:00 P.M.; the rest of the year, 9:00 A.M. to 3:30 P.M. Admission for either the walk-through or the drive-through: adults, under $6; ages 5–12 and seniors, under $5. During the summer, visitors have the option of taking both tours for an additional $2.

Take the Sequim exit off Highway 101, go south on Dunge Way to the first stop light, take a right on Ward Road, and follow the signs.

POINT DEFIANCE ZOO AND AQUARIUM

5400 North Pearl Street
Tacoma, WA (206) 591-5337

High on a hill, at the northernmost tip of Tacoma, sits Point Defiance Park, where visitors can take in the spectacular views of Puget Sound to the north, and Mount Rainier to the southeast. A small portion of the 700-acre park is occupied by the zoo and aquarium, which, most appropriately, have focused their collections on the Pacific Rim area.

If you can tear yourself away from the view long enough, there are a lot of other things to see while you're here, including walruses, beluga whales, arctic foxes, and Bengal tigers.

Season: Year-round, closed Thanksgiving and Christmas Day.

Hours: Memorial Day through Labor Day, daily, 10:00 A.M. to 7:00 P.M.; the rest of the year, 10:00 A.M. to 4:00 P.M.

Admission: Adults, under $8; seniors, 62 and older, under $7; ages 5–17, under $6; ages 3–4, under $4; under age 3, free. Additional fee: elephant rides, under $3.

The animals: More than 4,500 animals, more than 300 species, all displayed in naturalistic habitats or aquariums. Exhibits are divided into marine mammal, tundra, Southeast Asia, North Pacific, and South Pacific habitats.

Entertainment: During the summer there are bird shows twice daily (except Monday); marine mammal shows from 11:00 A.M. to 4:00 P.M.; daily unscheduled "talk and feed" demonstrations; and impromptu visits from some of the farm animals who are brought out among the visitors by their keepers.

Extras: Elephant rides in the summer; a children's zoo, which includes a petting farm and World of Adaptation exhibit. In other areas of the park are nature trails; a 5-mile drive-through road; Never Never Land, which depicts scenes from children's literature; rental boats and fishing gear; and Fort Nisqually, a replica of the first outpost of the Hudson Bay Company back in fur-trading days.

Special events: Various events, including summer concerts for both children and adults.

Food service: Year-round, the Chicken Coop Cafe serves a variety of fast foods, snacks, ice cream, and beverages. During the summer, the same food is available at the Plaza Cafe and at concession stands throughout the zoo.

Plan to stay: 2 hours for the zoo, more for the view.

Directions: Take I–5 to exit 132 (Highway 16). Take Highway 16 West to the 6th Avenue exit. At the end of the ramp, turn left on 6th Avenue and then make an immediate right onto Pearl Street. Follow Pearl straight into the park.

Nearby attractions: Fort Lewis Military Museum; Fireman's Park, containing a 105-foot-high totem pole carved from a single cedar tree by Alaskan Indians; boat tours of the Tacoma waterfront; McCormick Steamship Dock, a renovated warehouse containing shops, galleries, and boutiques; and the Tacoma Children's Museum, containing a model of a 13th-century English town.

SEATTLE AQUARIUM

Pier 59
Waterfront Park
Seattle, WA (206) 386–4320

Everywhere you look around here, there's water. Located on a pier, the aquarium building is surrounded by outdoor walkways that provide up-close and often spectacular views of Puget Sound.

In one of the exhibits, the Underwater Dome, you'll find yourself completely surrounded by more than 1000 fish, representing 34 different species, and if you're here during feeding time, you'll see the divers working with the specimens.

On the doorstep of one of the richest and most diverse aquatic habitats around, the facility features a wide collection of local fish and marine life. Don't miss the Salmon and People exhibit, where you'll travel along a working salmon ladder, leading to a hatchery where thousands of fish are released yearly.

Season: Year round, holidays too.

Hours: Opens 10:00 A.M., daily. Closes at 7:00 P.M., Memorial Day through Labor Day; at 5:00 P.M. the rest of the year.

Admission: Adults, under $7; ages 6–18, and seniors, under $4; ages 3–5, under $1; ages 2 and under, free.

The animals: More than 15,500 animals, more than 366 species, housed in indoor and outdoor exhibits. Top exhibits include: the Underwater Dome; four Northwest shoreline habitats (sandy beach, cobble beach, freshwater marsh, and rocky cliff); Pacific coral reef, simulated area with blacktip sharks; and Japanese fish.

Entertainment: Feeding times posted for diving birds, Underwater Dome fish, otters and harbor seals, and fur seals.

Extras: Touch tank with sea stars and featherduster worms, among other specimens; Omnidome Theater, adjacent to the aquarium, on the same pier.

Food service: None in the facility. The Steamers Restaurant is adjacent to aquarium, on the same pier.

Plan to stay: 3 hours.

Directions: In the downtown area, along Alaskan Way. Park in a garage downtown, walk down the Pike Street Hillclimb from Pike Place Market, and aquarium is across the street. The trolley runs along Alaskan Way from Pier 70 to the Pioneer Square area. Hop aboard and get off at Pier 59.

Nearby attractions: Pacific Science Center; tour of Underground Seattle; Kingdome tours; the Space Needle and adjacent Fun Forest amusement park; and the Museum of History and Industry.

Fauna Fun Facts

Maned wolves are often called "a fox on stilts."

WOODLAND PARK ZOOLOGICAL GARDENS

5500 Phinney Avenue North
Seattle, WA (206) 684–4800

If you like a wide variety of things to choose from, this place ought to make you happy. Plan to spend quite a bit of time here, and make sure you bring your walking shoes. The paths are somewhat flat and easy to walk, but the exhibits are spread out over ninety acres.

During the warmer months you can see elephant logging demonstrations, hear animal tales by a storyteller, and picnic while listening to concerts in the North Meadow.

Opened in 1904, this facility is currently updating its exhibit areas in accordance with a master plan that should be three-quarters complete by the end of 1997.

Season: Year-round, holidays too.

Hours: Mid-March through mid-October, daily, 9:30 A.M. to 6:00 P.M.; the remainder of the year, 9:30 A.M. to 4:00 P.M.

Admission: Adults, under $6; ages 6–17, seniors and handicapped, under $4; under age 6, free. Additional fees: parking, $1 for 4 hours; pony rides, under $2.

The animals: More than 2,400 animals, more than 250 species, displayed in both indoor and outdoor exhibits divided according to bioclimatic zones. Outstanding exhibits include the African Savannah, Tropical Asia, Australasia, Desert, Steppe, Temperate Forest, Northern Trail, and the new Tropical Rain Forest, in a geodesic dome.

Entertainment: Most of the shows and demonstrations take place during the warmer months and on a changing time schedule. Included are raptor shows, elephant logging demonstrations, elephant baths, animal tales by a storyteller, concerts in the North Meadow in July and August, as well as zoo tours and Discovery Carts operated by zoo docents.

Extras: Discovery Room educational center; Family Farm contact center, open Tuesdays through Sundays in the summer; extensive landscaping.

Special events: Endangered Species Month events, in March; Conservation Day activities, June 1; Wildlife Weekend, in August, featuring foods and dance groups from areas of the world represented by the animals in the zoo.

Food service: There are several food concessions on the grounds, offering standard fast-food fare, snacks, ice cream, frozen yogurt, and beverages. Picnicking is encouraged by staff members, who say the zoo is "picnic friendly."

Plan to stay: 5 hours.

Directions: From downtown Seattle, take I–5 North to Northeast 50th Street. Turn left and go west for 1.3 miles to North 50th Street and Fremont. South entrance to the zoo is on the immediate right.

Nearby attractions: Fun Forest amusement park; University of Washington Arboretum and Japanese Garden; Space Needle, a 605-foot-high landmark from the 1962 World's Fair offers spectacular views of the city, Puget Sound, and the Cascade and Olympic Mountains; Rainier Brewing Company offers free tours; Seattle Harbor tours; Seattle Aquarium; Nordic Heritage Museum; Omnidome Film Experience, featuring films on the eruption of Mount St. Helena and other subjects of natural history.

West Virginia

OGLEBAY'S GOOD CHILDREN'S ZOO
Oglebay Park
Wheeling, WV (304) 242–3000

Despite what the name would have you believe, all children, good and bad, are welcome at this zoo, which was built in memory of Philip Mayer Good by his parents after he died of leukemia at the age of 7.

You won't find any exotic animals, like lions and tigers, here because the focus is strictly on animals native to North America. You also won't find another facility quite like this one, the only accredited zoo in the state.

Originally a trailside facility in the wooded hills of Oglebay Park, it has come into its own, adding a planetarium/theater, model train layout, and miniature train ride around the grounds.

Season: Year-round, holidays too.

Hours: Memorial Day through Labor Day, weekdays, 10:00 A.M. to 6:00 P.M.; weekends till 7:00 P.M. September through May, daily, 11:00 A.M. to 5:00

P.M. During the last 11 days of October, the zoo is also open from 6:00 to 9:00 P.M. for Halloween festivities.

Admission: Adults, under $6; ages 2–17 and seniors, under $5; under age 2, free. There are additional charges for some special events. Additional fees: train ride, under $1.50; some shows in the planetarium also require an additional charge.

The animals: More than 200 animals, nearly 75 species, all from North America, are displayed in natural habitats. Highlights include the waterfowl exhibit, the river otter display, and the native aquarium.

Entertainment: Keeper Features on occasional weekends; animal feedings; concerts during warm weather; star shows, laser displays, and movies in the planetarium.

Extras: Train Ride around zoo grounds; 11,000-square-foot O-gauge model train layout; children's zoo, with domestic farmyard contact area.

Special events: Easter event, in the spring; Boo at the Zoo, the last week in October; Festival of Lights, held in the park and zoo from mid-November to early February.

Food service: A handful of refreshment stands offer a variety of fast foods, snacks, ice cream, and beverages. Picnics are not allowed in the zoo, but are permitted in the park.

Plan to stay: 3 hours.

Directions: I–70 to Oglebay Park exit. Travel north on Route 88 for 2½ miles. Park entrance will be on the right.

Nearby attractions: In other areas of the 1,500-acre Oglebay Park you will find gardens, greenhouses, golf, miniature golf, tennis, skiing, and tobogganing, and the Mansion Museum. In Wheeling there are the West Virginia Independence Hall Museum; cruises on the Ohio River; greyhound racing at Wheeling Downs; and the 900-foot-long Wheeling Suspension Bridge.

WEST VIRGINIA STATE WILDLIFE CENTER

State Route 20
French Creek, WV (304) 924–6211

Enjoy the beautiful Appalachian hardwood forest as you walk down a wooded 1¼-mile trail along which you can observe more than twenty-five different species of native West Virginia wildlife. Among the animals on display here are bears, elk, bison, timber wolves, white-tailed deer, wild turkeys, bobcats, and mountain lions.

Open every day of the year, the center's hours are 9:00 A.M. until sunset, weather permitting. Admission is less than $3 for adults, and less than $2 for children under age 15.

Located near the center of the state. Take I–79 to State Route 33. Travel east on Route 33 into the town of Buckhannon. In the center of town, make a right onto State Route 20/4. Go south on Route 20 for about 12 miles, to the entrance. Signs are prominently displayed on all major roads.

Wisconsin

HENRY VILAS ZOO

702 South Randall Avenue
Madison, WI (608) 266–4732

Scenic Lake Wingra and an adjoining lagoon form the backdrop to this twenty-eight-acre zoo that dates back to 1911. A pleasant eclectic blend of architecture and a lot of big old trees add to its charm and make a fitting memorial to the man for whom it is named.

When Henry Vilas died shortly after the turn of the century, he was only in his twenties, but his parents wanted his memory to live on. This they accomplished through their donation of about seventy-six acres to the city with the provision that a public park and zoo be built there in Henry's name. They further stipulated that there would never be an admission charge.

Season: Year-round, holidays too.

Hours: May through August, daily, 9:30 A.M. to 8:00 P.M.; September through

April, till 4:45 P.M. On New Year's Day, Good Friday, Thanksgiving and the day after, Christmas Eve, Christmas Day, and New Year's Eve, the zoo opens at the regular time but closes at noon.

Admission: Free.

The animals: More than 600 animals, more than 180 species, in indoor and outdoor exhibits. Highlights include the felines, birds, bears, African animals, harbor seals, and the Discovery Center/Herpetarium.

Entertainment: No regularly scheduled entertainment, but from time to time some of the zoo volunteers give talks on the animals in the children's zoo.

Extras: Free camel rides, most Sundays in June, July, and August, from 10:30 A.M. to noon; Discovery Center, with interactive exhibits; and children's zoo. In other areas of the park are athletic fields, a playground, and a bathing beach.

Food service: 2 main concessions and 2 portable ones are open from April to October. Menu includes hot dogs, hamburgers, fries, soda pop, cotton candy, ice cream, and bratwurst, which is quite popular in this part of the country. Picnics are also permitted.

Plan to stay: 1 hour.

Directions: I–90/94 to Highway 12/18 westbound. Get off Highway 12/18 at Park Street and turn right. Travel north on Park to Drake Street. Make a left on Drake. After the second stop sign, take the road that angles off to the left. It goes right into the parking area.

Nearby attractions: State Capitol, built in 1917, has free tours and a museum that illustrates Indian and pioneer life; Madison Children's Museum, with hands-on exhibits. The Washburn Observatory is open on certain clear nights and offers visitors free looks at the stars through a 15-inch telescope.

INTERNATIONAL CRANE FOUNDATION

E-11376 Shady Lane Road
Baraboo, WI (608) 356–9462

Cranes are the royalty here, and you'll find every species that exists on earth.

Just as its name indicates, the foundation is a worldwide organization dedicated to the preservation and propagation of cranes, two species of which are currently in danger of extinction. Through captive breeding, re-search, education, and habitat restoration and protection, the foundation aims to reintroduce all species to their natural surroundings.

There's a lot of walking here, but there's also a lot to see and learn. Dress comfortably and enjoy your visit.

Season: May through October.

Hours: Daily, 9:00 A.M. to 5:00 P.M. On Thursdays in July and August, till 8:30 P.M.

Admission: Adults, under $6, with discounts for seniors and children.

The animals: Approximately 145 cranes, of 15 different species; 13 of the species are in separate pens adjacent to the main building, while the re-maining 2, which are endangered, live in the African savanna habitat that has been created on the grounds. There is also a restored prairie habitat.

Entertainment: No entertainment per se, but there are guided tours that include a slide show, viewing of the bird runs and chick yard, an exhibit room, and a videotape about whooping cranes. Amusement is also pro-vided by the chicks, who manage to keep their keepers on the run.

Food service: No food concessions here, but picnicking is encouraged.

Plan to stay: 2 hours.

Directions: Located northwest of Madison. Take I–90/94 to exit 92 (U.S. Route 12). Go south on Route 12 for 1½ miles to Shady Lane Road. Turn left on Shady Lane and travel east for about a mile to the entrance.

Nearby attractions: Circus World Museum, the original winter quarters of the Ringling Brothers Circus. During the summer the museum offers live performances, magic shows, daily parades, and the world's largest col-lection of circus wagons. Also, there are a carousel museum and the House on the Rock, an architectural oddity.

JIM PECK'S WILDLIFE PARK AND NATURE CENTER

Highway 70 West
Minocqua, WI (715) 356–5588

If you like to meet and greet wildlife up close, here's a great place to do it. There are more than 7,000 animals here, including timber wolves, otter, bear, coyote, cougar, bobcat, badger, fox, beaver, buffalo, exotic birds, and birds of prey.

Bird and animal programs are held daily during the summer months, and the large gift shop, which specializes in environmental and nature items, is a great place to do some early Christmas shopping for the animal lover in your family. For a bit of different fun, you can rent small electric boats and tour the lake on your own.

A deer herd roams freely in the park, and there is a nursery area with baby animals where guests can have a hands-on adventure with various species, even porcupines.

Hours: May through mid-October, 9:00 A.M. to 5:00 P.M., daily. Admission: adults, under $6; ages 12 and under, under $4.

The park and nature center are located 2 miles west of Minocqua, on Highway 70.

MILWAUKEE COUNTY ZOOLOGICAL GARDENS

10001 West Bluemound Road
Milwaukee, WI (414) 771–3040

In keeping with its location in "America's Dairyland," this zoo has an elaborate dairy complex, where visitors can sample and purchase a variety of products made from the milk of the six varieties of dairy cattle that reside here. But the collection goes way beyond cows, with a total of more than 3,000 animals in residence.

The zoo originally opened in 1892 in downtown Washington Park, but was relocated to West Bluemound Road in the 1950s so it would have room to grow.

Season: Year-round, holidays too.

Hours: Memorial Day through Labor Day, 9:00 A.M. to 5:00 P.M., closing an hour later on Sundays and Holidays. The rest of the year, 9:00 A.M. to 4:30 P.M., daily.

Admission: April through October: adults, under $8; ages 3–12, under $6; seniors, under $7; under age 3, free. Rates drop by about $2 the rest of the year. Additional fees: parking, under $5 per car, year-round; train, under $2; Zoomobile, under $3 for adults, under $2 for ages 3–12; sea lion show, under $2.

The animals: More than 3,000 animals, more than 300 species, in outdoor exhibits grouped according to native continent. Highlights include a large walk-through tropical aviary; Aquarium/Reptile House, which contains a 65,000-gallon aquarium known as "Lake Wisconsin"; the Primate Building, or "Monkey House," containing one of the few families of pygmy chimpanzees in a U.S. zoo.

Entertainment: From May to October, Surfing Safari Sea Lion Show, with 4 performances daily by the show's stars, Fernando, Sport, and Ellie; Raptor Bird Show, featuring demonstrations by birds of prey; daily year-round slide and video presentations about the zoo and animal-related topics; "Animals in Action" talks are given at different times throughout the day, from Memorial Day to Labor Day, at the varying exhibit areas.

Extras: From May to October, weather permitting, the Zoofari Express offers train rides around the southern portion of the zoo; and the Zoomobile tram will take visitors for a 30-minute guided tour of the entire exhibit area. There are also camel, elephant, and pony rides available during the nicer weather.

Special events: From May through December, there is a special event going on at least 2 weekends each month. Included are Mother's Day and the Kite Fly-In, in May; Conservation/Earth Day and Father's Day, in June; Teddy Bear Day and the Wednesday Night Concerts, in July; Food Festival, in August; Senior Day and Harvest Jubilee, in September; Halloween events, in October; Behind-the-Scenes Tours and a Thanksgiving walk/run, in November; and a variety of Christmas events in December.

Food service: The Flamingo Cafe offers a variety of fast foods, snacks, and beverages on a year-round basis. During the warmer weather the Sea Lion Snack Shop, Woodland Retreat, Elk Stand, Lakeview Place, Snack and Cookie Shop, and Ice Cream Sundae Shop, located throughout the zoo, are also open for a quick bite. Picnics are permitted.

Fauna Fun Facts

An elephant is pregnant for about twenty-two months and gives birth to a 180–250–pound infant.

Plan to stay: 5 hours.

Directions: I–94 to I–894 (Zoo Freeway) northbound. Get off at Blue-mound Road exit. At the end of the exit ramp, go right on North 85th Street to Bluemound Road. Turn right on Bluemound and follow signs less than a mile to zoo entrance, on the left.

Nearby attractions: Mitchell Park features a modern horticultural conserva-tory and sunken gardens in 3 7-story glass domes; Pabst Mansion, for-mer home of Pabst Brewing Company founder; Miller and Pabst Brewing Companies both offer walking tours of their facilities.

RACINE ZOOLOGICAL GARDEN
2131 North Main Street
Racine, WI (414) 636–9189

If it's true that the more a zoo has to offer, the more fun it is to visit, then this place is sure to please. You'll want to take a little time to stroll around and take in the view, which is impressive virtually any time of the year, and adds to the tranquillity of the zoo's parklike setting. The facility itself, which premiered in 1925, is a happy mixture of old and new buildings, with a lot of mature trees and shrubs.

Although it's not far from downtown Racine, the zoo is surrounded by the lake, a park, and a residential neighborhood. On the west side of the grounds is a pond with a fountain. In the winter, the fountain is decorated with holiday lights and ice skating is permitted .

Season: Year-round, holidays too.

Hours: May through September, daily, 9:00 A.M. to 6:00 P.M. Remainder of the year, 9:00 A.M. to 4:30 P.M., except for Christmas Day, when gates close at noon.

Admission: Free. Additional fee: elephant rides (in summer only): adults, under $3.50; children, under $2.50.

The animals: More than 300 animals, more than 100 species, displayed in naturalistic habitats and enclosed areas. Highlights include the big cat and primate exhibits in the main buildings; a rare white Bengal tiger; South American exhibit; and bird exhibit.

Entertainment: No regularly scheduled shows, but on summer weekends and during special events, keepers talk about animals in the farm area.

Extras: Elephant rides in the summer; children's zoo, with a family farm and prairie dog exhibit, which contains an underground tunnel for children to crawl through and pop up in a plastic bubble in the middle of the exhibit.

Special events: Zoofari Day, in June, with entertainment and educational activities; Zoo Debut, a formal affair, for adults, in June; Summer Jazz Concerts; Halloween Hullabaloo; and a light display at Christmas. Some of the events require an extra charge.

Food service: 1 concession stand is open from April to October, offering fast foods, snacks, ice cream, and beverages. Picnics are permitted all year round.

Plan to stay: 1 hour.

Directions: I–94 to Highway 20 East. Follow Highway 20 to the downtown area. Make a left onto Main Street; go north on Main for about 1½ miles. Zoo will be on the right.

Nearby attractions: Johnson Wax main administration building, offering free tours, exhibits, and films; and Charles A. Wustum Museum of Fine Arts.

Wyoming

NATIONAL ELK REFUGE
Elk Refuge Road
Jackson, WY (307) 733–8084

More than 7,500 elk spend their winters on this 24,700-acre refuge, making it one of the largest gatherings of that beast in North America. Since the elk migrate northward in the spring, to the Grand Teton and Yellowstone parks, as well as to the Bridger-Teton National Forest, the best time to visit is between November and April.

While the refuge is open all year, the visitor's center and guided sleigh ride are in operation only from late December through March. The sleigh ride is a forty-minute trip through the refuge to the viewing area, and sleds operate continuously each day between 10:00 A.M. and 4:00 P.M. Displays and slide shows can be seen at the visitor's center during the same hours.

There is no charge to enter the refuge, but the sleigh ride costs under $10 for adults and under $5 for ages 6–12. Ages 5 and under ride free. No reservations are required, but make sure you dress warmly; and bring your camera.

Located near the western border of the state. Take U.S. 187 North into Jackson, where you'll pick up E. Broadway. At the end of E. Broadway make a left onto Elk Refuge Road. Follow signs for about 4 miles to the visitor's center.

CANADA

Canada, like the United States, has a varied selection of zoos, aquariums, and wildlife attractions. You'll find large municipal zoos and aquariums; you'll find wildlife safari parks; and you'll find some neat little privately owned zoological parks. Each has its own personality and its own following.

Due to its more northerly location, you'll find more seasonal animal facilities in Canada than in the United States, and those that are open year-round usually have fewer activities scheduled and fewer exhibits open during the winter.

Following is a sampling of Where the Animals Are in Canada, by province. It's far from a complete listing of facilities, but it will give you a good idea of what the country has to offer.

All references to fees, by the way, are in Canadian dollars.

Alberta

BROOKS PHEASANT HATCHERY

Trans-Canada Highway
Brooks, AB (403) 362–4122

A division of the Alberta Fish and Wildlife Agency, this facility hatches, raises, and releases nearly 100,000 ring-necked pheasants each year. Although pheasants do breed in the wild, changes in farming techniques, and the encroaching population, make a hatchery necessary to keep the numbers of the species up.

During the summer here you'll see pen after pen of young pheasants and wild turkeys. You can't touch or walk among the animals because they are being raised to be as wild as possible. Inside there is a fifteen-minute film that shows how the entire operation works. There are also displays of stuffed pheasants and egg collections.

Open year-round, Monday through Friday, 9:00 A.M. to 4:00 P.M. No charge. Located 6 miles east of Brooks on the Trans-Canada Highway (Highway 1). Look for signs: it's a small gravel road south off the highway. The hatchery is at the end of that road.

CALGARY ZOO, BOTANICAL GARDEN AND PREHISTORIC PARK

1300 Zoo Road
Calgary, AB (403) 232-9300

You get three for the price of one here. The zoo features over 1,400 animals in natural habitats; a botanical garden setting that comes alive each spring when 50,000 tulips bloom; and the 6½-acre prehistoric park presents twenty-eight life-size dinosaur re-creations and highlights of western Canada as it may have appeared when those critters reigned supreme.

Located on St. Georges Island in the middle of the Bow River, the 285-acre complex houses more than 300 species of animals from around the world. Some of the notable exhibits include the new Canadian Wilds, North America, Australia, the Polar Bear complex, a nocturnal facility, and a Eurasia compound. Each of the areas have been planted with native plants and trees, plus there are several formal gardens throughout the grounds, including an arid garden, a butterfly garden, and a tropical rain forest.

During the summer months, a series of interpretive talks and interactive presentations occur throughout the day; there's also an elephant encounter where you can come face-to-trunk with an elephant. There are four food-service locations and several picnic sites.

Open daily, year round, 9:00 A.M., to 4:00 P.M. in winter, till 6:30 P.M. in summer. Admission: adults, under $8; ages 2–15, and seniors, under $5.

Less than a five-minute drive from downtown. Take Memorial Drive eastbound and exit when you see the signs for zoo parking.

VALLEY ZOO

Buena Vista Road and 134th Street
Edmonton, AB (403) 496–6911

On the banks of the North Saskatchewan River, on the city's west end, this eighty-five-acre, municipally owned facility is part of the city's "Ribbon of Green," a series of parks that run the length of the city along the river.

Originally founded as a children's zoo, the facility has kept that emphasis while growing into a family park. It now houses more than 450 animals and approximately 125 species.

Two of the most popular exhibits are the sea lions and the elephants. Both are the subjects of training demonstrations several times each day. Other features here include: Siberian tigers, wolves, the endangered swift fox, a large indigenous collection of birds of prey, and a reptile collection.

Open daily, May through September, 10:00 A.M. to 6:00 P.M.; October through April, weekends only, noon to 4:00 P.M. Admission: adults, under $5; ages 3–12, under $3; under 3, free. A family pass, for four or more, costs $14.50. Winter admission is about half the regular price, and food service is closed during the winter.

To get here, take the 149th Street exit off the Whitemud Freeway. Get on 87th Avenue, which connects to Buena Vista. Follow signs to the zoo.

British Columbia

OKANAGAN GAME FARM

Highway 97
Penticton, BC (604) 497–5405

Deep inside the tourist area of Okanagan Valley, this facility rests on 550 acres, and has 900 animals representing 110 species.

The animals are located along a 3½-mile loop roadway within the facility, and you can drive around or walk around to see them. Unlike a lot of drive-through's, however, the animals here are behind fencing, separating them from the public.

There are numerous pull-off's where you can park and walk up to the exhibits, if you so desire, but you can also get a good look at the offerings

▼▼▼▼▼▼▼▼▼▼▼▼▼▼▼▼▼▼▼▼▼▼▼▼▼▼▼▼▼▼▼▼

Fauna Fun Facts

Spectacled bears get their name from the pattern around their eyes
that resembles a pair of tortoise-shell eyeglass frames.

from inside your car. Several small picnic areas are located along the loop.

Among the animals you'll see are giraffes, rhinos, tigers, lions, cougars, grizzlies, Himalayan and black bears, and three kinds of zebras. There are also numerous varieties of sheep, including the California big horn, which lives here in a natural area, complete with natural rock bluffs and pine trees.

In the central area, you'll find a nice playground for the kids, rest rooms, fast-food concessions, and a petting zoo.

Open year-round, daily, from 8:00 A.M. to dusk. The food and gift shops are open March through October only. Admission: adults, under $9; ages 5–15, under $7; 4 and under, free.

Located 5 miles south of Penticton on the west side of Highway 97. (NOTE: You're right in the middle of fruit-growing country here, so don't forget to load up before heading home.)

VANCOUVER GAME FARM

5048 264th Street
Aldergrove, BC (604) 856–6825

This preserve was a drive-through park until the summer of 1992; now you have to walk the 2-mile loop, or take the train ride, to see the animals. You can also do it by bicycle, if you wish. Located on 120 acres of rolling farmland, more than 750 animals, representing 115 species, live here.

The animals are living in large, fenced-in fields and paddocks until the owners complete the shift to zoological standards for natural habitats. There's a large picnic area, as well as a fast-food restaurant here. A jungle-theme playground has been created, and a colorful carousel, with exotic animals to ride instead of horses, was added in late 1992.

Open daily, year-round, 8:00 A.M. to dusk. Admission: adults, under $9; ages 5–15, under $7; and under 5, free. Located forty-five minutes east of Vancouver just 6 miles north of the U.S. border. Take exit 73, (264th

Street/Highway 13) off the Trans-Continental Highway. Go south 2,000 yards, to the entrance.

VANCOUVER PUBLIC AQUARIUM

In Stanley Park
West Georgia Avenue
Vancouver, BC (604) 682–1118

Nestled among the trees of world-famous Stanley Park, a few hundred yards from the Burrard Inlet, this facility holds the distinction of being the first aquarium accredited by the AAZPA, back in 1975. Today it is home to more than 8,000 creatures, representing nearly 600 species.

To provide a better understanding of the relationship between the flora, the fauna, and the overall environment, the facility is arranged in five separate galleries, each gallery being an exact replica of the habitat being represented.

The Amazon features poisonous frogs, piranhas, electric eels, tropical plants, and a large variety of free-flying tropical birds. The Tropical Gallery features marine and freshwater species from around the world, including Mexico, Florida, Australia, and the Red Sea. The Hall of the Fishes offers forty-three ecological displays depicting habitats from the exposed west coast of Vancouver Island, the Strait of Juan de Fuca, and the Gulf Islands.

The Arctic Canada Gallery is designed to increase your awareness of the marine environment of Canada's north. Beluga whales and a variety of arctic fish are on display. The Killer Whale Gallery is the largest of the five and houses two whales in a habitat that includes bays, beaches, rubbing areas, moving water, and water sounds. Ponds and tidal pools have also been incorporated into the area.

There are underwater viewing areas for the Beluga and killer whales, as well as surface viewing platforms. You will also find, among the galleries, specific exhibits featuring sugar seals and sea otters.

Open 365 days a year, doors open daily at 10:00 A.M. During July and August, closing time is 8:00 P.M., the rest of the year, 5:30 P.M. Admission: adults, under $10; ages 13–18 and seniors, under $8; ages 5–12, under $6; under 5, free. A family rate, which covers a maximum of two adults and 3 nonadults, is available for under $24.

Located on the 1,000-acre Stanley Park peninsula, five minutes from downtown Vancouver. West Georgia Avenue goes directly through the park. Follow the signs.

Manitoba

ASSINIBOINE PARK ZOO

2355 Corydon Avenue
Winnipeg, MB (204) 888-3634

You'll find some pretty hardy animals here at what officials call the coldest major zoo in the world. It's also one of the country's largest. Located in the Red River Valley of central Canada, the complex specializes in the Nearctic and Palearctic species and has the largest collection of northern endangered species of any zoo.

In all, you'll find about 1,200 animals here, from about 300 species, including reindeer, caribou, polar bears, Siberian tigers, snow leopards, northern leopard cats, and northern Chinese water deer. Because of the expense of keeping them warm in the winter, you won't find elephants, rhinos, or hippos.

Tim's Trivia

The dome lights of the New Jersey Aquarium in Camden provide local residents, and those driving by, with a forecast of the next day's weather. A blue dome—blue skies; white dome—overcast; red dome—storms; flashing red dome—severe weather.

There are, however, some indoor exhibits, which house certain tropical species, including the largest soft-billed bird collection in the country. The Discovery Center emphasizes interpretive exhibits for children as well as adults, and houses a large nocturnal room.

Open daily, year-round. Short hours on Christmas Day. During July and August, gates open at 10:00 A.M., and stay open until 9:00 P.M., closing the rest of the year at 4:00 P.M. Free admission. A cafeteria-style eatery is located indoors, while three fast-food stands are opened as needed.

Corydon Avenue is the major east-west artery through the city. From the Trans-Canada Highway, take the Roblin Boulevard exit from the west side of town. Take Roblin east 5 miles and follow the signs.

New Brunswick

CHERRY BROOK ZOO

In Rockwood Park
Sandy Point Road
St. John, NB (506) 634–1440

Positioned within the 2,000-acre city park in downtown St. John, this twenty-acre facility has quite a few endangered species among its residents.

Including several gnu, there are 160 animals, representing thirty-six species. The wooded terrain, with quite a few natural rock outcroppings, is ideal for the animals' natural habitat homes. Among the animals on exhibit are zebras, camels, deer, leopards, and monkeys.

Open daily, year-round, 8:00 A.M. to dusk. Admission: adults, under $4; seniors and teenage students, under $3; ages, 3–12, under $2; under 3, free. Take exit 116 (Sandy Point Road) 1½ miles west to the zoo, in downtown St. John.

Nova Scotia

FISHERIES MUSEUM OF THE ATLANTIC

Bluenose Drive
Lunenburg, NS (902) 634–4794

Dedicated to the fishing industry of the Canadian Atlantic Ocean, this complex has just about everything related to the sea you can think of. From a twenty-tank aquarium exhibit to boat building to vintage films of the sea, this place has something nautical for everyone in the family.

Located in a historic fishing village that dates back to 1753, the museum comprises four connected buildings and two former fishing schooners. The aquarium display features native fresh- and saltwater fish, highlighting indigenous species such as brook trout, salmon, eels, cod, and flounder.

In addition to the exhibits, there are several demonstrations offered on a daily basis, including lobster-trap making and fish fileting, and there are docent talks throughout.

Open daily, June through mid-October, 9:30 A.M. to 5:30 P.M. Admission: adults, under $3; ages 3–12, under $1. Restaurant on premises. Located 60 miles south of Halifax. Take exit 11 (Route 324) off Highway 103, and pick up Route 324 into Lunenburg. The complex is located on the waterfront at the head of the harbor, in red, turn-of-the-century buildings.

Ontario

AFRICAN LION SAFARI

Safari Road at Cooper Road
Cambridge, ON (519) 623–2620

Here's your chance to answer the call of the wild. By the time you finish your visit here, you'll feel like you've been on safaris to several countries. The drive-through encompasses six different lion habitats.

Once you take the drive, make sure you return to the central part of the complex—you've only just begun! There are four different animal shows daily, a petting zoo, elephant and pony rides, a jungle-theme playground for the kids, and a small, wet play area for the 3–12 age group that features sprinklers and small slides. You can also watch Calvin the elephant as he paints T-shirts.

The *African Queen* boatride takes you on a water safari where you'll see primates, all kinds of birds and ducks, and a Bactrian camel. On the Nature Boy Scenic Railway, you'll be taken into another small preserve where you'll see bison, elk, and rheas.

The 300 acres is home to more than 1,500 animals, representing about 136 species. For an additional fee, you can take the safari aboard an air-conditioned bus with tour narration. Gates to the safari open at 10:00 A.M.; the rest of the activities begin at noon. Gates close at 4:00 or 5:30 P.M., depending on the season, but the grounds remain open until 8:30 P.M. every evening.

Open daily, late-April through October. Admission: adults, under $15; ages 13–17 and seniors, under $13; ages 3–12, under $11; under 3, free. A cafeteria serves a wide variety of food, and there are plenty of picnic sites, if you choose to bring your own.

Take Highway 8 out of Cambridge to Safari Road, turn left, drive five minutes, and you're here.

MARINELAND OF CANADA

7657 Portage Road
Niagara Falls, ON (416) 356–8250

Originally a marine park, this facility, 1 mile upstream from the Falls, has added rides and other attractions through the years and is now a complete family experience.

Sea lions, dolphins, and killer whales are among the marine mammals who call this 300-acre park their home, and who are featured in hourly shows throughout the day. Additional, nonanimal shows are also featured throughout the summer months.

Among the many eateries are the Happy Lion Restaurant, featuring an all-you-can-eat buffet, and the Hungry Lion Restaurant, a full-menu, sit-down establishment. Food may be brought in, and there are numerous areas throughout the park to spread out a family picnic.

Elsewhere in the park are ten rides, including one of the longest roller coaster rides in the world. For children, there are four kiddie rides and a deer-petting park. The marine park is open year-round; the rides and other attractions operate seasonally. Admission: adults, under $20; children, under $17. Special, lower rates are in effect when the rides are not in operation. Open daily, 10 A.M. to dusk.

Located on Portage Road. Follow the numerous signs to the park from the middle of the other Niagara Falls attractions or take the Portage Road exit (actually a continuation) off Highway 18.

Fauna Fun Facts

The tree sloth is the slowest mammal, traveling an average of 6 feet per minute. If he hurries, however, he may be able to reach 14 feet per minute.

METRO TORONTO ZOO

Meadowvale Road
West Hill, ON (416) 392-5900

With more than 4,000 animals living in five habitat regions on 700 acres, this place is not only beautiful, it's huge!

You won't find rows of cages and pens here. Instead, you'll see acres of beautifully landscaped rolling hills studded with glass-roofed pavilions. All animals are exhibited in natural environments, surrounded by their native trees, flowers, and vines. And everything is arranged zoogeographically, which means that the mammals, birds, reptiles, fish, invertebrates, amphibians, and plants are grouped according to where they occur in the world.

As a unique service to visitors, officials have come up with five distinct trails through the park. Each is color coded and the guide book lists what you'll see along each trail and the approximate time it will take you to finish. One of the trails is the monorail ride that takes you into the Canadian Animal Domain. Catch the round-trip ride near the front gate.

In addition to the monorail trip, the other four trails are: Round the World, an all-weather tour that takes you to the major pavilions and exhibits (officials recommend this one for your first visit here); the Lion Trail, which takes you through the Indo-Malayan and African paddocks; the Camel Trail offers much more than a look at the camels (the children's zoo is also located here); and the Grizzly Bear Trail, which takes you into the Canadian Animal Domain where some of North America's largest mammals make their home.

Of all the zoos listed in this book, this facility wins the award for having the most comprehensive and helpful guide book. It's direct, educational, and full of photos. Nice work!

Open year-round, closed Christmas Day. Opens at 9:30 A.M. every morning, closes at 4:30 P.M. during the winter, 7:30 P.M. during the summer months (mid-May through August). Admission: adults, under $10; ages 12–17 and seniors, under $7; ages 5–11, under $5; under 5, free. Additional charges for monorail and pony and camel rides.

Year-round food service is provided by McDonald's, or you can bring your own.

From Toronto, head east on Highway 401. Take exit 389 and go north on Meadowvale Road to the zoo entrance.

NORTHERN FRONTIER ZOO

Highway 11 North
Earlton, ON (705) 563–8300

Almost hidden in the woods under big trees, this nice, little zoo complex has more than 200 animals, representing about 35 species. At the entrance, you'll be greeted by many of the small animals who call this place their home.

You'll find a nice variety of animals here, from moose to tigers to zebras. If you can't make the walk around the facility, there's a Zoomobile running on a regular basis, at no additional charge.

Open daily, May through October, 10:00 A.M. to 8:00 P.M. Admission: adults, under $8; ages 3–12, under $6. Located 2 miles north of Earlton, on Highway 11, on the left side.

Quebec

JARDIN ZOOLOGIQUE DE GRANBY

(The Granby Zoo)
347 Bourget Street
Granby, PQ (514) 372–9113

If you like snakes and such, you'll find plenty of them here to cheer you. Although they say they've never researched it, Granby officials are pretty certain they have the largest reptile collection in Canada.

Altogether, there are approximately 1,000 specimens and close to 300 species living here, surrounded by a great many flower gardens and huge, mature trees. Additional noteworthy exhibits include the Feline House, the red panda, and the African Plains exhibit, with elephants, giraffes, and rhinos.

A pair of Himalayan bears live in the new Mountain Bear exhibit, and bats, spiders, and a bunch of nocturnal species live in the adjacent cavern.

Open late May through September, daily from 10:00 A.M. Closes at 5:00 P.M. in May, June, and September, 7:00 P.M. in July and August. There are nine food outlets, but you can bring your own picnic if you wish. Admission: adults, under $15; ages 5–17, under $10; ages 1–4, under $3; under 1, free. Parking charge.

In addition to the animals, there are ten mechanical kiddie rides (requiring additional fee) and an aerial monorail that takes you over a few of the exhibits.

Located off Eastern Townships Highway, via Highway 10, exit 68, east of Montreal.

SAFARI PARK

850 Route 202
Hemmingford, PQ (514) 247–2727

It seems everyone wants to come here and drive through the 3-mile-long safari in the morning and see the rest of the offerings later in the day. So if you want to avoid the crowds, do it the other way around, and wait until late afternoon to make the drive.

The 300-acre park features more than 1,000 animals, representing some fifty-five species. You'll see the larger hoofstock of Africa, North America, and Eurasia on the safari, including giraffes, and zebra. Apart from the safari, you can take elevated walkways over carnivore and primate areas and hike through a six-acre deer park. There is also a petting area that features miniature animals. A Wild West show features actors and domestic trained animals in its production.

There are twelve family amusement rides, and a small water park featuring a wading pool and a lazy-river tube ride. Opens daily, mid-May through Labor Day, at 10:00 A.M. Although the gates close at 5:00 P.M., guests can stay for a couple more hours during July and the early part of August. Admission: adults, under $18; ages 3–12, under $15. The maximum price per family is $60.

Located south of Montreal, just 1½ miles from the U.S. border. Take exit 6 (Route 202) off Highway 15, and go west on Route 202 for 2½ miles to the safari.

Saskatchewan

MOOSE JAW
WILD ANIMAL PARK

9999 Seventh Avenue SW
Moose Jaw, SK (306) 691–0111

It's about a 2½-mile walk around the exhibit area here, and if you don't want to walk it, you can drive it. If you drive, you can see the animals from your car, or you can pull over and walk up to the various exhibits along the way.

Most of the hoofstock are quite friendly and were hand-raised right here, so they're used to people and will usually let you pet them. You'll find close to 200 animals representing eighty species living here, including Siberian tigers, black and grizzly bears, monkeys, lions, foxes, wolves, and panthers.

Sam the elk lives here and is well known for his "crown head," which consists of seven points of antlers, the best an elk can do. A walk-through aviary offers a colorful selection of birds, from tropicals to the bald and golden eagles. In addition, there's a petting zoo, six kiddie amusement rides, miniature golf, bumper boats, and an amphitheater where local entertainers perform every weekend in the summer.

Open daily, May to mid-September, 11:00 A.M. to 8:00 P.M.; but weekends only for the rest of the year, 11:00 A.M. to 5:00 P.M. Admission: adults, under

Fauna Fun Facts

The big bad wolf has a bad reputation it doesn't deserve. There are no proven cases of wolves killing human beings in North America.

$7; ages 3–12, under $6; under 3, free. Rides cost extra. Adult rates are reduced by about half during winter, and kids get in for $1, due to the fact that many animals are put into warm quarters and can't be seen.

Try the cross-country skiing on the grounds, past the hoofstock in their full winter coats; it's a nice way to spend a winter afternoon.

Within the city limits. Seventh Avenue SW deadends into the facility.

Indexes

General Index

A
AAZPA, 2
Acadia National Park, 116
American Quilt Showcase, 230
America's Dairyland, 274
America's first zoo, 215
America's largest
  crocodile, Gomek, 69
  urban zoo, 178
  gathering of elk, 277
America's most attended zoo, 89
America's oldest public aquarium, 52
amusement parks with zoos
  Busch Gardens, 55
  Cedar Point, 199
  Dollywood, 229
  Hersheypark, 220
  King Island, 202
  Marineland of Canada, 287
  Walt Disney World, 58
  York's, 118
Aqua Zoo, 218
Arabian oryx, 18
Arctic marmot, 14
Atlantic flyway, 52, 124

B
bat, Rodrigues fruit, 152
Big Sioux River, 228
Black Hills, 228
Budweiser Clydesdales, 56, 145, 158

C
Cannery Row, 32
Carousel Museum, 180
Cecil B. Day Butterfly Center, 75
Central Park, New York City, 173
cichlids, Lake Victorian, 198
Colo, 1

D
Delaware's only zoo, 50

Dentzel, William, 37

E
Eagle Mountain Sanctuary, 229

F
Falabella miniature horses, 215
First AAZPA accredited aquarium,
  283
Flipper, 66
Fortress of the Bears, 13

G
Gator wrestling, 61
Giant Pandas, only location in U.S.,
  53
Grant, Ulysses S., 145
Gulf of Mexico Exhibit, 252

H
how to enjoy your zoo visit, 6, 7, 8
humuhumunukunukuapuaa fish, 79
Hurricane Andrew, 65, 67

J
Jungle Larry Tetzlaff, 62, 199

K
Killer whales, 28, 42, 71, 200, 251,
  283, 287

L
Lied Jungle, 154
London, Jack, 81
Long Island Sound, 48
Louisiana World Expo, 113

M
manatees, 55
marmoset monkeys, 59
Mojave Desert, 26
Mount Rainier, 263, 265

N
National Crafts Festival, 230
National Wildlife Refuge System, 2
Nature Boy Scenic Railway, 286
North America's largest gathering
of bald eagles, 15

O
oldest zoo
Florida's, 61
Ohio's, 196
Texas's, 244
Olmstead, Frederick Law, architect,
50, 53, 126, 138, 173, 181, 185
Original Sea World, 42

P
Pacific flyway, 83
Panama-California International
Expo, 36
Parton, Dolly, 35, 229
Penguin Encounter, 42, 71, 200
Perkins, Marlin, 147
Pony Penning Week, 259
Prehistoric Park, 280
Puget Sound Exhibit, 266

R
Rhino Walk, 28
Roosevelt, Theodore, 191, 192
Rose Capital of the World, 238

S
Sam, the "Crown Head" elk, 291
Schroeder, Charles, 35
Shark Experience, 29
Shamu the Killer Whale, 42, 71, 200,
251
Spooky Zoo Spectacular, 90
Smoky Mountains, 229, 235

T
takins, Sichuan, 36

Tarzan Yell Contest, 63
Tennessee River, 236
Tom Mann's Outdoor Show, 12
Tongass National Forest, 23
Trumpeter swan, 150

V
vultures, Pondicherry, 61

W
white alligators, 113, 114
white rhino, 10, 198, 232
wholphin, 79
Whooping cranes, 249
World's coldest zoo, 284
World's Fair
1964, New York, 179
1904, St. Louis, 147
World's first-born liger, 255
World's first
freshwater life center, 236
test-tube tiger, 153
World's largest
alligator farm, 60
crocodilian collection, 69
World's last passenger pigeon,
Martha, 195
World's northernmost zoo, 14
WPA-built zoos, 22, 38, 95, 100, 106,
182, 201
Wright, Frank Lloyd, 134

Z
Zippity Zoo Days, 51
Zoo Boo, 12, 74, 84, 86, 91, 99, 108,
112, 133, 136, 139, 162, 197, 198,
214, 219, 250
Zoobilee Day, 11, 19, 125
Zoolie Ghoulies, 89
Zoo of the future, 35
Zoopermarket Restaurant, 23
Zpooktacular, 107, 185

Zoos, Aquariums, and Wildlife Attractions by State and Province

UNITED STATES

Alabama
Birmingham Zoo, Birmingham, 10
Montgomery Zoo, Montgomery, 11
Tom Mann's Fish World Aquarium, Eufaula, 12

Alaska
Admiralty Island National Monument, Juneau, 13
Alaska Zoo, Anchorage, 14
Chilkat Bald Eagle Preserve, Haines, 15
Kodiak National Wildlife Refuge, Kodiak, 15

Arizona
Arizona-Sonora Desert Museum, Tucson, 16
Grand Canyon Deer Farm, Williams, 17
Phoenix Zoo, Phoenix, 18
Reid Park Zoo, Tucson, 19
Wildlife World Zoo, Litchfield Park, 20

Arkansas
Arkansas Alligator Farm, Hot Springs, 21
Educated Animal Zoo, Hot Springs, 21
Little Rock Zoological Garden, Little Rock, 22

California
Chaffee Zoological Garden, Fresno, 23
Folsom City Park Zoo, Folsom, 24
Happy Hollow Park and Zoo, San Jose, 25
The Living Desert, Palm Desert, 26
Los Angeles Zoo, Los Angeles, 27
Marine World/Africa USA, Vallejo, 28
Micke Grove Zoo, Lodi, 30

Monterey Bay Aquarium, Monterey, 31
Oakland Zoo, Oakland, 32
Sacramento Zoo, Sacramento, 33
San Diego Wild Animal Park, Escondido, 34
San Diego Zoo, San Diego, 36
San Francisco Zoological Gardens, San Francisco, 37
Santa Ana Zoo, Santa Ana, 39
Santa Barbara Zoological Gardens, Santa Barbara, 40
Sea World of California, San Diego, 42

Colorado
Cheyenne Mountain Zoological Park, Colorado Springs, 43
Denver Zoological Gardens, Denver, 44
Pueblo Zoo, Pueblo, 46

Connecticut
Beardsley Zoological Gardens, Bridgeport, 47
Maritime Center, Norwalk, 48
Mystic Marinelife Aquarium, Mystic, 49
Wickham Park, Manchester, 50

Delaware
Brandywine Zoo, Wilmington, 50
Prime Hook National Wildlife Refuge, Lewes, 52

District of Columbia
National Aquarium, Washington, D.C., 52
National Zoological Park, Washington, D.C., 53

Florida
Blue Spring State Park, Orange City, 55

Busch Gardens, Tampa, 55
Central Florida Zoological Park,
　Monroe, 57
Discovery Island Zoological Park,
　Lake Buena Vista, 58
Dreher Park Zoo, West Palm Beach,
　59
Gatorland, Kissimmee, 60
Jacksonville Zoological Park, Jack-
　sonville, 61
Jungle Larry's Zoological Park,
　Naples, 62
Lowry Park Zoological Gardens,
　Tampa, 64
Miami MetroZoo, Miami, 65
Miami Seaquarium, Miami, 66
Monkey Jungle, Miami, 67
Parrot Jungle and Gardens, Miami,
　68
St. Augustine Alligator Farm, St.
　Augustine, 69
Santa Fe Teaching Zoo, Gainesville,
　70
Sea World of Florida, Orlando,
　71
Silver Springs, Ocala, 72
The Zoo, Gulf Breeze, 73
Weeki Wachee Spring, Spring Hill,
　74

Georgia
Aquarium of the University of Geor-
　gia, Savannah, 75
Day Butterfly Center, Pine Mountain,
　75
Stone Mountain Park, Stone Moun-
　tain, 76
Zoo Atlanta, Atlanta, 77

Hawaii
Honolulu Zoo, Honolulu, 78
Sea Life Park, Waimanalo, 79
Waikiki Aquarium, Honolulu, 81

Idaho
Deer Flat National Wildlife Refuge,
　Nampa, 82

Minidoka National Wildlife Refuge,
　Rupert, 83
Zoo Boise, Boise, 83

Illinois
Brookfield Zoo, Brookfield, 85
Glen Oak Zoo, Peoria, 87
Henson-Robinson Zoo, Springfield,
　88
Lincoln Park Zoological Gardens,
　Chicago, 89
Miller Park Zoo, Bloomington, 91
John G. Shedd Aquarium, Chicago,
　92
Wildlife Prairie Park, Peoria, 93

Indiana
Columbian Park Zoo, Lafayette,
　95
Fort Wayne Children's Zoo, Fort
　Wayne, 95
Indianapolis Zoo, Indianapolis, 96
Mesker Park Zoo, Evansville, 98
Potawatomi Zoo, South Bend, 99
Washington Park Zoo, Michigan
　City, 100

Iowa
Blank Park Zoo of Des Moines,
　Des Moines, 101
Greater Iowa Aquarium, Des
　Moines, 102

Kansas
Emporia Zoo, Emporia, 103
Lee Richardson Zoo, Garden City,
　104
Sedgwick County Zoo and Botanical
　Garden, Wichita, 105
Sunset Zoological Park, Manhattan,
　106
Topeka Zoo, Topeka, 107

Kentucky
Land Between the Lakes, Golden
　Pond, 109
Louisville Zoo, Louisville, 110

Louisiana
Alexandria Zoological Park, Alexandria, 111
Aquarium of the Americas, New Orleans, 113
Audubon Park and Zoological Garden, New Orleans, 114
Greater Baton Rouge Zoo, Baker, 115

Maine
Mount Desert Oceanarium, Bar Harbor, 116
Olde Orchard Beach Aquarium, Old Orchard Beach, 117
Rachel Carson National Wildlife Reserve, Wells, 118
York's Wild Kingdom Zoo & Amusement Park, York Beach, 118

Maryland
Assateague Island State Park, Berlin, 120
Baltimore Zoo, Baltimore, 121
Catoctin Mountain Zoological Park, Thurmont, 122
National Aquarium in Baltimore, Baltimore, 123
Salisbury Zoological Park, Salisbury, 124

Massachusetts
Cape Cod Aquarium, Brewster, 125
Franklin Park Zoo, Boston, 126
New England Aquarium, Boston, 127
Southwick's Wild Animal Farm, Mendon, 129

Michigan
Belle Isle Aquarium, Detroit, 130
Belle Isle Zoo, Detroit, 131
Binder Park Zoo, Battle Creek, 131
Clinch Park Zoo, Traverse City, 132
Detroit Zoological Park, Royal Oak, 133

Domino's Farms Petting Zoo, Ann Arbor, 134
John Ball Zoological Garden, Grand Rapids, 135
Potter Park Zoological Gardens, Lansing, 136
Sensey National Wildlife Refuge, Germfask, 137

Minnesota
Como Zoo, St. Paul, 138
Lake Superior Zoological Gardens, Duluth, 139
Minnesota Zoological Garden, Apple Valley, 141

Mississippi
Gulf Islands National Seashore, Ocean Springs, 142
Jackson Zoological Park, Jackson, 143

Missouri
Dickerson Park Zoo, Springfield, 144
Grant's Farm, St. Louis, 145
Kansas City Zoological Gardens, Kansas City, 146
St. Louis Zoological Park, St. Louis, 147
Wilderness Safari, Branson, 148

Montana
Bowdoin National Wildlife Refuge, Malta, 149
National Bison Range, Moiese, 149
Red Rock Lakes National Wildlife Refuge, Monida, 150

Nebraska
Ak-Sar-Ben Aquarium, Gretna, 151
Folsom Children's Zoo, Lincoln, 152
Grand Isle Heritage Zoo, Grand Island, 153
Omaha's Henry Doorly Zoo, Omaha, 153
Riverside Zoo, Scottsbluff, 155

Nevada
Anahoe Island National Wildlife Refuge, Reno, 156
Bonnie Springs Ranch/Old Nevada, Las Vegas, 157

New Hampshire
Anheuser-Busch, Inc., Merrimack, 158
Clark's Trading Post, Lincoln, 158
The Friendly Farm, Dublin, 159
New Hampshire Science Center, Holderness, 160
Paradise Point Nature Center and Hebron Marsh Sanctuary, Hebron, 160

New Jersey
Bergen County Zoological Park, Paramus, 161
Cape May County Park Zoo, Cape May Court House, 162
Cohanzick Zoo, Bridgeton, 163
Jenkinson's Aquarium, Point Pleasant Beach, 164
New Jersey State Aquarium at Camden, Camden, 164
Popcorn Park Zoo, Forked River, 166

New Mexico
Living Desert State Park, Carlsbad, 167
Rio Grande Zoological Park, Albuquerque, 167
Spring River Park and Zoo, Roswell, 168

New York
Animal Farm Petting Zoo, Manorville, 169
Aquarium at Niagara Falls, Niagara Falls, 170
Buffalo Zoological Gardens, Buffalo, 170
Burnet Park Zoo, Syracuse, 171
Catskill Game Farm, Cairo, 172

Central Park Zoo, New York City, 173
Clyde Peeling's Reptiland, Catskill, 174
Lake George Zoological Park, Lake George, 175
Long Island Game Farm, Manorville, 176
New York Aquarium, Coney Island (Brooklyn), 176
New York Zoological Park, Bronx, 178
Queens Zoo, Flushing, 179
Ross Park Zoo, Binghamton, 180
Seneca Park Zoo, Rochester, 181
Staten Island Zoo, Staten Island, 182
Trevor Zoo, Millbrook, 183
Utica Zoo, Utica, 185

North Carolina
North Carolina Aquarium at Fort Fisher, Fort Fisher, 186
North Carolina Aquarium on Pine Knoll Shores, Atlantic Beach, 186
North Carolina Aquarium on Roanoke Island, Roanoke Island, 187
North Carolina Zoological Park, Asheboro, 188
Western North Carolina Nature Center, Asheville, 189

North Dakota
Chahinkapa Zoo and Park, Wahpeton, 190
Dakota Zoo, Bismarck, 190
Roosevelt Zoo, Minot, 191
Theodore Roosevelt National Park, Medora, 192

Ohio
Akron Zoological Park, Akron, 193
Cincinnati Zoo and Botanical Garden, Cincinnati, 194
Cleveland Metroparks Zoological Park, Cleveland, 196
Columbus Zoo, Powell, 197

Jungle Larry's Safari, Sandusky, 199
Sea World of Ohio, Aurora, 200
Toledo Zoological Gardens, Toledo, 201
Wild Animal Habitat, Kings Island, 202

Oklahoma
Oklahoma City Zoological Park, Oklahoma City, 203
Tulsa Zoological Park and Living Museum, Tulsa, 205

Oregon
Metro Washington Park Zoo, Portland, 206
Noah's Ark Petting Zoo, Cave Junction, 207
Otter Crest Wayside, Otter Rock, 208
Wildlife Safari, Winston, 209

Pennsylvania
Animaland, Wellsboro, 210
Claws 'N' Paws Wild Animal Park, Hamlin, 211
Clyde Peeling's Reptiland, Allenwood, 212
Elmwood Park Zoo, Norristown, 213
Erie Zoological Gardens, Erie, 214
Land of the Little Horses, Gettysburg, 215
Philadelphia Zoological Garden, Philadelphia, 215
Pittsburgh Aviary, Pittsburgh, 217
Pittsburgh Zoo, Pittsburgh, 218
Pocono Snake and Animal Farm, Marshalls Creek, 219
ZooAmerica, Hershey, 220

Rhode Island
Roger Williams Park Zoo, Providence, 221

South Carolina
Brookgreen Gardens, Murrells Inlet, 223
Greenville Zoo, Greenville, 224

Riverbanks Zoological Park, Columbia, 225

South Dakota
Bear Country USA, Rapid City, 226
Gavins Point Aquarium and Hatchery, Yankton, 227
Great Plains Zoo, Sioux Falls, 228
Reptile Gardens, Rapid City, 228

Tennessee
Dollywood, Pigeon Forge, 229
Grassmere Wildlife Park, Nashville, 230
Knoxville Zoological Gardens, Knoxville, 232
Memphis Zoo and Aquarium, Memphis, 233
Nashville Zoo, Joelton, 234
Smoky Mountain Deer Farm and Petting Zoo, Sevierville, 235
Tennessee Aquarium, Chattanooga, 236

Texas
Abilene Zoological Gardens, Abilene, 237
Caldwell Zoo, Tyler, 238
Central Texas Zoological Park, Waco, 239
Dallas Aquarium, Dallas, 240
Dallas Zoo, Dallas, 241
Ellen Trout Zoo, Lufkin, 242
El Paso Zoo, El Paso, 243
Fort Worth Zoo, Fort Worth, 244
Fossil Rim Wildlife Center, Glen Rose, 246
Gladys Porter Zoo, Brownsville, 247
Houston Zoological Gardens, Houston, 248
San Antonio Zoological Gardens and Aquarium, San Antonio, 249
Sea World of Texas, San Antonio, 251
Texas State Aquarium, Corpus Christi, 252

The Texas Zoo, Victoria, 253

Utah
Hogle Zoological Garden, Salt Lake City, 254
Tracy Aviary, Salt Lake City, 256

Vermont
Morgan Horse Farm, Weybridge, 257
Vermont Raptor Center, Woodstock, 258

Virginia
Chincoteague National Wildlife Refuge, Chincoteague, 259
The Great Dismal Swamp, Suffolk, 260
Mill Mountain Zoological Park, Roanoke, 260
Virginia Zoological Park, Norfolk, 262

Washington
Northwest Trek Wildlife Park, Eatonville, 263
Olympic Game Farm, Sequim, 264

Point Defiance Zoo and Aquarium, Tacoma, 265
Seattle Aquarium, Seattle, 266
Woodland Park Zoological Gardens, Seattle, 268

West Virginia
Oglebay's Good Children's Zoo, Wheeling, 269
West Virginia State Wildlife Center, French Creek, 271

Wisconsin
Henry Vilas Zoo, Madison, 271
International Crane Foundation, Baraboo, 272
Jim Peck's Wildlife Park and Nature Center, Minocqua, 273
Milwaukee County Zoological Gardens, Milwaukee, 274
Racine Zoological Garden, Racine, 276

Wyoming
National Elk Refuge, Jackson, 277

CANADA

Alberta
Brooks Pheasant Hatchery, Brooks, 279
Calgary Zoo, Botanical Garden and Prehistoric Park, Calgary, 280
Valley Zoo, Edmonton, 281

British Columbia
Okanagan Game Farm, Penticton, 281
Vancouver Game Farm, Aldergrove, 282
Vancouver Public Aquarium, Vancouver, 283

Manitoba
Assiniboine Park Zoo, Winnipeg, 284

New Brunswick
Cherry Brook Zoo, St. John, 285

Nova Scotia
Fisheries Museum of the Atlantic, Lunenburg, 285

Ontario
African Lion Safari, Cambridge, 286
Marineland of Canada, Niagara Falls, 287
Metro Toronto Zoo, West Hill, 288

Northern Frontier Zoo, Earlton, 289

Quebec

Jardin Zoologique de Granby, Granby, 289

Safari Park, Hemmingford, 290

Saskatchewan

Moose Jaw Wild Animal Park, Moose Jaw, 291

About the Author

Tim O'Brien has what he calls the "world's best job." As Southeast editor for *Amusement Business Newsweekly*, an international trade publication for the outdoor mass entertainment industry, he travels the world's highways and byways, writing and taking pictures for a living.

His love affair with animals started when his grandparents took him to the Columbus (Ohio) Zoo to see Colo, the first gorilla to be born in captivity. Since then, he has visited zoos from coast to coast on assignment and "just for the fun of it."

When not traveling, he lives out in the country near Nashville, Tenn., with his wife Rosi; their two daughters, Carrie and Molly; and a menagerie of domestic animals.

He is also the author of *Tennessee: Off the Beaten Path* and *The Amusement Park Guide: Fun for the Whole Family at More than 250 Amusement Parks from Coast to Coast*, both published by The Globe Pequot Press.

Enjoying Nature

Here are some fine titles on nature and the environment. All Globe Pequot nature titles are written by experts in their fields and cover many aspects of nature, from identifying flora and fauna to conserving the environment. Please check your local bookstore for other fine Globe Pequot Press titles, which include:

Good Dirt, $19.95 HC
Animals in the Family, $11.95
Birding for the Amateur Naturalist, $8.95
River Reflections, $13.95
The Frail Ocean, $14.95
Private Lives of Garden Birds, $12.95
The World of Birds, $15.95
Where the Whales Are, $12.95
The Nocturnal Naturalist, $17.95 HC
Botany for All Ages, $12.95
A Guide to New England's Landscape, $9.95
Marine Wildlife of Puget Sound, $12.95
Birdwatching for All Ages, $13.95

To order any of these titles with MASTERCARD or VISA, call toll-free 1-800-243-0495; in Connecticut call 1-800-962-0973. Free shipping for orders of three or more books. Shipping charge of $3.00 per book for one or two books ordered. Connecticut residents add sales tax. Ask for your free catalogue of Globe Pequot's quality books on recreation, travel, nature, gardening, cooking, crafts, and more. Prices and availability subject to change.